EURASIAN UNIVERSISM:

SINITIC ORIENTATIONS
FOR RETHINKING THE WESTERN LOGOS

Xantio Ansprandi

2022

PRAV Publishing
www.pravpublishing.com
prav@pravpublishing.com

Copyright © 2022 Xantio Ansprandi

Edited by Lucas Griffin.

Cover image: "Finial with Garuda and Naga, Cambodian bronze, Bayon style, 12th century",
Honolulu Academy of Art
Source: Hiart via Wikimedia Commons

ISBN 978-1-952671-87-6 (Paperback)
ISBN 978-1-952671-88-3 (Hardcover)
ISBN 978-1-952671-89-0 (Ebook)

EURASIAN UNIVERSISM:

SINITIC ORIENTATIONS
FOR RETHINKING THE WESTERN LOGOS

The great square has no angles (says the Tao Te Ching § 41), and rotates whirlingly in this book which intends to blast the West, waiting for the moment when the dragon will crush the fixed cross and its dogs, while the eagle, the rotating cross, will shine again in the empire of Heaven.

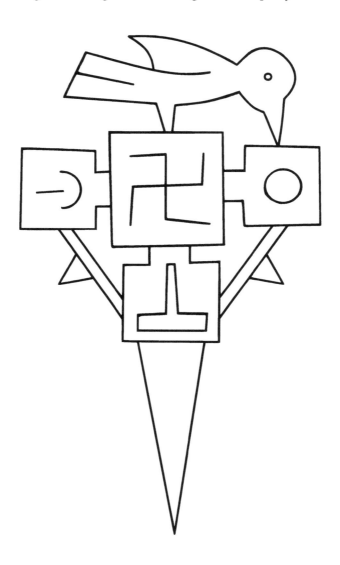

The figure on the foregoing page is my own rendition of a Nestorian cross of the Yuan dynasty (1272-1368). Cruciform artefacts of such kind, attributed to the Nestorians, were cast in the Ordos region of northern China. It is part of a collection, originally gathered by F.A. Nixon, a British postal commissioner who served in Beijing between the 1930s and the 1940s, preserved at the Museum and Art Gallery of the University of Hong Kong.

In my drawing, I have squared both the side wings, which in the original artefact are rounded. The wing below, which in the original artefact is a triangle, is here a square with an elongated triangle beneath it, making the whole figure in the guise of a dagger. All the other elements faithfully reproduce the original Ordos cross. I have chosen such a figure to introduce my essay because it shows at once various related symbols treated throughout the text. In other words, it is a thorough "symbol" in itself (in Greek, *σύμβολον súmbolon* means what "brings together/unites", acting in opposition to "diabolic" thinking; *διάβολον diábolon* means what "puts asunder/separates"), and at the same time is a symbol of the purpose of the essay, which is itself "symbolic". It is a synthetic visualisation of the religio-political philosophy that the essay is intended to present.

The drawing contains:

① The *swastika* at the core of the cross complex, which represents the wellspring of the world and its spiritual order (God; in Sinitic thinking, Heaven), outlining the moving patterns of the two Chariot constellations which rotate around the north celestial pole.

② A complete circle in the rightward wing (east) and an incomplete circle (semicircle) in the leftward wing (west). In Sinitic *yinyang* cosmology, broken lines represent *yin* while unbroken lines represent *yang*, respectively the powers of Earth and Heaven, *Chaos* and *Logos*, space (*yu*), and time (*zhou*). I interpret the circle and semicircle as such twofold reality, whose interplay begets the transformational dynamism for the reproduction of the order of Heaven.

③ A hammer or axe, a tool or weapon located in the downward wing (south), is an olden symbol of the wherewithals to reproduce the order of Heaven, the *Logos*, which is born in the gap of the twofold dynamism. The symbol itself portrays the Chariot asterisms, the sight of which endowed humanity with heavenly self-consciousness and craft, whence comes the associated symbolism of the thunderbolt. Ultimately, it represents divinely-empowered humanity, which by cooperating with Heaven and Earth, constitutes a threefold reality.

④ A raptor bird, another olden symbol associated with the Chariots, to divine inspiration, to the thunderbolt, occupies the vertex of the cross (north). In the figure, the bird emerges from the centre (*swastika*) and is turned rightwards, and with its beak, it grasps the complete circle. It represents those men who understand the appropriate ways to embody and use the heavenly measure, those whom in the essay are described as the sages/ethelings and, endly, the philosophers, divine men. As a symbol of Heaven and its *Logos* coming in the flesh, of a mankind which is aware of its heavenly gist, it is the fourth element of a fourfold reality.

Considering the centre as the unmanifested zero-grade of God, such theological, anthropological and cosmological scheme becomes fivefold. Within the two aspects of space and time, it is a sevenfold reality understandable as a sevenfold "hermeneutic circle".

TABLE OF CONTENTS

METHODOLOGICAL PREFACE

With the present essay, I intend to demonstrate how Sinitic thinking, especially in the form of "Ruism", may function as an efficacious framework for reconfiguring Western thought and the conception of the *Logos*, providing the underpinning for a palingenesis (i.e. regeneration) of European civilisation after the contemporary acknowledged socio-economic and political breakdown of the West. Reorienting Western thought by rethinking its *Logos* is a hermeneutic process; the wishable reformation of "Occidental" thought — the word "thought" comes from the Indo-European root **tong-/*teng-*, which means "to feel/to perceive" and to retain feelings/information[1] — has necessarily to pass through a re-apperception of the *Logos*, which may happen via the "Orient".[2] In other words, the purpose of the essay is to provide what the Canadian-American anthropologist Anthony F.C. Wallace calls a palingenetic "mazeway resynthesis", a new worldonshowing (*Weltanschauung*) devised for regenerating a society amidst, by means, and after a period of decadence, and created by integrating healthy elements inherited from the past into a new symbolism for the future.[3]

---

1   Pokorny (1959), p. 1088: **tong-*, **teng-*, which is also the root of "tongue". Note that etymological roots may be spelled in different ways according to the current conventions of philological linguistics and the style choices of manuals. Throughout the main body of the text, I predominantly employ the contemporary spelling conventions for Indo-European and Proto-Germanic roots, simplifying them in the case of Indo-European. On occasion, such as in this first case, I preserve Pokorny's (1959) forms. On other occasions I use Watkins' (2000) simplified forms.

2   It is worth highlighting that the Latinate word "occident", from the accusative of *occidēns*, means "falling down" and "passing away", secondly referring to the direction of the sunset; cf. verb *occidō*, *occidere*, also with the active meaning "killing". The English "west", instead, comes from the Indo-European root **ue-* via Germanic **westrą*, and denotes something that proceeds, "comes from", "departs" from something else, from "east". See: Pokorny (1959), pp. 72-73. Therefore, the meaning of "west" might be interpreted as less inauspicious than that of "occident". With such distinction, I want to betone the appropriateness of the term "Occidental civilisation" (i.e. "decadent civilisation") in defining the contemporary decadent Western societies. The meanings of its opposite, "orient", are explained later in the first chapter of the present essay (1.3.1). Besides, "north" and "south" etymologically mean "inside", "interiority" and "outside", "exteriority", respectively.

3   Cf. Wallace (1956), *passim*.

This work is conceived to be heuristic, experimental and seminal, articulated in four chapters, each of them dealing with a specific theme. The chapters may therefore be taken in themselves as independent argumentations; nevertheless, each contributes to the gist of the whole work. In line with the mode of Sinitic thinking, this work is "open" and multiperspective. It is open in the sense that it is inherently unfinished while leaving open and opening breaches where to start for further studies; it is multiperspective in the sense that each chapter represents a different facet and point of view of and on the whole. Moreover, concepts themselves are analysed from different outlooks and in dynamic relation with one another rather than as closed notions.

My endeavour is influenced by the work of the French philosopher and Sinologist François Jullien. Relying largely upon his compendium *De l'Être au vivre, lexique euro-chinois de la pensée* (2015), I try to employ the instruments of his philosophical praxis, working athwart "gaps" (*écarts*) between concepts, between Sinitic and Western thought. I share his view of China as the primary "heterotopia" (*hétérotopie*) of Europe, an external viewpoint wherefrom philosophers may investigate Western thought to discover its "unthought" (*impensé*; what has never been thought before) and therefore highlight the resources (*ressources*) upon which to draw for its regeneration. A gap is always also a "betwixt" (*entre*), a field wherein tension and inter-incitement among distant elements engender dynamic movement (energy). Such *entre* is the unutterable mystery that brings forth life and thinking.[4] The purpose of this essay is precisely what Jullien defines as "scanning the lines of potentiality" that are inchoately at work in the present state of things in order to forebode their future unfolding, that is to say, the possible future developments of thinking and civilisation — especially Western thought and European civilisation — after their contemporary dissolution.

---

4   Jullien (2016), pp. 246-247, 262 ff & 275-276 ff. For my work, I have relied upon the 2016 Italian translation of Jullien's book.

Another sway comes from the Traditionalist School, especially René Guénon, and from the Italian philosopher and historian of religions Ernesto de Martino, both of whom envisioned a reorientation of Western thought through the devices of Eastern thought.[5] A major inspiration is the Russian philosopher Aleksandr Dugin, who was influenced by the Traditionalist School and Martin Heidegger, amongst others. In his book *The Fourth Political Theory* (2009, first published in English in 2012), he foretells that the *Logos* will be reborn as *Dasein* once the degenerate liberal Western society of limitless chrematistics and its sclerotic metaphysics will be utterly disintegrated by their ultimate product, nihilism. Dugin says that thinkers living in the current, ending phase of the historical cycle of Western civilisation should work to hasten such destruction and help the resurrection of the *Logos* and of authentic European and broader Eurasian culture out of *Chaos*, elaborating together a new political theory.[6] This is precisely the purpose of my work, which is thus aligned with Dugin's Neo-Eurasianism, according to which the future of Europe rests on the constitution of a new Eurasian religio-political entity, spiritually led by Russia, the *Urheimat* of the Indo-Europeans (Aryans).[7] Dugin's philosophy karstically emerges here and there with regularity as a *Leitmotiv*, particularly, but not exclusively, through a sequence of excerpts from his 2012 book, working as a scaffold that thematises my essay in its entirety.

Some of my premises and conclusions differ from Jullien's. In my eyes, he might represent a Taoist stance, which favours

---

5   Cf. Guénon (1924), passim; De Martino (1977), p. 497.

6   Dugin (2012), passim. At p. 54, similarly to the spirit of the present work, Dugin says that, unlike other ideologies, the Fourth Political Theory "does not want to lie, soothe or seduce. [...] [It] trusts the fate of Being, and entrusts fate to Being. Any strictly constructed ideology is always a simulacrum and always inauthentic, that is to say, it always is the lack of freedom. Therefore, the Fourth Political Theory should not hurry in order to become a set of basic axioms. Perhaps, it is more important to leave some things unsaid, to be discovered in expectations and insinuations, in allegations and premonitions. The Fourth Political Theory should be completely open".

7   Dugin (2016), passim.

mystical contemplation and autochthonous conceptualisation of the origin of things rather than accentuating the study of the latter's manifestation in a hierarchical socio-political organism. In my work I espouse this last position, which is that of Ruism, concerned with humanity's origin and setting human society in harmony with divinity.[8] It is worthwhile to clarify at once that Ruism (儒教 *Rújiào*) is a more appropriate and far-reaching name for Confucianism (孔教 *Kǒngjiào*). The latter is indeed a misnomer since Confucius was not the founder but rather the reformer of the older *ru* philosophical and ritual system that goes back to the Shang dynasty. In recent years, the name "Ruism" has been increasingly adopted within academia.[9] I explain in detail the meaning of the word *ru* in the fourth chapter (4.4). Hereinafter, I employ the term "Ruism" when referring to the general *ru* tradition, a fluid cosmogenic system of concepts and rites,[10] which I see as potentially implementable within different cultural contexts, and extendable to all Eurasia as a common "Eurasian Universism".[11] The American Sinologist Robert Eno defines it as a "nonanalytic philosophy", a philosophy that is not concerned with a search for

---

8   Teiser (1996), pp. 2-6.

9   Eno (1990), p. 8.

10   Teiser (1996), p. 4. I have synthesised Teiser's definitions. I use the term "cosmogenic", a variant of "cosmogonic", in the acceptation of "generating a cosmos", an "ordered world".

11   Elsewise, it is possible to use the term **"Chinese Universism",** coined by the Dutch Sinologist J.J.M. de Groot, which is even wider in scope than "Ruism", also comprehending Taoism and all the other schools of thought and religion which have flourished in the Sinitic cultural sphere. Given that the concept of "Chinese" as it is intended in the West does not exist in Chinese language, and the ethnicity usually called "Chinese" (the Han) define the civilisation of which they are carriers (which includes other ethnicities) 中国 *Zhōngguó* ("Centred Nation"), it is also possible to speak in the terms of **"Universism of the Centred Nation"** or even better of **"Universism to Centre Countries".** Broadening it to Eurasia, it is possible to speak of "Eurasian Universism", which might, as we will see, find declination in the various local cultures of Eurasia, as Greco-Romanity in southern Europe, Germanic Heathenry in northern Europe, Orthodox Rodnovery in eastern Europe, or as a pan-European and Middle Eastern Zuism, and in the systems of contemporary China and Japan, integrating all of them into a common pan-Eurasian horizon of sense. Note it well, it is not a homologating horizontal "universalism" (globalism) like that of Western thought, but "universism" in the sense of a system which tends to vertical unity taking into account multiplicity, as it will be explained in detail throughout the essay.

"descriptive theories", but rather with "a search for the skills to configure the world according to its natural order", and endows the individual with the skills for behaving in the right way.[12] Consistently, I restrict the use of the term "Confucianism" to the post-Confucius historical and localised Chinese and East Asian forms of the tradition.

The essay, written between 2016 and 2017 and refined over the following years, is crowned by a postface, written in 2022, which constitutes a reflection on the previous work and opens up further ramifications of thought within and beyond the "Eurasian Universist" operative framework.

---

12   Eno (1990), p. 8.

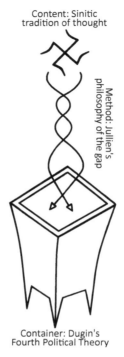

Content: Sinitic
tradition of thought

Method: Jullien's
philosophy of the gap

Container: Dugin's
Fourth Political Theory

Figure 0: Representation of the methodology and matters of
the present work. The content is Sinitic thinking, interacting with
Indo-European and broader Eurasian thinking. The methodology
per se is François Jullien's philosophy of the heterotopy and the
gap, through which I put into contrast and interoperation Sinitic
and Western concepts, in order to reactivate the latter, in many
cases recovering their original meaning, reinserting them into
a symbolic network. The container, or cauldron (the Chinese 鼎
ding, whose meanings will be explored in the essay), into which
this new symbolic network is cast, is Aleksandr Dugin's Fourth
Political Theory, which I aim to fulfil.

— ABRIDGEMENTS OF CHAPTERS

❶ In the first chapter of the essay, I try to outline a "pathological" reading of the deep crisis that is overwhelming the West, bringing to a swift downfall the vestiges of the erstwhile medieval European civilisation and of the lingering liberal democratic polities. I argue that the origin of such a crisis may be traced back to the rupture between human reason and the universal Reason of Heaven, itself a consequence of the abstraction of God and the objectification of the *Logos* which took shape in Christian theology.[13] The separation was later strengthened with Cartesianism and secularised within liberal democratic thought, ultimately leading to the hegemony of human reason and the negation and ousting of divine Reason from "rational" thinking. The outcome is a loss of meaning, a denial of qualities, and consequently a sclerosis of thought and its dive into material *Chaos*; whereas the remedy is to unfix the *Logos* by deconstructing its stiffened conceptualisations, preparing its rebirth and the rebirth of European civilisation, undergirding such palingenesis with a symbolic network aimed at the rectification towards Heaven, borrowed from Sinitic tradition and integrated within the discourse of Dugin's "Fourth Political Theory", fulfilling it.[14]

The chapter is introduced (1.1) by an analogy between the Hellenic concept of *thymos* and the Sinitic concept of *shen*. The purpose is to show that both these terms and their cognates

---

13 Throughout the essay, I uniformly capitalise the concept of *Logos* and its many translations, such as "Reason", as well as its Chinese equivalents and their translations, when they refer to the order of the universe. I use the lowercase (i.e. *logos*, reason) when they refer to human, particularised and localised incarnations of the universal Reason, or to nonspiritual and noncosmic, reductionist, narrower meanings of the word. Likewise, I capitalise the opposite of the *Logos*, that is to say *Chaos*, as well as the latter's translations in various systems of thought and its Chinese equivalents.

14 Alexey Belyaev-Gintovt, a contemporary Russian Neo-Eurasianist artist, winner of the Kandinsky Prize 2008, has created a series of banners entitled "Pax Russica", one of which depicts the Temple of Heaven of Beijing overflown by an eagle, that may well represent the integration of Ruism and the Fourth Political Theory into a "Eurasian Universism".

convey the idea of entity as "propensity" or "procession", a conception dear to Jullien that offers a fresh perspective on the ideas of "spirit" and "god", "reasoning" and "intelligence". I have chosen the analysis of *thymos* as the starting point of the essay also because it is a fundamental concept in the work of the American political scientist Francis Fukuyama. In the middle part of the chapter (1.2), I focus on the search for the "aetiology" of the degeneration of Western civilisation, developing some ideas contained in Fukuyama's keystone work *The End of History and the Last Man* (1992), namely: his thesis that the origins of Western moral dissolution are to be found in liberalism and Christianity, and his identification of Confucianism as the reason of the moral tenacity of East Asian cultures. In line with the anthropological-psychiatric essay *Did Christianity Lead to Schizophrenia?* (2013) written by the British scholars Roland Littlewood and Simon Dein, and with insights drawn from the work of Ernesto de Martino, I also identify the Christian abstraction as a form of psychopathology. In the last part of the first chapter (1.3), I start to deconstruct Western thought and its sclerotic Christian conception of the *Logos*, recovering the original meaning of "Reason" as attuning with Heaven and illustrating the Gnostic conception of the *Logos* as *Ktisma*, a spatiotemporal hierarchical and yet polycentric architecture, even shared by the early Christian thinker Origen, which is comparable to Sinitic cosmology. In the very last section (1.3.3), I point to Mesopotamian culture as the *trait d'union* between Sinitic and Indo-European thought.

❷ The second chapter is dedicated to noölogy. I use this term in a somewhat different way from its conventional acceptation. By the term "noölogy", I comprehensively mean the study of the universal *Logos* or *Nous*; its epistemology, that is to say, human awareness and knowledge of it; and also axiology, meaning the moralising praxis of the human mind and reasoning when it is in harmony with the *Logos*. The chapter is articulated into three major subsections, each dedicated to studying groundlaying concepts of Sino-Ruist thought that may serve as potent devices for unblocking Western thought and overcoming its dualisms. The main sources for this chapter are Geir Sigurdsson's dissertation *Learning and Li: The Confucian Process of Humanization Through Ritual Propriety* (2004) and Brook Ziporyn's essay *Form, Principle, Pattern or Coherence? Li in Chinese Philosophy* (2008).

The introductory part (2.1), which lays the epistemological basis for all the arguments thereunder, deals with the concepts of *Li* (corresponding to *Logos* or *Nous*) and *li* (rite) that, significantly, in the Chinese language are homophones and belong to the same semantic continuum, despite being represented by different graphemes.[15] The second and third parts (2.2/3) deal, respectively, with the concept of *zu* (patriarch) and with the concept of *ren* (humanisation). The former is examined through a lens manufactured by integrating Lacanianism and *yinyang* cosmology as an axiological device apt to handle primordial reality, which is full of potentiality and yet shapeless. The latter is studied as an anthropogogy,[16] a "human education" in the sense of a practice for the development of humanity's intrinsic heavenly gist, which is at the same time the teleology of human existence.

Both *zu* and *ren* are settings and modes of reasoning and ritualising. Throughout the parts of the chapter in which I unfurl such concepts, but especially in the very last section (2.3.4), which deals with human agency's "vertical" responsibility within Sinitic cosmology, I also outline how they are involved in the Sinitic conception of God. Indeed, such concepts represent the intimate relationship between God and humanity since both founding fathers of specific ways of being and the human

---

15 It is worth mentioning that Chinese words and graphemes are polysemantic, that is to say, they convey different meanings specialised according to the contexts, and they are connected in semantic networks with other words and graphemes on the planes of homophony and homography, that is to say, words/graphemes with similar sound and graphic construction belong to the same semantic fields, which are in turn interlaced on the aforesaid plains with other semantic fields.

16 "Anthropogogy" (ἄνθρωπος αγωγία *ánthrōpos agōgíā*, "leading/teaching/raising men"), "education of humanity", is a fresh coinage, not well-established in its usage and meaning. I use it to render the Sinitic concept of *ren*, otherwise translated as "humanisation".

figure itself are conceivable as a continuous embodiment of divinity. I highlight how such theology, which contemporary Ruist theologians define as "immanent transcendence",[17] offers ways for un-objectifying the *Logos*, rethinking it as manifold, and at the same time empowering human creative agency. The purpose of the chapter is precisely to dissolve the sedimented Western notion of the *Logos*, paving the way for the subsequent chapter that is dedicated to theological and theurgical devices for the *Logos'* re-apperception through an old-yet-new symbolic framework.

❸ The third chapter focuses on the centrality of the God of Heaven in Sinitic cosmotheanthropism, that is to say, the conception of the world (cosmology), divinity (theology), and humanity (anthropology), as a threefold synergic continuum. I borrow the term "cosmotheanthropism", which I consider particularly fitting for the Sinitic vision, from the work of the Spanish philosopher Raimon Panikkar, who coined it as a definition for his own theories.[18] The chapter largely relies upon John C. Didier's treatise *In and Outside the Square: The Sky and the Power of Belief in Ancient China and the World* (2009), supplementing it with other publications of the *Sino-Platonic Papers* and other authors' works about the same subjects, including the studies carried out by David W. Pankenier. Didier's treatise has been defined by the Sinologists Victor H. Mair and Michael Saso, respectively, as "one of the most remarkable achievements of Sinological research" and as surpassing "the work and methodology of the late nineteenth- and early twentieth-century anthropologist Franz Boas and the schools of social sciences and humanists who held the theory of mutually dependent cultural fertilization".[19]

---

17 Huang (2007), p. 462 ff.

18 Panikkar coined the term "cosmotheandrism" or "cosmotheanthropism", alternatively rendered "theoanthropocosmology", to define his "totally integrated intuition of the seamless fabric of all reality", that is the "original and primordial form of consciousness", the threefold synergy of world-divinity-humanity expressed by many other forms of trinity, overcoming all monisms and dualisms. See: Panikkar (1993), pp. viii, 1 & 54-55.

19 Saso (2009), p. 491.

The introductory part (3.1) presents a study of the Sino-Ruist conception of the God of Heaven by means of graphic and phonetic etymology. The discussion highlights the very physical symbolisation of God and its order as the northern pivot of the sky and the stars that revolve around it, and, therefore, the practicability of theurgical methods, that is to say, techniques whereby humanity may align with God and act according to its order, so that the times of men may take part in the great time of Heaven. Concisely said, I analyse the powerful devices that Sino-Ruist theology offers for reconciling human reason and divine Reason, theory and practice, reasoning and ritualising, to rectify towards Heaven. Then, I underline the ability of humans in general, and of some outstanding individuals in particular (sages/ethelings), to perceive and embody the order of God, and therewith to act as theurgical centres of space-time and as cosmogenic masters.

Throughout the first part and the subsequent ones, I also analyse the fourfold and foursquare symbolism of cosmogenic power, and I inspect some recently undertaken research about the analogy and possible common origin of Sino-Ruist and Indo-European theological and theurgical concepts.

The second part (3.2) deepens the analysis of the "bioastral" essence of human society, of the evolution of humanity as given by the attunement with the great time of Heaven, and further explores and represents the architecture of the divinely organised space-time as a threefold-cum-fourfold (ultimately sevenfold) system. In this part, I analogise Sino-Ruist cosmotheanthropism to Heideggerian phenomenology, especially Heidegger's vision of the "Fouring" as shown in his speech entitled *The Thing*.[20]

The third and last part (3.3) is dedicated to the analysis of the Yellow Deity, the Sinitic personified symbol of the theurgical/cosmogenic centre and archetype of the sage/etheling, and thus

---

20 Throughout the essay, I consistently capitalise Heidegger's core concepts, even when I use English translations, such as in the case of the "Therebeing" (*Dasein*) or of the "Thing" (*Das Ding*), in the latter case to fully distinguish the Heideggerian (and Lacanian) concept from the general "things" of the world.

of the incarnation of God. I compare it with the Heideggerian and Duginian concepts of "Therebeing" (*Dasein*), "Twice/Twist" (*Zwischen*), *Ort* and *Ereignis*, and I also highlight how it may work for a reinterpretation of the concept of Christ — of the *Logos* — as polycentrically always present/active. The analogy with the Christ, aimed primarily to the decomposition of the latter and its merger with the Eurasian figure of the cosmic sovereign, is also drawn by means of Bonaventuran theology as explained in Ilia Delio's essay *Theology, Metaphysics and the Centrality of Christ* (2007). In the very last section of this third part of the third chapter (3.3.3), I study how the Sino-Ruist cosmotheanthropic structure of space-time may be applied to Mesopotamian and Indo-European theologies.

Throughout the second and third chapters, I put in the spotlight, partly in disagreement with Jullien's views,[21] that the idea of God indeed plays a crucial role in Sinitic culture. I argue that the latter does not outflank subjectivisation as a relation with a universal absolute principle. Indeed, in Sinitic philosophy things are described as "self-so" (自然 *zìrán*), analogically to the *causa sui* of European philosophy, with the difference that such causality is not attributed exclusively to a transcendent God, but is always immanent/generated (生 *shēng*), is a power of continuous "self-determination".[22] Sinitic thinking prevents the abstraction and absolutisation of the subject that ensues when human reason and universal Reason are separated and the latter is denied. By conceiving the entity's bond with God as one of a continuous generation that is mediated by the patriarchal form, Sinitic thinking does not result in the dichotomy between transcendence and immanence, metaphysics, and physics. Yet, it maintains a distance and a tension between them, analogous to the Heideggerian notion of "ontological difference" between Being and entities. This gap between entities and the supreme God is what characterises the former as incomplete, but at the same

---

21 Jullien (2016), pp. 234-237.

22 Perkins (2016), § 3.2 – "Spontaneous Generation".

time it is the interstice (*entre*) wherein thought moves and the human being may continuously improve itself. Subjectivisation consists in the differentiation and individuation of entities depending on their functional roles within contexts.[23]

Besides being the primary heterotopy of Europe, Sinitic culture is also an inexhaustible source of coherent wisdom. Wang Mingming explains that with the breakdown of polities in the "Axial Age", new geometrical conceptions of the world were formulated by philosophers, both in the West and in China. However, while Hellenic philosophers sought to break away from traditional cosmology, Chinese philosophers presented their perspectives as a continuation of the knowledge inherited from the Neolithic and the Shang periods, which saw consistent geometrical patterns in the generation of the world and human society.[24] Furthermore, I believe that the ideogrammatic writing system and the strong emphasis on ancestrality upon which Sinitic culture builds itself have favoured the consistent preservation of such cosmotheanthropic vision; of divinity, humanity, and the world as a synergic continuum.

❹ In the fourth chapter of the essay I investigate the developments of Ruism in contemporary mainland China, giving centrality to the politological system formulated by Jiang Qing, that is to say, "Ruist constitutionalism". I handle Jiang's theories of the "Way of Humane Authority" and of the "Threefold Legitimacy of Power" (4.1), which reflect the cosmotheanthropism thoroughly explained thereinbefore and further deepened in the second part of the chapter, which discusses the statecraft model bewritten in the *Zhouli* (4.2).

Jiang, like Dugin,[25] rejects Fukuyama's hypothesis of the "end of history" and final triumph of liberal democracy, since, in accordance with Sinitic thinking, creation is continuous and never-fulfilled. Moreover, Jiang is fiercely critical of the Western

---

23   Ibidem, § 4 – "Impartiality and Differentiation".

24   Wang (2012), pp. 350-351.

25   Dugin (2012), passim.

liberal democratic system that he sees as decadent, founded on a maimed legitimacy, and subservient to the brutish desires of the amorphous masses. Sharing Jiang's vision about the urgency to reintegrate holy and cultural principles into politics for the restoration of true authority, I unfurl his formulation of a "Tricameral Parliament" (4.3) composed by representatives of the holy (*ru*), representatives and custodians of the national gist, and representatives of the folks. At the same time, I also sketch possible ways to translate and transpose such a system into European languages and contexts, believing in the opportunity of an integration of the Ruist system with Dugin's idea of the Fourth Political Theory, and devising the new mazeway for Europe's palingenesis within the broader building of a Eurasian religio-political entity aligned with Heaven. For instance, I draw a parallel between Jiang's Threefold Legitimacy and the distinction between "noöcracy", "aristocracy" and "democracy", one of the wordings for Indo-European trifunctionalism, which Georges Dumézil thoroughly studied.[26] Lastly (4.4), I set the starting point for an analogy, interplay, and possible overlap between the Sinitic figure of the *ru* and the Western figure of the philosopher. ≝

---

26   Dugin (2016), passim.

CHAPTER 1

HERMENEUTICS OF THE
DEGENERATION OF THE WEST

European modernity, which abolished religion, faith in the King and the Heavenly Father, the castes, the sacred understanding of the world, and essentially patriarchy, was the beginning of the fall of Indo-European civilization. Capitalism, materialism, egalitarianism, and economism are all the revenge of those societies against which the Indo-Europeans waged war, subjugated, and strove to remedy, which composed the essence of all Indo-European peoples' history. Modernity was the end of Indo-European civilization. It naturally corresponds to the *nadir*. [...] No compromises will help us. Either we will disappear and be dissolved, or we must restore our Indo-European civilization in its entirety, with all of its values, ways, and metaphysics. If we want to preserve ourselves as a people, as an Indo-European people, we must wake up and be reborn in contrast to all that has been taken for granted in the world of modernity. To hell with this world of modernity.

> Aleksandr Dugin, in a speech entitled
> "The Indo-Europeans", 28 December 2016.[27]

---

27 Dugin (2016), passim.

Figure 1: The eight-arrows star, the symbol of Dugin's Neo-Eurasianism and of the Fourth Political Theory. It is otherwise called the "Cross of *Chaos*" or "Cross of God". As a variation of the Mesopotamian grapheme ✳ *An* or *Dingir*, "God-Heaven", it is the "Gate of God" (𒆍𒀭𒊏 *Ka.dingir.ra* in Sumerian, *Babilu* in Akkadian), a name analogous to 天门 *Tiānmén*, one of the Chinese names of the north celestial pole. It is a symbol equivalent to the *swastika*.[28] The symbolism of crosses is deepened throughout the essay. What is relevant for this first chapter, is that in Dugin's philosophy it is a symbol of the unity of *Chaos* and *Logos*, or, better said, of the *Chaos* which hosts and makes possible the expression of a manifold *Logos*; a symbol of stars, God and the gods, of orthodoxy, verticality, and deification.[29]

— PROLEGOMENON: *CHAOS* AND *LOGOS*

Aleksandr Dugin expresses the relation between *Cháos* (Χάος) and *Lógos* (Λόγος) in the following terms:[30]

> The *Logos* regards itself as what is and as what is equal to it itself. [...] Beyond *Logos*, *Logos* asserts, lays nothing, not something. So the *Logos* excluding all other than itself excludes *Chaos*. The *Chaos* uses different strategies — it includes in itself all what it itself is but at the same time all what it itself is not. So, the all-inclusive *Chaos* includes also what is not inclusive as part of itself, and, more than that, what excludes *Chaos*. So, the *Chaos* doesn't perceive

---

28   Ingram (2001), p. 1034.

29   Nad (2014), passim.

30   Dugin (2012), pp. 204-211: Appendix II – "The Metaphysics of Chaos".

the *Logos* as other from itself or as something non-existent. The *Logos* as the first principle of exclusion is included in *Chaos*, present in it, enveloped by it and has a granted place inside of it. So does the mother bearing the baby, who bears in herself what is a part of her and even what is not a part of her at the same time. [...] The *Chaos* is eternal nascency of other from itself, that is to say of the *Logos*.

The idea of a fundamental complementarity of *Chaos* and *Logos* as constituents of reality underlies the present essay in its entirety, perfectly mirroring the very core of Sinitic philosophy, and will emerge here and there under various terminologies. Dugin describes the contemporary era as one in which *Chaos* is rampaging, all ties are unfastened and all categories are confused; the erstwhile dominating order of the Western and Westernised world is quickly dissolving, like the decomposing body of a configuration of the *Logos* that has expired. Yet, *Chaos*, as co-eternal with the *Logos* and necessary for the latter's existence like water for fish, is also a receptacle of infinite potentiality, wherein the *Logos* may be reborn. *Chaos* must complete its reabsorption of the wreck of the West, preparing the way for a new salvation. The palingenesis of the *Logos* may not come from within; "it needs something opposite to itself to be restored in the critical situation of postmodernity". Dugin calls for a recourse to archaic and Eastern theologico-mystical systems to trigger such regeneration; a "union with the East", which is also the path devised for Russia itself, before than the West, by the most radical Eurasianism and its precursors, such as Roman von Ungern Sternberg.[31]

In this first chapter of my essay, I try to give a hermeneutical reading of the pathology that has led to the sclerosis and death of the Western *Logos*, meanwhile describing the emergence of *Chaos* from its lingering vestiges. This is made by means of a

---

31 Ibidem, p. 210: "[...] We should explore other cultures, rather than Western [...]. We can find the real forms of such intellectual traditions in archaic societies, as well as in Eastern theology and mystical currents". Regarding radical Eurasianism and its precursors, see: Dugin (1992), pp. 41-42. Ernesto de Martino analogically envisioned a recourse to the Orient to stop the decadence of the West and the worldwide spread of its rottenness. See section 4.1 where I cite the exact sentence.

confrontation between Western and Sinitic concepts. In the last part, I provide means for the deconstruction of Western thought from its foundations, by making an etymological analysis of the word "Reason", by deconstructing the Christian *Logos* through a recovery of an alternative conception of it from Late Antiquity Gnosticism — a conception shared by an early Christian Father of the Church, Origen of Alexandria —, and lastly by finding the *trait d'union*, the common roots and point of convergence, between Sinitic and Indo-European thought in the ancient cultural tradition of Mesopotamia.

1.1. PHENOMENOLOGICAL ANALYSIS OF THE PATHOLOGICAL SYMPTOMS THROUGH A CONFRONTATION WITH SINITIC THINKING

1.1.1. *THYMOS* AND *SHEN*: IDEAS OF ENTITY AS PROPENSITY

The Greek word *thymos* (θῡμός; also Romanised *thūmós*) is one of those that in Hellenic philosophy and mythology denote the soul, the most common word being rather *psukhḗ* (ψυχή). *Thymos* — which covers a semantic field that besides "spirit/breath", also includes the meanings of "wrath", "heart", "mind" and "will" — particularly signifies the upsurging of the soul among other things in the world, the emotion (from Latin *ēmoveō*, "to move out") of the soul that is affected by, and in turn affects, other things. Put in another way, the *thymos* is a particularised coagulation of the *psyche*, within a given context, yearning for appropriate recognition and placement within such context.

According to the *Indogermanisches etymologisches Wörterbuch* (1959) compiled by Julius Pokorny, *thymos* derives from the Indo-European noun **dhuhmos*. The latter denotes "whirl", "smoke", "breath", and "wind", among other meanings which pertain to the same semantic field.[32] The same etymological branch gives rise to

---

32   Pokorny (1959), p. 261.

many cognate words in Indo-European languages, including the Latin *fūmus* and the Germanic "doom" — in modern English an inauspicious destiny — and "steam" (although both the Germanic derivations are also traced back to the roots *dheh-*, "to do"; cf. also "deed" and "to deem", the verbal form of "doom", varying according to the Germanic *umlaut*, and *dhew-*, "to die/to flow", which nevertheless belong to the same etymological stem).[33] The verbal root *dhewh-*, "to smoke", gives origin to the Greek *thúō* (θύω) — which, besides "smoke", Pokorny renders as well as *Stürm* ("storm"), *Woge* ("wave") and *Opfere* ("sacrifice") —, and to the Latin *suffiō* ("to blow") and *furō* ("to be furious").[34] Another derivation is the Slavic (for instance, Russian) дух *dukh* ("spirit", "soul").[35] Interestingly, Pokorny explains it through the German *Wut*,[36] a word that derives from another Indo-European stem, *weht-*,[37] which itself means "blow", "inspiration" and "rage", and in turn comes from *we-*, the semantic field of "wind".[38] It is the same etymological root of Latin *vātēs*, "seer", and related words, and also of *Wotan*, the original Germanic conception of God — i.e. Odin, whose name is rendered in Chinese, fascinatingly, 奥丁 *Àodīng*, meaning "Arcane/Abstruse Square"; the importance of the character *ding* is thoroughly explicated together with square symbolism, later in the present essay. Pokorny gives the root as *uat-/*uot-*, with the meaning of "prophet" and at the same time *Ursache*, that is to say, *Ursprung*.[39] Pokorny suggests that *dhewh-* is cognate with the root of *theós* (θεός),[40] that is *dhehs* — i.e. "god" — (noteworthily, Latin *deus* derives from a different root that denotes

33 Pokorny (1959), pp. 261-270: *dheu-*, *dheuə-*; Watkins (2000), pp. 18-19: *dhe-*, *dheu-1*, *dheu-2*, *dheu-3*.

34 Ibidem, pp. 268-269.

35 Rendich (2010), pp. LVII-LVIII.

36 Pokorny (1959), pp. 268-269.

37 Watkins (2000), p. 101: *wet-1*.

38 Pokorny (1959), pp. 81-84: *au(e)-*, *aue(o)-*, *ue-*; Watkins (2000), p. 95: *we-*.

39 Ibidem, p. 1113: *uat-*, *uot-*. In German, Pokorny's translation *Ursache* means "original sake", while *Ursprung* means "original spring". The cognate adjective *wüten* means "wroth", "obsessively wrathful", i.e. divinely inspired.

40 Watkins (2000), p. 270.

the act of "coming to light/shining", as well as "sky"[41]). *Dhehs in turn comes from *dheh- ("to do/to put/to give"), from which also originates the Latin *fās, fāstus* ("speech" and "divine order").[42]

In Chinese language and thought, 神 *shén* ("god/spirit") is a concept that may be regarded as analogous to the Indo-European notions of "spirit" and "god" hitherto explained. The "Great Compendium of Chinese Characters" (汉语大字典 *Hànyǔ Dà Zìdiǎn*) published in the 1980s, explains that the word *shen* may mean ① "god", "spirit", ② "mind", "consciousness" and "concentration", ③ "expression", ④ "portrait", ⑤ "ability to divine the unknown", ⑥ "esteem" and "respect", ⑦ "rule", ⑧ "display", "arrange" and "exhibit", ⑨ "dialect" and "dignity", "distinction", ⑩ "clever" and "intelligent", and ⑪ "surname", "family name". These definitions easily overlap with the Greek *thymos* interpreted as the soul that arises in the world and strives for affirming itself and for being appropriately recognised by other entities.

Another related Chinese concept is that of 氣 *qì*, which may be translated as "spirit", but expresses a non-dualistic idea of "energised-matter", and therefore may be more appropriately rendered as "psychophysical stuff". It has been sometimes translated as *pneuma* since according to etymology its earliest meaning is "steam" or "breath". Only within the twelfth-century interpretation of Confucianism promoted by Zhu Xi (1130-1200) and his contemporaries, *qì* is conceived in a way similar to the Western notion of "matter", as separated from, and informed by, the 理 *Lǐ* (universal "Reason").[43] It is worth pointing out straightaway that the latter is homophonous with 禮 *lǐ* (meaning "ritual"), and both pertain to the same semantic range.[44]

---

41 I discuss in depth the meaning of the Latin word *deus*, and derivations such as "deity", in section 3.1.

42 Pokorny (1959), p. 259: *dhes-*.

43 Teiser (1996), pp. 29-30.

44 *Li* 理 is at one time the Reason of Heaven and the multiplicity of reasons of things. Chinese language does not distinguish singular and plural. Hereinafter, I use capitalised *Li* when referring to its oneness, whereas I use lowercase *li* when referring to its particularisation, a particular *li* among the multiplicity of *li* of things. When I discuss *li* 禮 as "ritual" it is always lowercase. They are also pronounceable *ri*.

The etymological analysis hitherto explained demonstrates that both ancient Hellenic and Sinitic cultures inherited and elaborated concepts of "soul" and "god", conceived as principles that generate things, foster their growth, articulating them into categories (i.e. "dignities"); the *li* that harmoniously make the world.[45] On the plane of human society they are the patriarchs of kinships, whence comes the definition of *shen* as "surname". The words "deity" and "divinity", "phenomenon" (Greek for anything that "shows itself/comes to light/manifests itself"), and "entity",[46] themselves express the aforesaid vision of an energised reality. According to the definition given by the Sinologist Stephen F. Teiser, the spirits "make phenomena appear and cause things to extend themselves".[47]

The French Sinologist Elisabeth Rochat de la Vallée quotes the ancient Chinese dictionary *Shuōwén Jiězì* (說文解字) by defining the *shen* as "the spirits of Heaven, who lead all the beings to appear". She remarks that in literature they are often metaphorically identified as 風 *fēng*, "winds", and further clarifies the definition by saying that they "bring life from Heaven on Earth; they start the process of transformation leading things to take form according to their own qualities". In other words, they "are sent [...] on the four territories forming the Earth to bring life to each of them according to their natural position"; they "allow the manifestation on Earth of what is above".[48]

Rochat de la Vallée outlines the graphic etymology of the character *shen*: it is composed of the radical 示 *shì* (in the reduced form: 礻) on the left side, meaning "to manifest/to show"

---

45 Rochat de la Vallée (2012), p. 6: "The spirits are thus seen as what allows a life to take form and to integrate in the underlying patterns (*li*) which guide its natural development. The result is a universe where all the beings, things, and phenomena coexist in harmony and beauty".

46 Cf. *hes-, *hens-*, "to engender", "to produce", *hensus*, "energy", "life force"; from which also come the Germanic *ansuz*, North Germanic *óss, áss, æsir*, i.e. "spirits", "gods", Old English *ōs, ēse*, specifically defining the Ases/Anses of traditional Germanic religion, the spirits of Heaven. See: Adams (1997), p. 330.

47 Teiser (1996), pp. 31-32.

48 Rochat de la Vallée (2012), p. 3.

(analogously to "phenomenon"), but also "to worship", and by the near-homophonous radical 申 *shēn* on the right side, meaning "to grow/to extend".[49] A *shen* is therefore a thing that appears and extends itself in the world.

It is worthwhile to highlight that all spirits are conceived as part of *Tiān* (天 "Heaven"), which in Sinitic thinking is the source and the order of things, as well as the intrinsic moral power of mankind.[50] Whatever has the power to make things appear and raise them in accordance with the "Reason of Heaven" — 天理 *Tiān lǐ* and simply *Li*, as abovementioned; otherwise called 天道 *Tiāndào* and simply *Dao*, meaning the "Way of Heaven" —, ultimately belongs to Heaven.[51] Sigurdsson defines *li(s)* as the "dynamic patternings" that orchestrate the cosmos. From the perspective of Sinitic thought, "reasoning" and "reasonable" imply the capacity to harmonise and work together with such patternings.[52]

The graphemes of the phonetic and semantic series to which *shen* belongs are evidently composed of quadrilateral and cross shapes. As glimpsed in the description of the image shown in the frontispiece, and further elucidated throughout the chapters of the essay, square symbolism has a cosmological importance. In Sinitic cosmotheanthropism, the main gods proceeding from the supreme Heaven are four, and they express themselves as qualitatively different forms of life in the four directions of space, including four types of humanity (races).[53] A fifth major one, completing the cosmology, is the Yellow Deity representing the axle of a cosmos and those men who are

---

49   Ibidem, p. 4.

50   Perkins (2016), § 3.1 – "Monism". In Sinitic thinking the source of all spirits, of all things, is unique and is known by many names and epithets. I discuss some of them throughout the essay.

51   Rochat de la Vallée (2012), p. 6.

52   Sigurdsson (2004), pp. 108-109.

53   Rochat de la Vallée (2012), p. 3. "Races" here does not mean the great races of humanity as conceptualised in 18th-century anthropology, as the Sinitic concept historically refers to human groups internal to the Chinese population itself. It is a sort of "geosophical" and "geopolitical" concept.

able to act as cosmogenic centres.[54] Cosmologically, therefore, humanity should function as an intermediary between Heaven and Earth, constituting a trinity that vertically transfixes the four directions. At the same time part-heavenly and part-earthly, humanity is endowed with the responsibility to be in the "likeness of the spirits", "helping the emergence of beings" and maintaining the balance between Heaven and Earth. This cosmotheanthropic architecture has great importance in early Confucianism. For instance, Xunzi (298-235 BCE) says that whenever mankind refuses its role or longs to take the role of the other two cosmic powers, it goes astray.[55]

1.1.2. DIAGNOSIS OF DEGENERATION AS DEPOLITICISATION AND DESPIRITUALISATION

Rochat de la Vallée points out that depravity and distortion of reality, destruction of goodness and beauty, and even mental regression and bodily decay of individuals, ensue when humanity is disconnected from the life of the universe and therefore does not participate in its patterns of functional order. Contrariwise, when humanity is consonant with the order of Heaven, it acknowledges and grasps the patterns of things, the "reasons" (*li*) of things; this is the meaning of "reasoning". *Li* are also defined as the "traces" of the spirits; they are what we may know about them, but also the limit beyond which the human mind may not venture, since the spirits are "not probed by *yin* and *yang*". They are beyond duality even though they manifest themselves through and by means of it. Acknowledging the limits of human reason is the essence of wisdom.[56]

At the present time, we Westerners are living amidst a deep crisis of our own moral and political traditions; it may be frankly

---

54 I thoroughly discuss what I call Sinitic "cosmotheanthropism", i.e. the synergic continuum of cosmology, theology and anthropology, including the symbology of fourfold figures, the Four Deities and the Yellow Deity, in the third chapter of the present essay.

55 Rochat de la Vallée (2012), p. 7.

56 Ibidem, p. 16.

said that we are witnessing the swift meltdown of the vestiges, of erstwhile forms, of Western thought and civilisation. Many philosophers in the recent past foresaw the ominous nature of processes that were then already underway and are now in full swing. Authors like Oswald Spengler (1880-1936), René Guénon (1886-1951), and Julius Evola (1898-1974)[57] — among whom the latter two belong to the Traditionalist School of philosophy, also called Perennialism or Integral Traditionalism — share a morphology of history and civilisation which holds that human societies and cultures undergo life cycles of birth, growth, decline, and death. Spengler views civilisations as "superorganisms", that is to say, organisms made up of mereologically specialised and cooperating constituent smaller organisms.[58] According to the Traditionalists, each phase of a civilisation is characterised by the hegemony of certain races, human groups, and thought systems that they represent and that, in turn, represent them. The phase of decadence, immediately preceding death, is dominated by the third/fourth race,[59] dysgenic egalitarianism, and mass ideologies essentially characterised by abstract quantity and materialism, denying any spiritual principle of hierarchy and functional differentiation. The Western civilisation is now in the phase of such pathological degenerescence. Having lost any constitutive axial principle of morality, the West has ceased to be an organic culture and it is quickly dissolving. Yet, the

---

57 Cf. Oswald Spengler's *The Decline of the West* (1922), René Guénon's *The Crisis of the Modern World* (1927), Julius Evola's *Revolt Against the Modern World* (1934).

58 Spengler conceptually distinguishes the terms "culture" (*Kultur*) and "civilisation" (*Zivilization*), giving to them the meanings, respectively, of the phases of birth and growth of human society, and of the phases of decadence and death which according to him are also phases of a civilisation's spatial expansion. I do not adopt such distinction in my essay; rather, I generally use "civilisation" when referring to an actual manifestation of a "culture", while I use the latter to mean a character or style of human cultivation.

59 The three traditional forms of being, races, or classes, are discussed in the prolegomenon to the fourth chapter of the present essay. The fourth race is the indistinct one which emerges in the end cycles, after the hegemony of the third race and the consequential implosion of all the races.

Gestell of "emancipated technology" sustains and reproduces with deceitful efficiency its lifeless wreck.[60]

Within such machinery, what follows is the fragmentation of knowledge into purportedly independent disciplines, the disconnection of language and thought, and at the same time their detachment from reality — where a loss of "terms" translates itself as a loss of "boundaries" and "ends". The American political scientist Francis Fukuyama, in his 1992 book entitled *The End of History and the Last Man*, proposed that the modern triumph of egalitarian and liberal democratic ideology within Western cultures, and its worldwide influence conveyed by the West's technological hegemony, might mark the deadlock of history and of the evolution of humanity.

According to Aleksandr Dugin, who continues in the wake of Heidegger and of the Traditionalist School, the phase of decadence of the Western civilisation reached its peak in the twentieth century, when mass ideologies produced by the Enlightenment — the three systems of liberalism, communism, and fascism — completely replaced the erstwhile European civilisation built upon hierarchic religious principles. Dugin calls the contemporary state of degeneration, of the godless, amoral, and mechanical fiend of global market society, of unbridled *Chaos*, postmodern "postliberalism". Liberalism apparently triumphed after the early death of fascism and the death of communism in the 1990s, but after its victory, it immediately transformed into something else that no longer is a political ideology, but rather a diffuse "existential fact", or a lifestyle characterised by consumerism and individualism within the framework of egalitarianism.

Postliberalism is also moving "from the sphere of the subject to the sphere of the object", replacing reality with virtuality. It has become "biopolitical", using Michel Foucault's definition, so that true politics is no longer possible and those disagreeing

---

60 Dugin (2012), p. 30. The author mentions Spengler. *Gestell* means "frame", "superstructure". Heidegger used it defining the technological framework that hides reality in the modern world.

with liberalism find themselves unable to react politically. Liberalism's founding idea, that of the individual "freed from all forms of collective identities" and from any kind of limit (reason, morality, and identity; social, ethnic, and even so-called "gender"[61] ties), has become a deterministic destiny haunting entire states and their populations, which may be defined as a whirl that swallows and grinds races and cultures,[62] all together in the "melting pot of world globalisation" in which polities become logistic entities, container-machines, and individuals are treated as "masses of identical objects" that function as their fuel.[63] Since it is politics that constitutes the subject (this last is *causa sui* but it is always shaped by the context), functioning as an anthropological structure, the shift of political forms brings about a change in the shape of man itself. In postmodern postliberalism, the true, vertical, axial, polar, political power — in the original Greco-Latin meaning of a power which brings to unity acknowledging and politicising multiplicity; which guides, cleans, purifies (*polītus*), making the polity, the city out of the many (πόλις *pólis*)[64] — is liquidated,[65] and man is not regarded as a whole but as a conglomerate of independent desires and emotions (emotivism; the "individual" is rather regarded as "dividual") which at one time dissolve themselves in clouds of dust and collapse together in "trans-individual" multitudes. As long as

---

61 A term misused by contemporary delirious nonsensical ideologies of sex, whose true meaning is explained just hereinafter.

62 Dugin (2012), pp. 46-48. Dugin rejects geneticistic conceptions of race typical of 18th-century racism. Rather, he, and the Fourth Political Theory, espouse the idea of *ethnos* and, as its political reflection, Richard Thurnwald's concept of *Dorfstaat*, "village-state", which gives an idea of polycentric politics. I myself do not consider the term "race" exactly in the acceptation of 18th-century racism, i.e. the great races of humanity as monoblocks, but in that of "kinship", which, while maintaining a genetic undertone, intends humanity as framed and educated in well-ordered families and cultural lineages.

63 Ibidem, pp. 12-21.

64 Pokorny (1959), p. 798 ff: *pel-, *pelə-, *plē-.

65 We may therefore speak of a despiritualisation accompanied by a depoliticisation intended as a "decentring", "deaxialisation", "depolarisation", loss of the centre, axle or pole.

vertical lines of political power are denied, "all forms of vertical symmetry are subject to destruction, and everything becomes horizontal"; man itself becomes horizontal.[66]

Yet, once liberalism has achieved its goals and has realised itself in practice, its tenets lose their logical meaning; the "ideological shell" weakens, and holes begin to appear in the fabric of postmodernity. The task of those who fight postliberalism is to hack through its holes and hijack the system using its own awesome technological weapons, the same ones that liberalism used to win against its adversaries.[67]

"Degeneration" is the word that best expresses the outburst of *Chaos* from the decomposing body of an order of being, a configuration of the *Logos* which has come to its saturation and death. "Degeneration" literally means "without generation", "denial of generation", an uprooting from the genealogical structure of being. The Latin verb *generō*, *generāre* shares the same root of *genus* and *gēns* ("ilk", "kin[d]", "race"), *genuīnus* ("genuine/innate", "germane"), and *genius* ("ilk spirit", "inborn quality").[68] A degenerate state necessarily involves the denial of different spiritual qualities, the disconnection from the spirits, and their consequent self-concealment and withdrawal from reality. Western civilisation is dying because it has become a "despiritualised" and "despiritualising" machinery, having rejected the "reasons" of reality and the order of Heaven which they represent.

As expressed by Alain Soral in his foreword to Aleksandr Dugin's *The Fourth Political Theory*, "the only worthwhile international" that may counterweight the forces of the ultimate degeneration of the West, of such forces' representatives, of the "morbid blend of the society of the spectacle and consumerism" that results from the decomposition of the erstwhile Western order, "is

---

66 Dugin (2012), pp. 169-171.

67 Ibidem, pp. 22-23.

68 Pokorny (1959), p. 373 ff: *gen-, *genə, *gne, *gno; Watkins (2000), p. 26: *genə-. From the same root come the Greek *gignomai* (γίγνομαι, "to come into being"), *génos* (γένος) and other related words, and the Germanic root *kunją* ("race"), from which comes for instance the English "kin", "kind".

that of the spirit", incarnated by the geopolitical sovereignty of the Eurasian powers, chiefly Russia and China, "which safeguard the freedom" and the health of "all other peoples on the planet".[69]

According to Dugin, in the Fourth Political Theory, "the stone that builders rejected (i.e. spirituality and theology) becomes the cornerstone" for the new project aimed at overcoming the dictatorship of objectification (and virtual objectification) that with postliberalism swiftly replaces the dictatorship of liberalism and other post-Enlightenment ideologies.[70]

1.1.3. DUALISM AND THE OBJECTIFICATION OF ENTITIES

As explained hereinbefore, there are conceptual devices pertaining either to Western (*thymos*) or Sinitic thought (*shen*) that may be regarded as expressing the same notion: entity as propensity. The French philosopher and Sinologist François Jullien dedicates the very first chapter of *De l'Être au vivre* (2015) to the notion of "propensity". He himself explains that Sinitic thinking conceives an "entity" as the upsurge, growth, and transformation of a spirit that interacts with a given situation, which in turn contains the potential for the spirit's own development.[71]

Jullien contrasts this notion of the entity as a process with that of causal dualism. The latter, which entails the conception of causes and effects as separated, has long been prevalent in Western thought characterising a notion of intelligence as the ability to find the links between such separated causes and effects. Causal dualism, which is just another aspect of metaphysics-physics and mind-body dualism (Cartesianism), has ultimately paved the way for a separation of the iity (also ihood or

69   Dugin (2012), p. 10.

70   Ibidem, pp. 22-23. Dugin quotes *Mark* 12:10.

71   Jullien (2016), pp. 20-24.

ichhood, German *Ichheit*)[72] from the context regarded as a set of objects.[73] Through the conception of entity as propensity, Jullien proffers an alternative definition of intelligence, similar to the aforementioned notion of reasoning provided by Rochat de la Vallée. According to Jullien, intelligence is the ability "to discern the outlines" of the configurations of reality.[74]

I argue that the dualistic way of thinking causes and effects has its earliest roots in the Christian conception of God as an abstract, otherworldly entity, that is to say, as a transcendent cause that is separated from its creation. The reification, or objectification, of generated things, the view of them as static, and therefore the negation of their spirit, is an immediate consequence of the dualism inaugurated by Christian theology. On the contrary, Sinitic theology never conceived God, its universal order, and the generated things, as separate powers or entities. This last perspective has been defined by contemporary Ruist theologians as "transcendental immanence" or "immanent transcendence".[75]

From a non-dualistic outlook, an iity's ability to recognise the spirits — that is to say, to perceive their traces — shows itself to be the same as the reciprocal recognition among spirits. Words pertaining to the semantic field of spirituality, as hereinabove seen, depict "spirits" as agents that produce categories of beings and live within them. Jullien bespeaks the notion of trust/faith, as it is conceived in Sinitic philosophy, as the only basis upon which it is possible to build cohesive communities. Trust should not be put in a presumed abstract truth, whose timelessness

---

72 "Iity": the pronoun "I" plus the Latin suffix of essence *-itas* ("-ity"), renders the German term *Ichheit*, coined in German philosophy. I use it on some occasions to define the "I", or the subject, or the individual entity. Other possible calques of the German term are "ihood", "ichhood" or "ikhood", with the English suffix of essence "-hood", and the latter two with *"ich"* or *"ik"* as the root word, which are Middle English forms (the former also used in some occurrences up to the 18th century), respectively of southern and northern England, of the pronoun "I".

73 Jullien (2016), pp. 11-20.

74 Ibidem, p. 15.

75 Huang (2007), p. 462 ff.

smothers the intrinsically temporal development of an entity. Rather, trust should be put in the very process of development, in other words in the long time, or duration, of a thing. At the same time, it should be put in the conformity between words and works, instead of putting it in timeless "sincerity".[76]

Interestingly, Sinitic thinking may be approached by means of Indo-European concepts whose etymology provides the basis for an identification of "truth" as an entity's propension. The Germanic words "trust" and "true" are traced back to the Indo-European *derw-/*drew-/*dru-, which is the same root of "tree", originally meaning a "strength" or a "tenacity", conveying the idea of an entity that is firmly rooted in the ground and yet stretches itself out in multiple directions; that grows protensively. Latin words like *dūrō, dūrāre* ("to last/to persist"), but also *indūrō, indūrāre* ("to harden/to endure"), ultimately come from the same root.[77] Jullien conceives trust as resultative rather than *a priori*; trust depends on the effectiveness of the process of past forces that have come true and have the potential to grow towards a future.[78]

Remarkably, in the Chinese language the concept of "truth" may be expressed through various compounds containing 真 *zhēn* ("true") as the first character (including, for instance, 真相 *zhēnxiàng*, "true figure/appearance/phenomenon"), which belongs to the same semantic series of 正 *zhèng* ("right"),[79] but may also be expressed by the already introduced concept of 理 *lǐ* (which primarily means "reason", "logic", "texture", and also "science") and by 谛 *dì* ("meaning", "significance"), the latter being a homophone and belonging to the same semantic group of 帝 *dì*, "deity". All these concepts that, among their various yet related meanings, express the Sinitic concept of "truth" will have a cardinal role throughout the forthcoming parts of the essay.

---

76   Jullien (2016), pp. 42-45.

77   Watkins (2000), pp. 16-17: *deru-*.

78   Jullien (2016), p. 44.

79   Pankenier (2013), pp. 140-142.

1.1.4. OBJECTIFICATION AND SCLEROTISATION OF THE *LOGOS*

The architecture of the postmodern world is completely fragmented, perverse and confused. It is a labyrinth without an exit, as folded and twisted as a Moebius strip. *Logos*, which was the guarantor of strictness and order, serves here instead to grant curvature and crookedness, being used to preserve the impassability of the ontological border with nothing from the eventual and inevitable trespassers seeking to escape into the beyond.

Aleksandr Dugin[80]

Logos, possibly the most important concept of Hellenic philosophy, defining the order of self-unfolding of things, is usually translated as cosmic performative "Word" and "Reason", *Oratio* and *Ratio* in Latin. A nearly equivalent concept is that of *Noûs* (Νοῦς), meaning cosmic "Intelligence" or "Mind". The verbal root *légō, légein* (λέγω, λέγειν; "to say/to speak"), comes from the Indo-European **leg-* and means "to arrange/to put in order"; it is also related to the semantic field of "linking" and "binding" (cf. Latin *ligō, ligāre*), and in Romance languages also "reading" (cf. Latin *legō, legere*). The words "intelligence" and "religion" come from the same root, via, respectively, Latin *intelligō, intelligere* (*inter+ligere*, i.e. "linking together") and *religiō, religiōnis* ("relinking", "rereading" or "remembrance").[81]

Heraclitus (c. 535-475 BCE), was the first attested Hellenic pre-Socratic philosopher to deal with the *Logos* as the order of the universe. His thought prevented the development of a dualistic logic by conceiving opposite things and qualities as contending forces working within a coherent whole (Latin *co+haereō, co+haerēre*, "to stick together"), rather than as unchanging separated entities or abstract qualities of a substance. Heraclitus says that "God is day-night", presenting duality as the dynamism of the unity, as the dynamism through which the oneness, that

---

80   Dugin (2012), p. 209.

81   Pokorny (1959), p. 658: **leg-*.

is the source of all things, works and manifests itself. Another Heraclitean concept is that "war (*Polemos*) is the father of all things", meaning that competing forces are necessary to one another, and the tension between them produces the energy of the oneness. Notwithstanding Heraclitean thought, dualistic logic would have later prevailed in the form of the law of non-contradiction formulated by Aristotle.

The non-dualistic pre-Socratic style of thought, Jullien says, is analogical to that which has always been prevalent in Sinitic philosophy.[82] Sinitic thought is founded upon the idea of a *Tian* whose *Li* or *Dao* manifests itself through the interplay between the 阴 *yīn* and 阳 *yang*. These latter are usually rendered, respectively, as "dark" and "bright", "waning" and "waxing", or "absorption" and "emanation", but they cover a still wider semantic range. They are the modality of differentiation working between the original oneness and the many things of the world.[83] Heaven and its Reason, the source and the way of configuration of the universe, are well expressed in Jullien's terms as the "upstream" and "downstream" of the same manifestation process. Sinitic thought does not create an unbridgeable schism between metaphysics and physics, being and becoming, or between God and the *Logos*, so that any modality of configuration (*shen* and their *li*) is at the same time a way of communication with the source (源 *yuán*) of all things.[84] *Tian* and the *shen* and their *li* are reciprocally and complementarily related, since oneness manifests itself in duality and multiplicity, and in turn oneness is continuously reassembled and reconfirmed by the multiplicity's coherence. It is a system that allows for both unity and multiplicity, without denying the latter. Denying the oneness's manifoldness is therefore the same as denying the oneness itself that is at work in the multiplicity.

The Hellenic *Logos* and the Sinitic *Dao* are often compared and contrasted, especially when the former is perceived to be

---

82   Jullien (2016), pp. 92-96.

83   Perkins (2016), § 3.4 – "Polarity and Cycles".

84   Jullien (2016), p. 99.

"fixed" while the latter is considered to have preserved "flexibility".[85] Rather, the tauter opposition is not that between the *Logos* and the *Dao*, but between them and the Christian conception of the *Logos* as "Christ". This last is a reification/objectification of the *Logos* as one single entity, spatiotemporally confined in the person of Jesus (ישוע, *Yeshua*, "*Ya* who Saves") of Nazareth.

I argue that the objectification of the *Logos* should be recognised as the ultimate cause of the degenerative pathology that plagues Western civilisation. The abstraction of the universal God — conceived as an otherworldly entity, an entity existing outside the universe that it created as a separate object — is the first step towards the separation between, and the objectification of both, God and the *Logos*. The latter's fixation into one specific historical entity marks the critical point of its objectification, and at the same time its separation from the rest of the world and from humanity, which in turn are despiritualised and bereft of value.[86] Once it is deprived of flexible and multifarious creativity, the *Logos* sclerotises and petrifies into an empty simulacrum, then plunging back into inorganic matter. Starting from the splitting between human reason and the *Logos*, it takes only one step for the complete denial of the latter and the unrestrainable hypertrophy of the former (rationalism) and its complete materialisation, its identification with matter itself.

We may identify the multiplex *Logos* or *Li* with the Lacanian concept of "Symbolic Order", which is accessible by means of the "Name of the Father". According to Jacques Lacan, symbols, and words which they represent, "umbelap the life of man in a network so total that they join together [...] the shape of his destiny".[87]

---

85   Cf. Zhang (1985), passim.

86   Similar critiques are advanced by Porphyry of Tyre (233/234-305) in his *Against the Christians* (*Contra Christianos*). According to him, because of its reduction of the utmost God and of the many ways to understand it to a historical person, spatiotemporally determined, Christianity is arrogance, violence and madness; it is a principle of *Chaos* in the world.

87   Lacan (2007), p. 231. In Lacanianism, the human psyche and its experience are threefold: the "Symbolic Order" represents the Freudian superior layer (the

Symbols constitute a web that, since the dawn of history, permits humanity to rise above undifferentiated matter by building languages and civilisations. The Name of the Father is the wherewithal that moulds and sublimates the otherwise shapeless Thing (*Das Ding*), the original undifferentiated oneness that at one time generates and reabsorbs individual things. In other words, the Name of the Father opens a gap between the individual and the Thing within which thought may develop.

Christianity's reduction of symbols to one historicised person corresponds to what Lacanians define as an "obduracy" or "network sclerosis", that is the stiffening of the Symbolic Order and its infestation with the deathly aspect of the Thing. In this process, the network of symbols ceases to be dynamic, it becomes saturated, and it protractedly reproduces itself as a machine-like empty shell.[88]

All forms of totalising egalitarian ideology produced by the Enlightenment, together with the whirl of postliberalism discussed by Dugin — i.e. ideologies denying the existence of functional differences in the organisation of reality, that is to say, the hierarchical manifestation of the *Logos* as a multiplicity of degrees or orders of being (*thymoi* or *shen* and *li*), or even actively trying to destroy such qualitative differentiation — are pathological symptoms of the same illness that, once embryonically contained in Christian theology, became wholly manifested with the latter's secularisation in the modern era. I argue that the remedy for such Western sclerosis must start from a deconstruction of the sclerotised *Logos*, rethinking it with the purpose of onsetting its palingenesis. This may be done by means of operative frameworks offered by Sinitic thinking.

Freudian *superego*), the "Imaginary Order" is the middle layer (the *ego*) and moves through dualities, while the "Real Order" (that is *Das Ding* as such) is the inferior layer (the *id*). Lacanian orders, contrariwise to Freudian ones, have not to be interpreted as a hierarchy or a mereology of the psyche; rather, they fluidly coexist within the individual and manifest themselves as linguistic registers. They may be compared to the threefold articulation of the iity according to Aleksandr Dugin, explained further onwards.

88 Nobus (2000), p. 87. For deepenings regarding the Thing see the section 2.2.2 of the present essay.

1.2. LIBERAL DEMOCRACY: THE TRIUMPH OF THE "LAST MAN" AT THE "END OF HISTORY"

In liberal ideology the historical subject is the individual [...] conceived as a unit that is rational and endowed with a will [...]. The individual is both a given and the goal of liberalism. It is a given, but one that is often unaware of its identity as an individual. All forms of collective identity [...] impede an individual's awareness of its individuality. Liberalism encourages the individual [...] to be free of all those identities and dependencies that constrain and define the individual from outside. This is the meaning of liberalism (in English, liberty; in Latin, *libertas*): the call to become "liberated" (Latin: *liber*) from all things external to oneself. [...] As for what the purpose of this freedom is, liberals remain silent. To assert some kind of normative goal is, in their eyes, to restrict the individual and his freedom. Therefore, they strictly separate a "freedom from", which they regard as a moral imperative of social development, from the "freedom for" — the normativisation of how, why and for what purpose this freedom should be used. The latter remains at the discretion of [liberalism's] historical subject — in other words, the individual.

Aleksandr Dugin[89]

In 1992, Francis Fukuyama published *The End of History and the Last Man*, a book that deals with philosophy of history and morphology of civilisation from a politological perspective. He analyses the underlying processes of modern history after the French Revolution of 1789, the event that brought to reality for the first time the purportedly universal homogeneous nation-state based on the ideology of egalitarian human rights, that is to say, the liberal state.

Building upon the theoretical systems of Hegel, Nietzsche, and Alexandre Kojève, among others, Fukuyama gives an insightful analysis about the roots and the possible outcomes of the processes of modernity. The book has been oftentimes, and perhaps superficially, read as endorsing liberal democracy. Rather, it merely shows why such a political system has been

---

89   Dugin (2012), p. 37.

so successful in the modern era, and forecasts its triumph, identifying it with the Kojèvean "end of history" and the hegemony of the Nietzschean "Last Man" (*der Letzte Mensch*). This triumph would mark the arrest of the dynamic evolution of humanity through competition and reciprocal recognition and would start the involution of man into a beastly entity yearning only for material pleasure.[90]

Fukuyama says that, as opposed to lower animals that are driven only by selfish instincts of bodily survival, men primarily long for dignity, honour, and value, which depend on being recognised by others (by other worthy men) as peers, as men of the same worth.[91] Such longing for recognition is what Fukuyama calls *thymos*. He bases his idea on the theory of the tripartite soul found in Plato's Republic, in which the *thymoeidés* (θυμοειδές, "spiritedness") is the life force driven either by the *logistikón* (λογιστικόν, human reason informed by the sight of the metaphysical Sun, the Form of the Good, the One that begets all lesser forms) or by the *epithymitikón* (ἐπιθυμητικόν, the chthonic part of the soul that longs for the satisfaction of bodily needs of sustenance and reproduction).[92] In accordance with Hegel's dialectic of lordship and thralldom (*Herrschaft und Knechtschaft*), one who qualifies as a true man, that is to say, a lord, is willing to risk his own life in order to quieten and sublimate his lower instincts for the sake of dignity and higher truths. At the dawn of history, the desire for dignity provoked wars for life or death. Those who overcame the fear of death emerged as lords and masters of those who were whelmed by it.[93] The former were the aristocrats, whose life and culture was shaped by an ethic of war and honour, while the latter became the classes of serfs.[94]

Fukuyama believes that liberal democracy is destined to be the ultimate political form in a globalised economy. This is

---

90   Fukuyama (1992), pp. 20-21.

91   Ibidem, p. 14.

92   Ibidem, p. 15.

93   Ibidem, pp. 14-15.

94   Ibidem, p. 202.

because liberal democracy has the power to satisfy, by egalitarian means, the type of desire of recognition common to the majority of human beings, at the same time defusing what Fukuyama calls *megalothymia*, that is to say the stronger spirituality of superior men. Liberal democracy smothers *megalothymia* by strengthening *isothymia*, the desire for equality based on the only type of spiritual longing that is shared by all humanity, i.e., the lower instincts of sustenance, thus working for a downward levelling of all men.

Purportedly (pseudo-)universal human rights, based on the idea of equality, may be traced back to the seventeenth-century philosophy of Thomas Hobbes, famous for the hypothesis of the "social contract".[95] The American Revolution, and especially the later French Revolution of 1789, were the first large-scale political actualisations of these hypotheses.[96] They are brought to the extreme in today's pervasive nihilistic relativism, which questions any norm based on higher principles and, by doing so, opens the way for the actualisation of any abnormality. We are living in a period in which morality is on the wane, distinctions between right and wrong are denied, limits and boundaries are questioned, and the very existence of any community is threatened.[97]

The French sociologist Émile Durkheim (1858-1917) introduced the concept of "anomy" to describe such a state of things, in his book *Suicide* (1897). Anomy, the absence of *nomos*, means the breakdown of society, of the bonds that hold together individuals and groups. According to Durkheim's definition, anomy ensues when a mismatch occurs between individual aspirations and social standards so that individuals are no longer involved in the life of society. I proffer that "anomy" might also be employed to define an active denial of the norm (antinomy) preceding and initiating the process and the condition of dissolution. Liberalism, believed by its supporters to be a "rational" way of living, is merely a product of

---

95 Ibidem, pp. 174-175.

96 Ibidem, p. 16.

97 Ibidem, pp. 336-337.

human *ratio inferior*, that is to say calculative reason (logism),[98] which arises when the latter separates itself from the *Logos*. As explained hereinbefore, the denial of spiritual qualities is intrinsically related to the denial of the hierarchy of the *Logos* itself. Egalitarian and liberal ideologies, quantitative indistinction, and anomy threaten the very essence of humanity and its role within the cosmos.[99]

Instead of working in the dynamic interaction between the *megalothymia* of the warrior aristocrats and the *isothymia* of the masses, early liberalism tried to deaden the thymotic impetus by overwhelming it with the unchaining of primordial instincts.[100] According to Nietzsche, liberal democracy represents the unconditional victory of the lower types of humanity and their twisted moralism, *Sklavenmoral*, which glorifies weakness and fault.[101] Such a type of humanity, devoid of any pride and dignity, is what Nietzsche calls the "Last Man".[102] Nietzsche believed that nihilistic relativism would have ultimately eroded the foundations of the same *Sklavenmoral*, opening a new era of freedom for the superior spirits (*Übermenschen*) and their creative reaffirmation of true values (*Herrenmoral*).[103]

The liberal state, based upon the separation of powers and legal positivism, which confers the same rights and citizenship to anyone, and its liberal economy, joined by modern techno-science which has removed any constraint to the production and the accumulation of wealth and money (capitalism, limitless chrematistics), constitute the machinery and the merely material growth that has made possible the actualisation of any earthly desire and the exponential reproduction of the

---

98 Augustine of Hippo distinguished *ratio superior* or *sapientia* or "intellect" as the human reason capable of ascending to the highest good, i.e. God, and *ratio inferior* or *scientia* or "calculative reason".

99 Fukuyama (1992), 309-313.

100 Ibidem, pp. 201-202.

101 Ibidem, pp. 20-21.

102 Ibidem, pp. 314-315.

103 Ibidem, pp. 346-347.

amoral masses of kinless men teeming in the urban centres,[104] and the transcription of any lies useful for oiling the anomic machination channelling the chthonic forces thanks to the popularisation of printing and "journalism", outcomes of the Protestant world. Alexis de Tocqueville believed the organisation of true communities of sense to be the way to curb the overflow of inferior humanity.[105]

Notwithstanding his acknowledgement of the evils of liberalism, Francis Fukuyama apparently maintains a sociological perspective on facts, neither approving nor disapproving of the tendency of modern politics. He indeed seems to lack a deeper understanding of the events and a spiritual notion of reason, especially when he defines phenomena such as ethnicity as "irrational".[106]

Aleksandr Dugin lucidly analyses the political anthropology of postmodern postliberalism (which he characterises as post-politics and post-anthropology[107]) as an overturning of Hegel's lord-thrall dialectic: those whom Dugin calls "political soldiers", the creators of traditional societies willing to kill or die for politics, are nowadays swamped within the decomposing horizontal multitudes, the debris of collapsed political structures; instead, modern "politicians", those endowed with power in postmodern postliberal society, are people willing to change or give up their ideas whenever they confront risks and threats.[108]

Dugin studies the three post-Enlightenment mass ideologies as "hermeneutic circles", each one spinning around a

---

104 Ibidem, pp. 344-347. "Degeneration", as a fall outside the generation of the spirits according to the axle of Heaven, is also senseless and endless merely material breeding; production of offspring bereft of any reason of being, without genealogy, roots and history. The crisis of Europe and the West is also the deluge of merely earthen, spiritless individuals (mere children of *Gaia*, a Greco-Latin name of the Earth), who have nothing to do with the kinships which constructed European civilisation and who will submerge and dissolve what remains of the medieval European civilisation.

105 Ibidem, p. 337.

106 Ibidem, p. 217.

107 What I have characterised as "depoliticisation", "deaxialisation" or "depolarisation".

108 Dugin (2012), p. 173.

different subject. While the subject of fascism was the racial state, and the subject of communism was class, the subject of liberalism is the atomised, isolated individual, freed from all historical and contextual bounds and roles; the "idiot", as the Greeks would have called it. Such "freedom from" is fictitious freedom, since it reveals itself as limited to the microscopic orbit of individuality as such, to the "small people" (the only ones that liberalism tolerates, revealing its totalitarian flip side). The hermeneutic circle of liberalism has the smallest orbit in comparison with the other two ideologies; within it, the small men are allowed to do anything they want, but they are actually made unable to do anything since they are deprived of the ability to interact with the world. To break this circle, anomic individuality has to be stricken; the individual has to be recontextualised, and thence reëndowed with meaning. Champions of liberalism, such as Karl Popper with his *The Open Society and its Enemies*, fought any kind of ideology that integrates the individual in supra-individual communities (even anachronistically labelling Plato and Aristotle as "totalitarian fascists").[109]

Real freedom, the "freedom for" (true *libertas*) that the Fourth Political Theory wants to bring into play once again, may be achieved by leaving the small circle of individuality. One who leaves individuality finds itself, at first, "crushed by the elements of life and by dangerous *Chaos*", and thence acquires the will and ability to establish order. Such a man may be embodied in individual forms; this is not anomic individuality, but rather "individuation"; not the fictitious liberty granted by the liberal machination, but liberty to act authentically, taming oneself and one's context. This is the *Dasein*.[110]

---

109 Ibidem, pp. 51-52.

110 Ibidem, p. 53.

1.2.1. GLOBALISM AND THE IMPLOSION OF TIMES

Dugin construes the *Dasein* as comprehending both Edmund Husserl's "transcendental subjectivity" and a deeper state of consciousness, which he calls "radical subjectivity" (or better "radical self"). In Husserlian terminology, transcendental subjectivity is the deep layer of the "subject" that emerges in the experience of the "short-circuit", the experience of the source of reality. Such experience is a trauma, in which consciousness perceives nothing else than itself in the present time, and is explained by Dugin as a tensional void. In order to escape the present and the unbearable confrontation with itself, self-referential pure present perception, and to discharge its tension, the transcendental subjectivity articulates as the Heideggerian three ecstasies of time (past, present, and future; Dugin ontologically characterises them as, respectively, "documentary", "immediate" and "probabilistic"), and at the same time in dual logics (yes-no, subject-object, before-after, and any other dualities that thread reality) and intentionality. Thus, time is the entity and the entity is time, the phenomenon is intrinsically temporal, and it is intrinsically future (projection); it is Kant's "thing as such" (*Ding an sich*) which establishes itself in "practical reason", Husserl's "continuous instance" and the metaphor of time as music (the past resonates in the present, which in turn projects the future), and Heidegger's "thrownness" (*Geworfenheit*).[111] It is the Italian philosopher and historian of religions Ernesto de Martino's "presentification", his own reading of the *Dasein* which emphasises its world-making activity.[112] It is also Jullien's "propensity", discussed hereinbefore.

111 Ibidem, pp. 156-160.

112 Ernesto de Martino laid the foundations for an enterprise very similar, in its purposes, to the present essay, with his unfinished (or open) *La fine del mondo* (1977), in which he compares the experience of the "dissolution of the world" in religious mysticism and psychopathological documentation, linking them to the experience of the structure of time, to rite as a device to restart it, and advancing interesting insights about the crisis of the West. Similarly to the present work, which finds a way for reintegration after the dissolution through Sinitic conceptual tools, De Martino proposes a new "integral humanism" as an overcoming of the religions of abstract theism.

The short-circuit of consciousness is an eternal refrain pattern, a return of the same, or a "circular time" in which past and future overlap, with the iity placed in the centre as the spring and doer of all times. Emerging out of this circular time, the three ecstasies may be interwoven in different ways, through the schemes of different looms. Dugin proposes three constructions of time: ① "traditional time", in which the short-circuit is placed in the past and is reëvoked through Platonic *anamnesis* and steadily reproduced in the present; ② "chiliastic time", in which the short-circuit is placed in the future, and history is a "perpetual state of waiting" for a future fulfilment; and ultimately ③ "material time", in which time melts in the objective world, which in turn is fixed. This last is the "time of slaughter" and the death of the subject.[113]

Consciousness needs the future in order to escape from the encounter with itself; otherwise, without a future as in the case of the frozen material time, the subject does not find space to extend itself, and it short-circuits. As already explained, this is at the same time the experience of death, of the primordial source of reality, but also of the potentiality of *novum*, of new construction.[114] Since the future is subjective, societies — as organisms, emerging spatiotemporally from different acts of consciousness and united by the "structures of the collective consciousness of the individuals" who belong to the "expanding forces of the constituent subject" — have their own distinguishing futures. What follows from this understanding is that "global humanity" as a whole (it itself an abstract concept) may not have an objective future.[115]

The "end of history", ultimately coming in the form of globalism (globalisation of liberal democracy), "the logical conclusion of universalism", erases history and abolishes the future. By blocking the future, space-time collapses in the present, short-circuits in a whirl that Dugin (building upon

113 Dugin (2012), p. 161.

114 Ibidem, pp. 158-160.

115 Ibidem, p. 162.

Husserl's metaphorisation of time as music) compares to a senseless cacophony in which all notes play simultaneously, ultimately being the same as absolute silence. In such a state there is no space for the temporalisation of the inner tension of the transcendental subjectivity, which grows exponentially towards a conflagration. According to Dugin, the forces of globalisation are trying to extinguish the *Dasein* in order to prevent the blaze, by trapping consciousnesses into the virtual web of a "world machine", ensnaring it in what he calls "simulacra" of the past, that is to say false, fabricated, unnatural memories. Future is thence petrified and semantics, which should say the truth of reality, "blur, fork and multiply"[116] in a loss of meaning, perversion of language and proliferation of lies which do not address the reality of things. For De Martino, "the repetition compulsion which in nature is without drama [...] in mankind manifests itself as psychic illness",[117] a whirl of inner and private descent, which in those societies provided with tradition is reintegrated in publicity by means of mytho-ritual symbolism; the latter is an operation of *imitatio naturae*, of remoulding the circle of the eternal return of nature within the spiral dynamic of a culturalising time, which frees human consciousness from matter, avoiding its petrification, establishing a being-in-the-world (the Heideggerian *in-der-Welt-Sein*), a common world,[118] and a syntonisation of all participating particular times into a greater time-being.

Then, Dugin introduces a deeper layer of the iity that Husserl did not reckon: the radical subject. While the transcendental subject establishes reality in the three times as a manifestation of its self-awareness, the radical subject, the deepest *Dasein*, shows itself only "in the moment of the ultimate historic catastrophe", the implosion of space-time,

116 Ibidem, pp. 164-166.

117 De Martino (1977), p. 223. Regarding the whirl of descent about which is described, it is worth noting that the logo of George Soros' Open Society Foundations, one of the promoters of worldwide liberalisation, has contained for long time a sinister vortex.

118 Ibidem.

in the strongest and longest short-circuit, enduring it. While the transcendental subjectivity reacts to the experience of the short-circuit by creating time, the radical subject reacts to it by withdrawing into non-time (the same as eternity), non-duality, and ultimately non-identity, since reality and time itself are, for it, a torturous trap. The radical subject, incompatible with any form of time, awaits the "end of history" (and of humanity, the last men) as its "drastic gesture", and the anti-time rebirth of the radical light.[119] The radical subject is the "first man", and the *novum*, remaining after the end.

---

119 Dugin (2012), pp. 167-168.

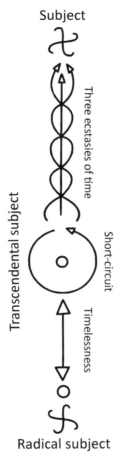

Figure 2: Representation of the structure of the iity according to Dugin. Up from below, there are the two modalities of *Dasein*, namely ① its deepest foundation, the "radical subjectivity" which dwells in timelessness/eternity, and ② the Husserlian "transcendental subjectivity". As explained hereinabove, the radical subjectivity withdraws within itself when it lives the short-circuit, manifesting itself only after the end of times as new light; the transcendental subjectivity, otherwise, while experiencing the short-circuit, escapes from the encounter with itself by projecting its experience in the three ecstasies of past, present, and future, according to dual logics. Such projection forms ③ steadfast subjectivities in space-time.

1.2.2. FINDING THE AETIOLOGY IN CHRISTIANITY SO AS TO SHED IT

Both Fukuyama and Jullien provide further evidence for tracing the rupture between human reason and the *Logos* well before the seventeenth century, back to ideas that were already present in early Christianity. Jullien focuses on the Western conception of liberty that has turned into an illusory absolutisation and hypertrophy of the iity, which, under the influence of Christianity, establishes itself as such by infringing the universal order. Jullien contrasts such hypertrophy with the attitude of availability and adjustment of the iity that is stressed in Sinitic philosophy. It consists in the ability to set oneself in harmony with the given situation, grasping the latter's patterns (*li*) and their potential for development.[120] This approach, which is not a passive renunciation of initiative but rather an active craft for prosperity, may also be described as openness — what Heidegger calls *Offenständigkeit*, staying open and letting things be what they are — to the perception of the dynamics that are at work in a given configuration of the world.[121]

Fukuyama, in the wake of Hegel and Nietzsche, defines Christianity as the "most prominent ideology of slavery" and the foundation of deceptive ideologies of indiscriminate freedom and equality useful for bridling masses of humble slaves.[122] Fukuyama clarifies, however, that in the historical Christian religion, which focused on otherworldliness, these principles remained unactualised. Equality merely consisted in all humans' possibility to have a direct relationship with God and in the abstract idea that all men are created equal; liberty merely consisted in one's willingness to engage in the relationship with God, choosing good over evil. Christianity paradoxically consists in the rejection of natural dignities and at the same time in the postponement of the complete realisation of equality. In other

---

120 Jullien (2016), pp. 27-37.

121 Ibidem, pp. 29-30.

122 Fukuyama (1992), p. 211.

words, Christianity at the same time rejects actual potentiality and drives the intelligence of individuals toward an otherworldly future, resulting in anomy and alienation.[123]

The problem of the decontextualisation of the iity and its hypertrophy within the framework of Christianity has been well-discussed by two British scholars, the anthropologist Roland Littlewood and the psychiatrist Simon Dein. In a joint work in which they highlight similarities between the Christian belief and the states of psychosis, schizophrenia in particular (i.e. the separation of the self from the world and the inner fragmentation of the self), they put forth the idea that Christianity itself may have given rise to schizophrenic psychoses in the Western world. Elements of the Christian modality of thought, including "a delocated omniscient deity, a decontexualised self, ambiguous agency, a downplaying of immediate sensory data, and a scrutiny of the self and its reconstitution in conversion", are the same found in schizophrenic psychopathologies.[124] According to Littlewood and Dein, the uprooting of the individual from context (the anomic internalised subject), the loss of the being-in-the-world, of the interaction with its potentialities, which leads to an illusory hypertrophic omnipotentisation of the iity and to its objectification of the world,[125] began in early Christianity, was reinforced with the Protestant Reformation and the secular processes which it triggered, including

---

123 Ibidem, p. 213.

124 Littlewood & Dein (2013), passim. According to the authors, Christianity consists in "[...] an emphasis on scrutinising and questioning the convoluted workings of a hidden and immaterial self, seen as distinct from other similar selves and from the natural world, now with private communication with an omniscient presence who already knows one's thoughts and emotions, and with ambiguous agency for personal actions and experience in the world which are no longer to be taken as tacit and unproblematic [...]".

125 Ibidem: "As agency is withdrawn from the natural world, from others, from animals, plants, stars, and spirits, our individual agency appears enhanced and yet there remains the uneasy balance between the 'is it me?' and the 'is it something external?'. Many external causes, spirits, and stars, not only no longer have agency but are no longer validated by our society, so any personal explanations of an external locus of control become increasingly idiosyncratic and divorced from our common social life."

industrial capitalism, and is fully concomitant with modern "Westernisation". Due to excessive self-analysis, to the internal splitting of the consciousness, and to its reconstitution only through the relationship with the "delocated and omniscient" God of Christianity, the individual loses "any sense of naturalness or capacity for spontaneous action, thus exacerbating self-alienation". After the loss of the world (worsened in modern industrialised societies, which are senseless as they have arisen from the Christian objectification of the world), the individual "is plunged into an idiosyncratic internalised experience, into a set of fragmented pluralistic alternatives in which the act of choice itself becomes problematic, and in which the individual self is increasingly restricted to its processes, indeed it itself becoming an object for scrutiny".[126]

Interestingly, Ernesto de Martino comes to similar insights in his unfinished work *La fine del mondo* (1977). Through his study of the different structures of time to which different religious worldviews give access, De Martino found that the modern West is subject to a loss of meaning (even on the plane of language, which always reflects the relationship between humanity and the world), psychopathological stiffening, sclerotisation of the system within a horizontal relativism, and a relativistic fragmentation launched into a linear materialist progress. He attributes this state of things to a "paradoxy" of time introduced by Christianity, that is the historicisation of myth and fixation of it in time (the life of Jesus, which is placed at the centre of history; the implosion of myth and history), which pretends to be the final solution of all being, thus blocking and ousting the creativity of the symbol (myth and rite), the device traditionally used to renovate time (the spiral time of traditional societies), and projecting a linear time, or teleological plan, waiting for an otherworldly "Kingdom of God", which, having utterly failed, has become secularised and has turned into a purposeless fall into material *Chaos*, a reification of becoming (historical time) bereft of being; the ultimate schizophrenia without possible

---

126 Ibidem.

reintegration; the "material time" of Dugin; the "end of the world", of the Western world.[127] As a recoagulation, De Martino proposed the establishment of an "integral humanism", both a "religion of man" and a new "unifying discipline which ever-renews itself in order to adapt to the ever-changing multiplicity", meant to overcome the Christian theological abstraction and its purposeless temporal projection, putting at the centre the *Dasein* as a "presentification", the conscious symbolising, time-renewing, space-ordering, world-making, cosmifying activity of the creative transcendental subject.[128] De Martino's outcomes are similar to those of the present essay: his integral humanism may be easily found in the man-centred and man-centring Sino-Ruist thought, while his idea of the presentification is similar to Dugin's conception of the return of the *Logos* as *Dasein* in the *Ereignis*, as it is explained further onwards in the present essay.

The actualisation of indiscriminate freedom and equality, which crush differences and breed horizontal amorphous masses, occurred with the secularisation of Christianity, triggered by the diabolic (even by name) "Protestantism", and the incorporation of its principles into modern political theory.[129] The fathers of liberalism were regurgitations of the Protestant nations. Thomas Hobbes postulated the "right to life" as the foundation of equality, reducing the value of human life to mere survival. Hobbes ousted any holy and moral foundation from his hypothesis of the social contract and excluded any dynamism of reciprocal difference and recognition from his idea of social peace as a common interest.[130] At the same time, while his ideal state continued to be a monarchy, Hobbes rejected any idea of divine legitimacy and laid the foundations of democracy, by introducing the principle of election through popular consensus.[131]

---

127 De Martino (1977), pp. 294-296, 311-321, 329-335, 466-470, 472-474 & 482-483.

128 Ibidem, pp. 327, 332, 351-353, 356-357, 396-397, 406-407 & 412-413.

129 Fukuyama (1992), p. 214.

130 Ibidem, pp. 174-175.

131 Ibidem, p. 175.

John Locke, who refined the thesis of the social contract, introduced the model of parliamentary sovereignty based on an electoral majority. Furthermore, Locke postulated that the primary propellant of man is not simply survival, but material wealth and accumulation — the right of possession. These principles, based on mere material quantity and excluding any spiritual quality for measuring human life and its sense, are the foundations of liberal democracy.[132]

Such fundamental errors were already contained in early Christianity with its fixation of the *Logos* in space-time, and its claim to be the only way to a delocated God for all humanity. It was one of the directions of Gnosticism, the dissolution and transformation of ideas that took place in the critical Late Antiquity, during the collapse of the Roman Empire. However, those errors were prevented from becoming practice as the psychotic crisis was gradually reintegrated when "Christianity" was created as a newly established religion unifying all previously existing religions and movements of thought, first at the hands of the Roman emperors by the fourth century CE and then throughout the Germanic Middle Ages. Roman Catholicism (i.e. Roman Universalism), thus, as the stabilised outcome of the Gnostic transition — which mixed traditional state theology with the original Christian ideas, Jewish, Hellenistic, Zoroastrian, and even Buddhist ideas which had penetrated the Roman world —, may be interpreted a recoalescence of society and a new vision of the world, a "mazeway resynthesis", which took shape during the collapse of the Roman Empire, and also became the essential character of the medieval Germanic civilisation. The fundamental errors contained in the original Christian theology remained dormant, to become manifest only in modernity, when Christianity revealed its true face, fully transmuting into (or reverting into) the *Sklavenmoral* harshly criticised by Nietzsche.

---

132 Ibidem, p. 177.

1.2.3. THE TENACITY OF CONFUCIAN CIVILISATIONS

Fukuyama acknowledges the moral tenacity of certain East Asian cultures, even of those which have adopted liberal democracy, as a condition that sharply contrasts with the degeneration haunting Western cultures. These Eastern cultures, Fukuyama observes, are those historically or even today influenced by Confucianism, and they have been able to integrate Western models of development with indigenous cultures.[133] Western modes of production combined with Confucian work ethics and embedded in traditional communities have resulted in outstanding economic growth that has not implied erosion of morality. Rather, in Confucian societies, economic growth and traditional morality corroborate one another, as in the Greek concept of *oikonomía* (οἰκονομία).[134] These societies are characterised by hierarchical, patriarchal structures, and individuals are entrusted from birth to the care of community networks and concentric and correlated groups, stretching from the microcosm of the extended family to the macrocosm of the ethnic community and the nation.[135]

In other words, these societies are organically structured; individuals and their groups functionally participate in a wider organism. Fukuyama recognises that European civilisation itself, in the past, was structured according to similar patriarchal models.[136] Fukuyama foresees that if Western cultures continue on their road to moral disintegration and individual atomisation in the name of liberal ideologies, the outcome will be their

---

133 Ibidem, pp. 253-254.

134 The meaning of "morality" and *nomos* is discussed later. Here is important to note how in the West, in line with the degeneration of language, "morality" and even "economy" have become abstract concepts and have lost their original meaning. "Economy" in the West is no longer perceived as a synonym of "family", as in the Greek original *oikonomía* (οἰκονομία), but as an unembedded, abstract, concept for the processes of production, consumption and chrematistic accumulation.

135 Fukuyama (1992), pp. 254-255.

136 Ibidem, p. 255.

economic breakdown, and Eastern models of political authority will emerge as viable alternatives to postliberal wreckage.[137]

Fukuyama fine-tuned such observations throughout the 1990s and 2000s, witnessing the unrestrainable crisis of liberal democracies and the economic rise of China. In his 1995 short essay *Confucianism and Democracy*, he argues that Confucianism, with its emphasis on education and meritocracy, has the potential to accommodate egalitarian stances and democratic political forms. This would be especially true for Chinese Confucianism, whose doctrine of the "Mandate of Heaven" legitimises or delegitimises political authority on the basis of its efficiency or deficiency in upholding morality to make the social organism thrive, and leaves open space for the spontaneous development of grassroots civil society, as opposed to Japanese Neo-Confucianism which incorporates the doctrine of the divine right of the unbroken imperial dynasty, which is at the same time the foundation of a monolithic national identity that takes precedence over local and kinship identities.[138] Fukuyama acknowledges Confucianism's potential to build "well-ordained societies from the ground up, rather than the top down", articulating a hierarchy of concentric groups that starting from the familial and local authority rise up to the highest authorities of the social body.[139] The German Confucian philosopher Thorsten J. Pattberg, in his *The East-West Dichotomy* (2009), argues that the East is characterised by a prevalence of inductive thinking (i.e. from the many to the one; seeing eternal unity always operating in plurality, thus integrating many truths, continuous articulations of the unity, as parts of the whole), while the West by a prevalence of deductive thinking (i.e. from the one to the many; explaining plurality as a departure from the unity, thus accepting just one truth and its linear development in time, and exclusively its line of time, denying other ones).[140]

---

137 Ibidem, pp. 258-259.

138 Fukuyama (1995), p. 3.

139 Ibidem.

140 Pattberg (2009), pp. 17-18.

As I clarify later in my essay, the Sino-Ruist conception of political authority is more complex than what it appears to be in Fukuyama's analysis. Chinese and Japanese Confucianism represent two manifestations of the same system of ideas. In Japan, what I have previously introduced as the *Li*, or the *Logos*, is incarnated by the emperor (Japanese: 天皇 *Ten'nō*, "Ruler of Heaven"), who as such gathers and represents the national society as one body; and he is such because the imperial kin is the genealogical point of convergence of all kins. In historical Chinese Confucianism and broader Ruism, the *Logos* maintains its dynamic policentricity and manifoldness, since it is embodied by different entities, in different ways, in different spatiotemporal conditions. Chinese Confucianism is therefore an always-adapting open system.

In his most recent works, Fukuyama dedicates attention to Russia and especially China as political entities that have risen as powerful rivals of liberal democratic polities. In *Political Order and Political Decay* (2014) he writes that China with her "two-millennia-long tradition of strong centralised government [...] never to have developed an indigenous tradition of rule of law" (the indiscriminate legal positivism, disconnected from the order of Heaven and thus bereft of any higher sense and meaning, of the Western liberal states) poses "the most serious challenge to the idea that liberal democracy constitutes a universal evolutionary model".[141]

Sinitic culture is not only one of the oldest uninterrupted traditions of human society, but it is also constantly changing and renewing itself by drawing from and reinventing its historical heritage and spiritual source. From the perspective of Spenglerian and Traditionalist philosophy, the extraordinarily hardwearing Sinitic culture may be regarded as a reservoir of knowledge about the practice of civilisation. Noteworthily,

---

141 Fukuyama (2014), pp. 542-543. Regarding the development of the "Chinese Model" (of economy) in Central Asia and potentially elsewhere see Fukuyama's article "Exporting the Chinese model" (5 January 2016) published on *Project Syndicate*'s 2015 Year-End Supplement (12 January 2016), and on *New Europe* (10 November 2016).

the Chinese concept usually rendered as "culture", 文化 *wénhuà*, expresses the idea of an ever-living and ever-changing organism.[142] The grapheme 文 *wén* means "writing/literature", "rite", "character" and "natural phenomenon", and as a verb it means "to paint", implying the idea of a constructive activity that comes from nature and is reproduced and confirmed by humanity; the grapheme 化 *huà*, means "to turn/to transform", and belongs to the phonetic series and semantic field of 花 *huā*, which means "flower(ing)" and "to invest". The same De Martino wrote that a "culture is such to the extent that it guarantees the possibility of initiatives, innovations, readjustments or reshapings at the hands of single individuals more gifted than others", and every true culture is threatened by its petrification in a codified system, close and dead.[143]

Articulate condemnations of liberal democracy, together with alternative political models which may replace it, have been put forward by many contemporary Ruist thinkers. Such models and their potential functionality for the regeneration of European civilisation are the subjects of fourth chapter of this essay.

1.3. INITIATING THE DECONSTRUCTION OF WESTERN THOUGHT

1.3.1. RECOVERING THE ORIGINAL MEANING OF REASON: THE *AR* ROOT, INDICATING ALIGNMENT WITH HEAVEN

If names be not correct, language is not in accordance with the truth of things. If language be not in accordance with the truth of things, affairs cannot be carried on to success. When affairs cannot be carried on to success, proprieties and music do not flourish. When proprieties and music do not flourish, punishments will not be properly awarded. When punishments are not properly awarded, the people do not know how to move hand or foot. Therefore a superior man considers it necessary that

---

142 Jullien (2016), p. 267.

143 De Martino (1977), p. 175.

the names he uses may be spoken appropriately, and also that what he speaks may be carried out appropriately. What the superior man requires is just that in his words there may be nothing incorrect.

Confucius[144]

Sinitic philosophy relates the corruption of society to that of language, and to the loss of the meaning of names. Confucius sees language corruption as a consequence of the separation of the human mind from the order of the universe. When names are inappropriate, they fail to address things and things do not reveal themselves for what they are, men do not know how to relate to things and to one another, and ultimately actions are blocked and may not be accomplished. This is based on the belief that the etymological composition of words demarks accurately the natural formation of the things that they signify. The treatment prescribed by Confucius for healing the corruption of language is the "rectification of names" (正名 zhèngmíng), which may be likened to the practice of etymological analysis, reconstruction, and interpretation; in one word, the "redeeming"[145] of things. This section deals with the redemption of reason.

Etymologically, the term "Reason", a Latinate from *Ratio* (in the sense of "order", "rule"; "ration" and "race" are alterations of the same word) or *Oratio* ("word", "speech", cf. the verbal *ōrō*, *ōrāre*, but also "kind" and "style"), comes from the Indo-European root *her-, *hreh-. The latter primarily means a "movement" aimed at "putting together properly", whence the derivative meaning of "well composed" or "well joined". Such root is otherwise spelled *Ar* or simply *R-*, and refers to the principle and mode of unfolding of the universe. It continues in modern German *Ur* ("Origin"), in *Er*, or in *Or*, the latter contained as the radical element in many Greco-Latinate words. It is therefore the same concept expressed by the Hellenic *Logos* or *Nous*.

---

144 Excerpt from the *Analects* (book XIII, chapter 3, verses 4-7) in the translation of James Legge (1815-1897), published in 1861 and revised in a second edition published in 1893.

145 In English, "to deem" is the verbal form of "doom", destiny, and related to the verb "to do" and to "deed", as analysed in the first section of this first chapter of the essay (1.1.1).

Specialised through various suffixes, the *Ar* root gives rise to many words of common usage that originally have a cosmic and axial significance.[146] There are, for instance, the Latin *ordō* ("order"), as well as *ars, artis* ("art"), *artus* ("fit", "apt", "appropriate", "right time"), *arma* ("tool/device/gear", "weapon/defensive arm", "armour") and *rītus* ("rite"), and also, significantly, the verbs *orior, orīrī* ("to rise") — which begets *orīgō* ("origin"), *ortus* ("risen", "sprung", "appeared") and *oriēns* ("east/orient", "daybreak"; meaning "rising", "originating" when used as a participle) — and *arō, arāre* ("to plough").

In the Greek language, there are *Arkhḗ* (Ἀρχή, "beginning/ origin") and *Orthótes* (Ὀρθότης, "rightness"; cf. also the adjective ὀρθός *orthós*, "right") — uppercase when meaning the origin and order of the cosmos — and all their derivatives such as "archaic", the prefix "arch(i)-", and *hierárkhēs* (ἱεράρχης, "holy principle"), and also *armonía* (ἁρμονία), *arithmós* (ἀριθμός, "number", "rhyme", "right time"), and *aretḗ* (ἀρετή, "virtue"), the latter being the quality of the *áristoi* (ἄριστοι; a superlative meaning "the rightest/the best").[147]

In Germanic languages, one of the branches of **hreh-* produces all the words pertaining to the semantic field of "right" (straight, correct, appropriate movement and direction, appropriately ordered behaviour, juridical right) and "rich" (originally it itself meaning "to be right"). The same stem, in Latin, produces the verbal *rego, regere, rēxī, rectum* ("to rule, to reign, to righten, to straighten"), and the noun *rex* ("king").[148]

In Vedic Sanskrit, the root **her-* produces ऋत *R̥tá*, otherwise spelled *Rita* or *Arta*, the second form being the Iranian rendition, and

---

146 For *Ar* and its derivatives see Pokorny (1959), p. 55 ff: **ar-*; p. 59: *reor, ratio*; p. 67: **ario-*; pp. 326-327: **er-, *or-, *r-*, av. **ar-*; Watkins (2000), p. 5: **ar-*. Also see: Pianigiani (1907), entries: *ario, aristocrazia, arte, ordine, oriente, origine, orto2, reggere, ricco.*

147 The Greek word *aristoi* has its most appropriate rendition in modern Western languages as "aryan", a term today shunned by mass ideologies, which is a relatively recent borrowing from Vedic Sanskrit: आर्य *ārya*, which corresponds to the Latin *arius*. As one of the derivatives of the root *Ar* it means "one who moves in a fitting manner (in accordance with *Ar*)", "artful". Also see: Mahony (1998), p. 3.

148 Pokorny (1959), pp. 854-857 ff: **reg-, *rek-*.

ऋतु *ṛtú*, referring to the "right timing" for sacrificing in attunement with the *Rita*. The latter has preserved, in Vedic literature, its original meaning of "Holy Reason" or "Holy Right",[149] and in later religious literature was replaced by the concept of *Dharma* (the cosmic "Law"; Latin *Firmus, Firma*), which originally indicates a mere specialisation of the *Rita*. William K. Mahony corroborates the meaning of "moving in a fitting manner", and highlights its relation to "rites" interpreted as movements that dramatically establish order in space-time. He defines the *Rita* as the way of things coming together in a "structured yet dynamic whole".[150] As I clarify in the following sections and chapters, this cosmic Reason, the *Logos*, is the second person of a triune vision of the God of Heaven shared by all the cultures of Eurasia, and the attunement with such Reason, implying to be right and thus prosper, means to steer human activities in vertical accord with the time of Heaven.

1.3.2. DESTROYING THE CHRISTIAN CONCEPTION OF THE *LOGOS* BY RECOVERING THE GNOSTIC *KTISMA*

As seen hereinbefore, Christianity arose in the fourth century as a codification of the Gnostic climate of Late Antiquity. Once the Roman Empire had defined the official creed, all other religions, traditions of thought, and alternative Gnostic and Christian doctrines, were outlawed and suppressed. These included alternative conceptions of the *Logos*, even intended as Christ, that differed from the official one, which, as I have enunciated, enshrined the errors of exclusivity and spatiotemporal fixation which have led to the pathological sclerotisation and degeneration of Western thought. In this part of the essay, I propose to demolish the sclerotised Christian conception of the *Logos* as a historicised spatiotemporal person by mining its foundations, illustrating how a Gnostic cosmological polycentric conception of the *Logos*, the *Ktisma*, was shared even

---

149 Pokorny (1959), p. 56: **rt-, *art-*.

150 Mahony (1998), p. 3.

by the officially anti-Gnostic Fathers of the Church, including the Meso-Platonic Origen of Alexandria (184/185-253/254).

An excerpt from Origen's *Commentary on John* (1:22) says:[151]

> Now God is altogether one and simple, but our Savior, for many reasons, since God set Him forth as a propitiation and a first fruit of the whole creation, is made of many things, or perhaps all these things; the whole creation, so far as capable of redemption, stands in need of Him.

What is described in these lines is a conception of the Christ as the word of God that enlivens the many things of creation and at the same time, is composed of the many things of creation. The Christ shows itself in created things and renews those things which need it and are capable of receiving its redemption. In *Homilies on Jeremiah* (9:4) and other works of Origen's, we read that God continually generates the *Logos*, and that creation is an eternally ongoing process. The *Logos* is eternally at work in the multiplicity of things, and is not "a thought in the mind of God" as described by Philo and Justin.[152]

Amongst contemporary Western thinkers, there are some who attempt to move beyond a static logic and anthropocentric conception of the cosmos, identifying the divine not with something ontologically determined but rather as a power that inspires lines of transformation, enabling new coherences among humans and other entities.[153] Some theologians have recovered the Gnostic concept of the *Logos* as *Ktisma*, also present in Origen, which means "creation/created thing", "building", or "foundation".[154] Patricia Cox Miller defines it as "God's binding structure in which all things are made new".[155] The *Ktisma* represents what Luke B. Higgins calls a "cosmology of transformation".[156]

---

151 Higgins (2010), p. 141.

152 Bargeliotes (1972), p. 206.

153 Higgins (2010), p. 141.

154 Ibidem, p. 144.

155 Cox Miller (2001), p. 115.

156 Higgins (2010), passim. Higgins provides "a Deleuze-Guattarian reading of the ancient Christian *Logos*".

In Origen's terms, the *Logos*, the Christ, occupies a mediatory position between the unity of God and the dynamic multiplicity of creation. In Meso-Platonic terms, the *Logos* organises itself as a natural hierarchy in which creatures emerge on different levels according to their ability to relate to God and be in its likeness. The Gnostic *Ktisma* is not an ontological monolith but rather a dynamic cosmological architecture, a dynamic ontology within which souls condense into different directions and places and combine with various material media, driven by their own choice of what they want to become, as well as by their own impulses and merits.[157]

The *Ktisma* is the image of God, in turn, composed of multiple images of it itself. It is a multifaceted manifestation of God, articulated in spiral layers of "rooms", "spheres", or "dwellings" through which souls move. Souls are engaged in a pedagogical journey of self-transformation through the experience of the various spheres, proceeding threshold by threshold to get closer to God's perfection. In each sphere, they must understand a particular facet of divinity and their own nature. Spiritual perfectibility consists in an intensification of psychophysical coherence, that is to say, in an increasing functional harmony of one's mental and bodily parts, and at the same time an increasing freedom to move through the layers of the *Ktisma*, and an increasing ability to understand, incorporate and manage its various elements. This increasing coherentisation of oneself and one's context means to get closer and closer to the *Logos'* perfection.[158]

Higgins compares the Gnostic *Ktisma* to Gilles Deleuze and Félix Guattari's cosmology of the "Plane of Consistency", made up of various "plateaus", which represent the receptacles or crossroads where all directions and concrete forms intersect in a "rhizome". He defines this conception of the *Logos* as an "intensive architecture of the manifold", where structural oppositions generate intensities and dynamics of transformation. Much like

157 Ibidem, pp. 142-144.

158 Ibidem, pp. 144-147.

in the Gnostic theory of the *Ktisma*, in the Plane of Consistency, material differences are means of transformation, the vehicles for approaching the ultimate "Body without Organs", and are not to be rejected for the sake of whatsoever presumed transcendent abstraction. A complete "deterritorialisation" (i.e. anomy and uprooting) brings the breakdown of all intensities opening the way to a deadly "black hole".[159]

According to Higgins, the Gnostic *Ktisma* and the Deleuze-Guattarian Plane of Consistency provide an understanding of the *Logos* or *Lógos Spermatikós* (Λόγος Σπερματικός), in the Stoic definition, as a scattered "Germinal Word" which works as a polycentric receptacle of connections of multiplicity.[160] These conceptions are very similar to the Sinitic cosmological models that I unfurl in the next chapters; the difference is that Sinitic models are polycentric and yet not horizontal, but vertically, polarly hoisted; hinged at the northern top of the sky.

Indeed, Aleksandr Dugin criticises postmodern post-structuralist philosophers like Deleuze and Guattari, and especially their concepts such as the rhizome and the Body without Organs (a term coined by the playwright Antonin Artaud), representing the underlying not yet functionally differentiated oneness, as a "mockery of Heidegger's *Dasein*"; they offer multiple ingangs and outgangs for the representation and interpretation of knowledge, but they do not provide a verticality, rather emphasising the diffusion of polarity and the horizontality of the ensuing schizoid "rhizomatic dusts" of fragmented humanity.[161] They are symptomatic of a "loss of Heaven".

---

159 Ibidem, p. 148.

160 Ibidem, p. 151.

161 Dugin (2012), pp. 171 & 182-183.

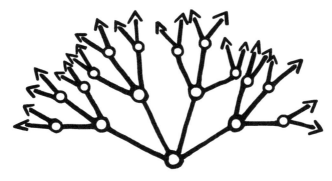

Figure 3: Representation of the morphology of time and truth in Sinitic thought (above: unity articulates in a multiplicity of truths which reflect it by adapting it to diverse spatiotemporal contexts) and Western thought (below: truth is one and has a monolinear development in time), according to Thorsten J. Pattberg's descriptions.

1.3.3. THE MESOPOTAMIAN CONNECTION: THE COMMON ROOTS OF SINITIC AND INDO-EUROPEAN THOUGHT

John C. Didier, whose treatise *In and Outside the Square* (2009) is the primary source of inspiration for the third chapter of my essay, writes in the wake of Sino-Babylonianism, the school of academic research according to which the Sinitic civilisation directly originated from the diffusion of Mesopotamian culture.[162] Didier finds a common "centre-plus-

---

162 On the basis of these presuppositions, Eurasian Universism might find declination even in a recovery of Mesopotamian religio-cosmology, especially as an interpretative platform wherefrom to start for the reunderstanding of the meaning of Indo-European traditions. Zuism, or Mesopotamian Neopaganism, has already found expression since the 1960s and 1970s among Hungarian groups led by Turanist ideologues and Assyriologists such as Ferenc Badiny Jós, the author of the *Magyar Biblia* (1985) of Hungarian Zuism, during the same years with the development of the Gate-Walking rituals based on the *Simon Necronomicon* (1977) and its later ancillary manuals published in the United States, since the mid 2000s in Mardukite (Babylonian) Zuism, developed by the American philosopher and esotericist Joshua Free, among groups in Israel (professing the Canaanite, West Semitic versions of the religion), and even in Iceland (where in 2013 it was officially recognised by the state as a legitimate religion).

agency structure" that "ancient proto-Chinese and Chinese may have inherited from a transmitted Sumerian-Babylonian religion".[163] This transmission may have occurred from the 4th millennium BC onwards, mediated by the migrations of the Indo-Europeans. Such spiritual knowledge is ultimately shared by a common pan-Eurasian religion,[164] whose most ancient core is to be found in the myths of Siberia.[165]

In this Eurasian religio-cosmological knowledge, the supreme God of Heaven is identified as the north celestial pole, "the creative source of all energy and thus also the patriarch of the entire cosmos"; specifically, the ecliptic North Pole of the sky when representing the God's quiescent and hidden aspect — in the European tradition corresponding to the *Empyrium*, and in the Indian one to the *Brahma-loka* ("Place of Brahma") or "Solar Gate" —, and the precessional North Pole of the sky and the seven-stars constellations of the Dippers (also known as the Chariots or the She-bears) revolving around it when representing the God's active and manifested aspect or offspring which "helps as an agent to produce and/or govern further evolutionary developments of the cosmos" — in the European tradition it is the *Elysium*, and in the Indian one the *Svarga* or *Indra-loka* ("Place of Indra"), or the "Lunar Gate".[166] A third aspect is the earthly manifestation of the God of Heaven, embodied by the sovereign of a celestially-ordered civilisation, the father of a celestially-ordered family, and the same generative spirit of the individuals. The sovereign (as we have seen, the

---

163 Didier (2009), vol. I, p. ix.

164 Ibidem, vol. III, p. 257 ff.

165 Ibidem, vol. III, p. 264. Aleksandr Dugin, in his writings about Siberia, identifies the Sumerians as having originated from the Turanian (Finno-Ugrian and Turko-Mongol, or more broadly Uralo-Altaic) branch of the Aryans, who ultimately came from Siberia. The most ancient Turanian/Siberian traditions are the most essential "right way" (shortest but dangerous, not walkable by everyone) to the North Pole, very similar to the sacral models of pre-Vedic and pre-Zoroastrian Indo-Europeans (especially the Germanics, and especially the Goths amongst the Germanics), but also to the earliest layers of Sino-Tibetan sacral models. See: Dugin (1992), pp. 27-35 & 128-132.

166 Ibidem.

74

Latin *rex*, bringer of divine Reason; the etymology of the Germanic word "king", as well as that of the broader concept of "emperor", are explained further onward in the essay[167]) is the shaft of transmission between Heaven and Earth, the axle of the world (*axis mundi*), whose grace-giving active force enlightens darkness and ousts wicked forms of being (rectifying being).[168] The second aspect is identified as the *Logos*, the Reason (*Ratio*) and Word (*Oratio*) of God, which is the mode of development of things according to the patterns of Heaven, while the third is the *Anima Mundi* ("World Soul"), the earthly reflected image of the *Logos*.[169] In this section, I highlight the precise correspondences which may be found between the Mesopotamian, the Sinitic, and cursorily also the Indo-European and broader Eurasian religio-cosmological traditions; the Sinitic and Indo-European concepts are further treated throughout the entire essay.

In the Mesopotamian tradition — that is to say Sumerian religious culture, later continued by the Semitic peoples with whom the Sumerians intermingled — the supreme power of the ecliptic North Pole, the God of Heaven in its quiescent and hidden aspect, is ✳ *An* ("Heaven"; also vocalised *Dingir*, "Deity", similar to the Siberian *Tengri*, *Tenger*; *Anu* or *Ilu/El* in Semitic), identified as manifesting itself as the entire vault of the sky. As the north ecliptic pole is coiled by the constellation of the Dragon (*Draco*), *An* is also identified as the Dragon itself.[170] The precise equivalent in Sinitic thought is 天 *Tiān* ("Heaven"), (*Shàng*)*dì* (上)帝 (["Supreme"] "Deity"), or 口 *Dīng* ("Square"), having the same astral correspondences as in Mesopotamia, as explained further onward in the essay.[171] As enunciated by the Finnish Assyriologist Simo Parpola, the Mesopotamian tradition, at least in its Assyrian variation, also conceives a pre-Heaven or hyper-Heaven, a wholly transcendent, unmanifest

---

167 Section 3.3.1 of the present essay.

168 Mander (2011), pp. 16-18.

169 Ibidem, p. 6.

170 Vv.Aa. (1951), pp. 300-301.

171 Section 3.1 of the present essay.

and unknowable aspect of *An*, ✴ — ᭠Ѱ *Ashur* or ✴ ● *Anshar*, which Parpola translates as "Whole Heaven", "God as Many", "Flowing One", while the sky vault would be its reflection as *An* in the flesh, the proceeding as the "tree of life" in all entities and most perfectly in the body of the sovereign.[172] *Anshar* may be compared to the Sinitic concept of 一 *Yī*, the transcendental "One" already discussed by the Warring States (5th to 3rd century BCE) and Qin-Han theology (3rd century BCE to 3rd century CE).[173]

The Mesopotamian grapheme ✴ *An* is the "Gate of God" or "Gate of Heaven" (𒅗 ✴ 𒊏 *Ka.dingir.ra* in Sumerian, *Babilu* in Akkadian; later *Ianua Caeli* in Latin), a designation analogous to 天门 *Tiānmén*, one of the Chinese names of the north celestial pole,[174] otherwise called 天樞 *Tiānshū* ("Pivot of Heaven"),[175] and is also equivalent of the pan-Eurasian 卍 swastika (*wàn* in the Chinese language, alternatively represented by the grapheme 萬, meaning "myriad", a metaphor for "all things" and "universe"). They are all representations of the constellations of the north celestial pole, and at the same time of the unmovable centre of all things, still and not affected by the entropic flows of chaotic matter, yet giving order to it.[176] The Mesopotamian grapheme is also analogous to the eight-arrows star symbol of Dugin's Neo-Eurasianism and of the Fourth Political Theory. It represents "the compass, something that provides orientation, introducing order in the seemingly chaotic space", and is ultimately a geometric symbol of the universe, of orthodoxy, verticality, and deification.[177]

The Italian Assyriologist Pietro Mander explains that ✴ *An* means "Heaven", but also more general "divinity" (*dingir* in Sumerian, *ilum* in Akkadian), and also has the meanings of

---

172 Parpola (1993), p. 191, note 113 & pp. 206-207.

173 For further insights see the section 3.2.1 of the present essay.

174 Reiter (2007), p. 190.

175 Milburn (2016), p. 343, note 17.

176 Dugin (1992), p. 144; Didier (2009), vol. I, pp. 257-259; vol. III, p. 256.

177 Nad (2014), passim.

"spike", "cluster", "petiole", and is frequently interpreted as meaning "star", "asterism", though this, *mul* in Sumerian, is more precisely represented by doubling (✳ ✳) or tripling the *An* grapheme. On a philosophical level, its most appropriate rendition is "centre of irradiation" and "navel of the world" (a concept treated by Mircea Eliade), which emanates the web of the world, which connects all things; it is the sacred centre shared by all entities. This is well represented by the Sumerian figurative meanings of the spike composed of many spikelets, the bunch of grapes, and the petiole from which the fruit (metaphor of the world) hangs.[178] As highlighted later in the essay, the Sinitic grapheme 帝 *Dì* has identical etymological meanings as the footstalk of a fruit or an inflorescence.

As aforeseen, the second aspect of the God of Heaven, active and manifested, is identified as the precessional North Pole, or the pole star (currently α *Ursae Minoris*) and the constellations spinning around it (the Big and Little Dipper, also called the Great and Small Chariot or the Great and Little She-bear, *Ursa Major* and *Ursa Minor*),[179] functioning as a proxy of the unmanifested, unintelligible supreme pole. In the Mesopotamian tradition, this second aspect is 𒂗𒇸 *Enlil* (*Ellil* or *Bel/Baal* in Semitic), meaning the "Lord of Breath/Spirit", who is forthwith identified as the *Logos*, the "Universal Intellect", by Mander.[180] The 𒇸 *Lil* is the "Breath", the "Spirit", the power of the *Logos*, thus also the magical "Word" (*Utu* 𒌓, which is also the Sun in the Mesopotamian tradition) begetting, shaping and linking all things, which is also the human power of "naming" entities, forging their fate.[181] It is also analogised with the Greek concept

---

178 Mander (2011), pp. 5-6.

179 In medieval Germanic culture also called, respectively, the Man's Wain or Charles' Wain (*karl* in Norse, or *churl* in English, is a Germanic concept of free man; *Karl* is also another name of Thor, and with the Carolingian dynasty of the Frankish Empire [481-888] was identified as the emperor Charlemagne [747-814]), or *Irmin*'s Wain in older times and among non-Christianised Saxons (*Irmin* being another name of Odin), and the Woman's Wain. See: Allen (1963), pp. 419-460, where the author explains the symbolisms of *Ursa Major* and *Ursa Minor*.

180 Mander (2011), p. 6.

181 Ibidem, pp. 6 & 12.

of *pneuma*, as the *Lil* is also the substance of which all things are made, which connects Heaven and Earth; especially the substance of reality in its shifting state prior to any formal coalescence.[182] In the Sinitic tradition, *Enlil* corresponds to the Yellow Deity (黄帝 *Huángdì*), the chief manifestation of the supreme God of Heaven at the North Pole, who is both the Thunder God and the Sun God, central master of the four directions, cosmogenic organiser of space-time, the axle of the world, model of the sage. The Mesopotamian *Lil* is the same as the Sinitic concept of 理 *Lǐ* or 天理 *Tiānlǐ*, the "Reason of Heaven", which informs all things, and also when intended as the substance of reality, the same as the 氣 *qì*, the "psychophysical stuff". The seven stars (*septemtriones*) of the Dipper constellations (or, to better say, the Chariots, as they are represented as the "Chariots of God" in pan-Eurasian mysticism), both in the Mesopotamian and the Sinitic tradition, are identified as the operating powers of the God of Heaven's *Logos*, associated to the seven planets of the Sun system, that is five planets plus the two luminaries, the Sun itself and the Moon, representing seven planes of ascension towards the God of Heaven, and personified as seven gods (*Anunnaki* in Mesopotamia).[183]

The third aspect of the God of Heaven, which as we have seen is the *Logos* coming in the flesh, the *Anima Mundi*, manifesting itself as the sovereign, the father and even the generative spirit of the individual, functioning as the bridge between Heaven and Earth, the antenna for the communication of the order of Heaven to human society,[184] is 𒀭𒂗𒆠 *Enki* (*Ea* or *Ya* in Semitic) in the Mesopotamian tradition, meaning the "Lord of the Earth/Squared Earth", the god of craft and production, the fish-god shaper of the waters of primordial matter, as well as god of the male spermatic power (he is the

---

182 Kramer (1956), p. 47.

183 Kasak & Veede (2001), *passim*. Also see: Didier (2009), vol. I, pp. 113-119. The seven deities and their associations are deepened in the section 3.3.3 of the present essay.

184 Mander (2011), p. 18.

god with the erected phallus), personified by the sovereign *lugal* (the "great man"). The latter corresponds to the general Sinitic concept of 王 *wáng* ("ruler", "king") — which, as explained later in the essay, is a concept related to the knowledge and practice of heavenly craft — and to the polysignifying concept of 皇帝 *huángdì*, the "divus emperor" of a celestially-ordered kingdom, whose graphic and phonetic etymology gives the meaning of a perfect *wang* who fully impersonates the central Yellow Deity. The concept also corresponds, on the level of the family and the social group, to the *zǔ* 祖, the Sinitic idea of patriarchal ancestrality. In broader religio-cosmological symbolism, the Mesopotamian *Enki* corresponds to the Red Deity (赤帝 *Chìdì*) or Fiery Deity (炎帝 *Yándì*), or Divine Farmer/Factor (神农 *Shénnóng*), the god of humanity, craft and agriculture in Sinitic religious culture.

As seen in the first section of this first chapter, according to the Sinitic tradition, the potency of Heaven manifests itself in space as fourfold directionality, i.e. the four directions, identified as 風 *fēng*, "winds", but also described as 方 *fāng*, a concept with the multiple meanings of "square", "phase", "direction", "way" and "power", and having complex historical and cosmological implications further elucidated later in the essay.[185] These four "faces" correspond to the Mesopotamian *lamassu* who manifest and protect the *Logos*, the fulgor of God descending from the axle of the world, as illustrated by Mander, as four forms of being: the divine man, the bull, the lion and the eagle. The same fourfold cosmology was later reformulated in Biblical literature and in the Christian religion as the Four Evangelists (Mark, Matthew, Luke, John),[186] corresponding to the Four Archangels (Michael, Gabriel, Raphael, Uriel) part of the Seven Archangels (the seven gods of the Eurasian tradition), and is also bewritten in John's *Apocalypse*; in earlier Hebrew literature this cosmology is found expressed as the Jewish mysticism of the *Merkabah* (הבכרמ; the "Chariot"),

---

185 Section 3.1.1 of the present essay.

186 Mander (2011), p. 10.

Hayyoth (חיות; the four "Forms of Being") and *Heikhaloth* (תולכיה; the seven "Palaces" or "Halls" of God).

In the Mesopotamian tradition, the Earth, or the material plane which Heaven impregnates with its forms, is 𒆠 *ki*. The analogous Sinitic concept is 地 *dì*, or 地方 *dìfāng* ("squared Earth") when cosmically wrought by the power of Heaven. The concept of "cosmos", ordered world or space-time, is expressed in the Mesopotamian tradition as the union of "Heaven-Earth", 𒀭 𒆠 *Anki*,[187] which finds a precise equivalence in the Sinitic 天地 *Tiāndì*. The ordered world constantly emerges out of primordial confusion, 混沌 *Hùndùn* ("muddled confusion", "turbid waters") in Sinitic thought, corresponding to the Mesopotamian idea of 𒍪 𒀊 *Abzu* (the "Abyss"; literally the graphemes mean "watery/dissolved knowledge", otherwise "before knowledge"), also called 𒇉 *Engur*,[188] *Nammu/Mummu* (the primordial "Mother/Matrix", also rendered "Noise", "Confusion", "Scream"),[189] which is the same as the later *Tiamat* 𒀭𒋾𒊩𒆳 or *Tamtum* 𒀭𒀜𒆳𒄖, the primordial "Sea" of formless matter/earth, which may take the role of either the moulded surface (the Mesopotamian *Ninhursag*, the Chinese *Demu*) or the still unmoulded underground substance (the Mesopotamian *Ereshkigal*, the Chinese *Houtu*) of the Earth. In the Mesopotamian tradition, like in the Sinitic tradition, creation is not *ex nihilo* but *Ordo ab Chao*, an ordering process of configuration enacted by the power of the performative, magical word.[190]

Within Heaven-Earth, humanity has a central role in both cultures. In the Sinitic tradition, this centrality is expressed in the concept of 天地人 *tiāndìrén*, the unity of "Heaven-Earth-mankind", which later in my essay I render, through Greek concepts, as "ouranogeoanthropism".[191] Humanity has

---

187 Kramer (1956), pp. 46-47.

188 Black & Green (1992), p. 134.

189 Gabrieli (2017), p. 88 ff.

190 Ibidem, p. 128.

191 Section 2.3.4 of the present essay.

the duty to be "in the likeness of the spirits", in the words of Rochat de la Vallée quoted hereinbefore, and to co-work with the spirits through the 礼 lǐ, the patterns of development of things which always have to conform to the supreme Reason of Heaven. In the Mesopotamian tradition, too, humanity has the divine duty to co-work with the gods through the ⊢ *me* (the "measures", "means", "manners", or "morals", which are also performative words, magical words which outline entities), for the continuous realisation of the cosmos; to co-create with the gods.[192] Besides the analogy with the Sinitic concept of *li*, the *me* also correspond to the *zu* in their value as the "names" — 名 *míng* —, and thus the "destinies" — the near-homophone 命 *mìng* —, of the entities.[193]

In the Mesopotamian tradition, the three aspects of the God of Heaven are also clearly identified with three concentric rings of the physical sky seen from the Earth and hinged at the ecliptic North Pole, and with the star-gods (constellations) moving within such rings, drawing the scheme of time (the calendar).[194] The three aspects of the God of Heaven, and their three skies, are also associated with a colour symbolism. The inner sky, closer to the pole, of *An* as *Enlil* (wherein *Enlil* himself is [MUL]*Apin*, i.e. "[STAR]Plough", that is *Triangulum* in modern astronomy;[195] while his female aspect, *Ninlil*, is [MUL]*Mar.gid.da*, "[STAR]Chariot", the Big Dipper[196]), is conceived as white, red and black,[197] representing the threefoldness withheld in potence in the quiescent and hidden supreme. These three colours are together known as *luludanitu*. The middle sky is lapis lazuli-blue, the colour of *An*

192 Mander (2011), p. 11.

193 The etymology of the words "morality" (Latin *mos, mores*), "measure", "mean", "middle", "man" and "mind", from an Indo-European root *me- possibly related to the Mesopotamian *me*, as well as that of "name", "norm" and *numen*, from *nem-*, both pertinent to the discourse expressed in this section, are deepened, respectively, in the sections 2.1.1.3 and 2.2.1 of the essay.

194 Didier (2009), vol. I, p. 95.

195 Kramer (1956), p. 52.

196 Rogers (1998), p. 18.

197 Ataç (2018), p. 78.

as *Inanna* ("Lady of Heaven", implying the union of Heaven with material Earth, which is thus sublimated, becoming the "Celestial Virgin"; within Heaven, *Inanna* herself is $^{MUL}Dili.$ *bat*, which may mean "^{STAR}Forbearing"[198] or "^{STAR}Daisy",[199] the constellation *Virgo* and the planet Venus). The outer sky of *An* as *Enki*, farther from the pole, is jasper-green (wherein *Enki* himself is ^{MUL}Iku, "^{STAR}Field", that is the Square of Pegasus,[200] a constellation which has high importance also in the Sinitic representation of the supreme power, as explained further onward).[201] The three colours as transmitted in Indo-European cultures (white, red and black), as it will be enunciated later in the essay, are also related to a trifunctional structuration of society as a reflection of Heaven.[202]

In broader Eurasian religio-cosmology, throughout various more or less localised cultures, mostly Indo-European, the three aspects of the God of Heaven have been variously expressed as: *Taranis* (*Dis Pater*), *Esus* and *Toutatis* (synthesised as one in *Lug*) in Celtic cultures;[203] 𒀭 *Amun*, ☉ *Ra* and *Ptah* in Egyptian culture;[204] *Odin*, *Thor* and *Ingfrey* in Germanic cultures;[205] *Jupiter* (*Deus Pater*), *Mars* and *Quirinus* in Latin

---

198 "Enduring Star" is the commonly accepted meaning of the Semitic rendition of the name of *Inanna*, that is *Ishtar* (Hellenised: *Astarte*).

199 Kasak & Veede (2001), p. 23.

200 Rogers (1998), p. 21. About the Square of Pegasus, see the section 3.1.3 of the present essay.

201 Wright (2002), pp. 34-35; Didier (2009), vol. I, p. 78.

202 See the prolegomenon to the fourth chapter.

203 Duval (1989), passim. In the later medieval Celtic mythology, in the *Arthurian Cycle*, the hidden supreme is *Uther Pendragon* ("Head of the Dragon"), father of the owner of divine right, *Arthur* ("Guardian of the She-bear").

204 Van den Dungen (2002), passim. The Belgian philosopher Wim van den Dungen explains *Amun* ("Hidden [One]") as the hidden presence and principle of unity, *Ra* ("Radiant/Shining [One]") as the luminous presence and principle of filiation, and *Ptah* ("Fathering/Begetting [One]") as the physical solidity and principle of realisation of the supreme God of the universe.

205 The three aspects of the supreme God in Germanic and Vedic cultures, in association with the trifunctional organisation of society, are deepened in the prolegomenon to the fourth chapter of the present essay. Tacitus' *Germania* also attests the supreme God as *Tuisto*, the human archetype emanated by it as *Mannus*,

culture;[206] *Deivos* or *Svarog, Perun* and *Veles* in Slavic cultures;[207] *Varuna, Indra* or *Mitra* and *Aryaman* in Vedic Sanskrit culture.[208] In Hellenic popular culture, *Zeus Pater* represents the first aspect, *Ares* the second one, while the third has no univocal equivalents, probably as it was occupied by the various terrestrial heroes, sons of God, or likely by *Apollo*, the god of the *Apélla* (Ἀπέλλα, the "assembly within the square"). In another more intellectualised tradition, the triad is rather represented by *Ouranos-Khronos* ("Space-Time"), *Zeus* and *Poseidon* ("Lord of the Earth"; Latin *Neptunus*, the "Wet" or "Covered One"), with *Ouranos* ("Heaven"; Latin *Uranus*) and *Khronos/Kronos* ("Time"; Latin *Chronus/Cronus* or *Saturnus*) representing the first aspect of the God-Heaven as God-Space-Time, and *Zeus* (Latin *Deus*; which as we will see means both "Heaven" and "Day") representing the time most closely and easily lived by humanity, that of the year and the day, determined by the Sun. In Hellenic philosophy, the three aspects are variously rendered in intellectualised ways, such as the Form of Good of Platonism and *Primum Movens* of Aristotelianism, and the already exhaustively explained concepts of *Logos* and *Anima Mundi*.

Christianity appropriated the triune conception of the God of Heaven, which ultimately belongs to pan-Eurasian

and *Mannus'* three sons and progenitors of the three major genealogical categories of the ancient Germanic peoples as *Irmin* ("Great [One]"; corresponding to Odin), *Ist* ("Being/Flowing [One]"; corresponding to Thor) and *Ing* ("Begetting/ Begotten [One]"; corresponding to Ingfrey).

206 Cf. Dumézil (1941), passim. The Greco-Latin concept of *Zeus Pater/Deus Pater* is further etymologised in the section 3.1.2 of the present essay.

207 Kushnir (2016), p. 40, where the three aspects of God (*Rod*, "Generator/ Generation" of reality, in modern Rodnovery, or Slavic Neopaganism), and the three colours (white, red and black), are also associated to the three aspects of reality: *Prav* ("Rightness"), *Yav* ("Actuality") and *Nav* ("Potentiality"). Below *Deivos/Svarog* ("Heaven"), which in the Slavic tradition is already the first manifestation of God (*Rod*) as the visible vault of the sky, the three phases of reality are also represented by *Perun* ("Thunderer"), *Svetovit* ("Lord of Power") and *Veles* ("Coverer"), and collaterally the three colours are white, green and black. See the section 3.3.3 of the present essay.

208 In Hinduism, the original Vedic trinity composed by *Varuna, Indra* or *Mitra*, and *Aryaman* has been variously reformulated throughout history. The well-known trinity of modern Hinduism is composed by *Brahma, Vishnu*, and *Shiva*. See: Achuthananda (2018), pp. 21-22.

religio-cosmology, reformulating it as God as the Father, God as the Holy Spirit, and God as the Son. However, due to its intrinsic errors, and Biblical confusion, which included the spatiotemporal fixation of the *Logos* and the abstraction of God from the world, all these concepts have degenerated, losing their original meaning. Due to the same corruption of ideas, in Christianity, God was no longer Heaven, and the latter became an imaginary transcendent and future realm rather than an order to be realised in this world. The loss of Heaven and the psychotic maddening of human reason, projected into an endless becoming and exempting mankind from its role of co-creation of the cosmos, had become an established movement, ready to become secularised as the nonsensical and horizontal fidgeting of all forces in the machination of Western modernity.[209] The abstraction of God brought about the loss of Heaven; the fixation of the *Logos* into space-time (in a space-time pretending to be globally applicable) brought about the loss of reason, which consequently has plunged into the *Chaos* of horizontal afinalistic operativity.

BABILU = TIANMEN = IANUA CAELI:

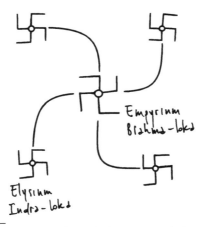

209 An afinalistic, returning waggling, which is proper of *Chaos*, and, as it is already understandable but we will see more in detail further onwards (especially in 2.2), of the black phase of reality, of femininity. A nonsensical fidgeting of the teeming forces of the West in full necrotisation, femininisation and infantilisation, which is like a female awaiting to be fecundated by a new *Logos*.

Figure 4: Represented hereunder are the three concentric bands of constellations spinning around the ecliptic North Pole centered in the constellation of the Dragon, the quiet heart of the supreme God of Heaven (*An* in Mesopotamian religio-cosmology, *Tian* or *Shangdi* in the Sinitic one, and *Dyeus* in Indo-European ones), according to the Nippur calendar of the Mesopotamian tradition. The three rings, from the innermost one to the outermost one, are associated with the three stages of manifestation, or three faces, of the God; each triplet of aligned constellations in the three circles is associated with a month of the year. The innermost circle, which is white-red-black, is the Path of *Enlil*, with *Enlil* himself (the Chinese *Huangdi*) identified as the asterism of the Plough (*Apin*), even comprehending the Great Chariot (*Margidda*) as his female *Ninlil*, and in general, representing the precessional North Pole; the midway circle, which is blue, is the Path of *An* joining *Inanna*, the "Lady of Heaven", with *Inanna* herself identified as the asterism of the Daisy (*Dilibat* or *Dilipat*); endly, the outermost circle, which is green, is the Path of *Enki*, with *Enki* himself (the Chinese *Yandi*) identified as the asterism of the Field or Square (*Iku*).

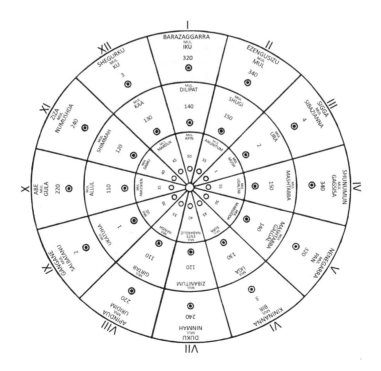

Figure 5: Representation of the constellations of the Dragon and the Great Chariot and Small Chariot, or Big Dipper and Little Dipper, or Great She-bear and Little She-bear, or Wain of the Male (or Charles, or Odin) and Wain of the Female. The Dragon coils the north ecliptic pole (NEP), represented by a fictional dot, in its first bight. The two Chariots represent, in the cultures of Eurasia, the vehicle (chariot) or tool (dipper) of distribution of the rotatory energy of the supreme God of Heaven; their seven stars represent the seven operative powers of the God, also reflected as the seven planets of the Sun system, and seven planes for ascending to the comprehension of the supreme power, and are personified as seven deities, in Mesopotamian culture and in the Chinese one as well. The Chariots spin according to the north precessional pole (NPP) and are here represented in the positions that they acquire in the four phases of the year. As it will be described more detailedly further onwards in the essay, the Small Chariot is the female or absorbing aspect, or *yin*, while the Great Chariot is the male or emanating aspect, or *yang*, of the energy of the God, which is the Mesopotamian *Lil*, the Hellenic *Logos*, the Sinitic *Li*.

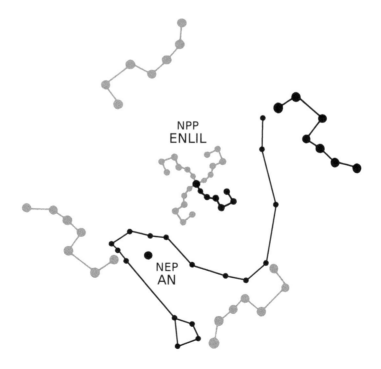

CHAPTER 2

SINO-RUIST NOÖLOGY

The Fourth Political Theory has opened a unique perspective: if we comprehend the principle of the reversibility of time, we are not only able to compose the project of a future society, but we will also be able to compose a whole range of projects of different future societies, thus we would be able to suggest some non-linear strategies for a new institutionalisation of the world. || [...] Time as the evasion of the present, and the unbearable tension of the pure presence of the same. This tension is immediately relieved by the expansion of all the imaginable types of dualities that constitute the textures of the continuous process of time. The model of this process is the creation of the three moments of time. The logical and spatial symmetries follow [...] yes/no, true/false, high/low, right/left, here/there, and so on. Before/after belongs to the same cadence. Time constitutes consciousness running from the unbearable confrontation with itself. But this confrontation is inevitable, so the present, and the high precision of its existential perception, is born. What is most important in this interpretation of the morphology of time? [...] The world around us becomes what it is by the fundamental action of presencing accomplished by the mind. When the mind sleeps, reality lacks the sense of present experience. It is fully immersed in a continuous dream. The world is created by time, and time, in its turn, is the manifestation of self-aware subjectivity, an intrasubjectivity. [...] Time is that which is inside us, and what makes us who we are. Time is man's ultimate identity.

Aleksandr Dugin[210]

— PROLEGOMENON: OVERCOMING DUALISM

This second chapter deals with noölogy, intended as ① the study of the *Logos* as *Nous*, or, otherwise said, the study of the universal ordering and intelligence intrinsic to reality; ② epistemology, i.e., human awareness and knowledge of the *Logos*; and ultimately ③ axiology, i.e., the moralising organisation of

---

210 Dugin (2012), pp. 70 & 159.

humanity when it is harmonised with the universal mind. The discussion focuses on the concepts of "reasoning" and "ritualising" that in the Chinese language are represented by two homophonous graphemes, respectively lǐ 理 and lǐ 礼, expressing two aspects of the same semantic field (of which the second contains the already encountered radical for "showing" and "worshipping", 礻 shì). According to Robert Eno, the analogy between the two rests upon the fact that "rituals are, in essence, the extension of natural reasons into the human sphere".[211] As aforesaid, the *Li* is the Sinitic equivalent of the *Logos*. It is the underlying pattern of the cosmos, which may be grasped by humanity and cast into instruments of moralisation, and, at the same time, it is the law of established morality itself. As such, the *Li* is central to any discourse about the nature of human mind and the axiology of human society. Epistemologically speaking, as demonstrated throughout the text, the knowledge of the *Li* is at the same time and complementarily both deductive and inductive, both intuitive (*a priori*) and empirical (*a posteriori*), both subjective and objective, both spatial and temporal (in one word, it is spatiotemporal). Amongst its meanings, *li* may also signify "science" and "natural science".[212]

Through the dynamic interplay between Sinitic and Western concepts, in this chapter, I present theoretical conceptions and representations of the manifold structure of the *Li*, reconciling the dichotomy between "ritual" and "reason" which has occurred in Western thinking in the wake of the split between human reason and the universal *Logos*, and all the other aforementioned dualisms. Afterwards, I explore the Sinitic concept of the patriarch (*zu*) as the personified embodiment of the *Li* on the plane of human experience, equivalent to the figure of the sage, and then the Ruist teleology of humanisation (*ren*), which is a process of anthropogogy, i.e., education as continuous and open-ended cultivation of the heavenly gist of humanity.

---

211 Sigurdsson (2004), p. 141. Sigurdsson quotes: Eno (1990), p. 152. I have slightly altered the words of the quote to avoid redundancies in my context.

212 So that, alternatively to "noology", I could have also used "scientology", besides "logology", "lilogy", "ratiology", and, for the part about *li* as rite, "ritology", "oratiology", "nomology".

The models of the *Li* that are proposed throughout the chapter demonstrate its spatiotemporality; ultimately, they show the identifiability of *Li* with space-time itself, and show that time itself is institutionalised by, and as, the *Dasein/Traiectum*, as discussed by Aleksandr Dugin and deepened later in the present essay.[213] Such models discard any linear, unidirectional, monotonic, and irreversible conceptions of time and the "topography of progress" (modernisation) upon which liberalism and the other post-Enlightenment ideologies, as well as Hegelianism and the philosophies of thinkers like Fukuyama and Kojève, are based. Within the Fourth Political Theory, such processes are reckoned as real but relative to certain coalescences of space-time, not as absolute trends. The Fourth Political Theory espouses a "systematised occasionalism": time coagulates around the *Dasein* into different complexes, establishing topographies in which concepts combine and recombine in a nonlinear and reversible way. Concepts from the past may be reëvoked, providing the foundations for the composition of projects for the future and the strategies for their institutionalisation.[214]

"Noölogy" is, therefore, the discourse about both thinking and acting. Thought, the character of *Dasein*, foregoes the duality of theory and practice and generates them both. "Thought is the only thing that crosses worlds", and magically builds and changes them. In the light of this pre-dualistic view, the Fourth Political Theory and the Fourth Political Practice are one and the same.[215] As Dugin says:[216]

> The important concept of *Nous* (Intellect) developed by the Greek philosopher Plotinus corresponds to our ideal. The intellect is one and multiple at the same time, because it has multiple differences in itself — it is not uniform nor an amalgam, but taken as such with many parts, and with all their distinct particularities. The future should be noetic in some way [...] many poles, many centres, [...] many worlds.

213 Section 3.3 of the present essay.

214 Dugin (2012), pp. 67-70: Chapter 4 – "The Reversibility of Time".

215 Ibidem, pp. 181-182.

216 Ibidem, p. 197.

2.1. EPISTEMOLOGY AND PRAXIS OF *LI* 理 AND *LI* 礼

The separation of human reason from the *Logos* in Western thinking entails at the same time a dichotomisation between "reasoning" and "ritualising", even despite the etymological affinity of the two words. As explained in the foregoing chapter, the modern manifestation of this separation may be traced back to the seventeenth century, but its earliest roots are to be found in Christian metaphysics. The philosophy of the Enlightenment explicitly rejected whatsoever ritual tradition as a stagnant reproduction of the "old order". According to the Icelandic philosopher Geir Sigurdsson, based on the historian Peter Burke, an articulate opposition of reason to rite was first laid out with the Protestant Reformation. The reformers' doctrines despised ritual as an illusory artifice that hides true spirituality.[217]

Sigurdsson alters a dictum of Kant's in the light of the concept of *Li*, saying that "tradition without reason would be blind, and reason without tradition would be empty". Analogously, the *Analects* of Confucius say that "learning without reflection results in confusion, reflection without learning results in peril". Reason is not an abstract entity but is always incarnated in a cultural context, in which reason itself enlivens and moralises. Conversely, whenever human reason is deprived of its background, it results in meaningless abstraction. Reason and cultural tradition are concurrently complementary in both their epistemology and praxis. When reason does not consider the forces at play in the context in which it works, it threatens the existence of both itself and the context. Alienated reasoning is immoral since it fails to measure the potential inchoately working in the present time and to behave appropriately towards them.[218]

In Lacanian terminology, as explained in the foregoing chapter, the *Li* may be identified as the Symbolic Order

217 Sigurdsson (2004), pp. 21-22. As part of the loss of the world, formerly "organised through myth and ritual", as discussed in: Littlewood & Dein (2013), passim; and treated in the section 1.2.2 of the present essay.

218 Sigurdsson (2004), pp. 42-43.

established by the Name of the Father, a mode of reasoning to deal with reality. Rite may therefore be regarded as a mould that gives shape to the Thing, the original indistinct oneness. At this point, it is worthwhile making a distinction between the Thing in its structured symbolisation, which I call the *Yang*-Thing by integrating Lacanianism with Sinitic cosmology, and the Thing in its primordial shapeless state, which I call the *Yin*-Thing. Rite is the device aimed at creating a *Yang*-Thing, while the abstraction of the Symbolic Order from any context marks the beginning of its sclerotisation, obdurate senseless repetition. When this happens, as it is the case in the modern Western civilisation, the Symbolic Order becomes asphyxiated and overrun by the *Yin*-Thing, which reëmerges from the network's sclerosis and dissolution. An obdurate Symbolic Order is the *Yin*-Thing disguised as *Yang*-Thing, comparable to the perversion of the fatherly function, that is to say, the Lacanian concept of the "Father of Pleasure", the "Father of the Horde", of anomic undifferentiation and of the "Hatred of God".[219] This is comparable as well to the "inversion of sign" which takes place in dying civilisations, of which Ernesto de Martino spoke, by which the anabasis/anastrophe or ascending and public-wise movement turns into the katabasis/catastrophe or descending and private-wise movement, corresponding, in the life of individuals, to a turn from healing altruistic publicisation to a shattering egoistic privatisation.[220] Due to this inversion, the world as a "temple", as a "hodology", a common project of operativity and usability, crystallises and then collapses.[221]

2.1.1. *LI* 理: REASON AND REASONING AS MAPPING SPACE-TIME

As previously stated, the *Lǐ* 理 is simultaneously the universal *Logos* generated by Heaven and its manifold incarnations, that is, the plurality of *li* or *logoi*, which enliven the things in the world.

219 Recalcati (2007), p. 6 for a cursory description of the Lacanian "Evil Father", that is the Thing disguised as father.

220 De Martino (1977), pp. 62-67 & 256.

221 Ibidem, p. 94.

The American Sinologist Brook Ziporyn paraphrases Zhu Xi describing the *Li* as simultaneously one and many: "Particularised *li* are one and the same *Li*", and "the entire supreme *Li* is contained in each differentiated entity".[222] Hereinafter, I portray a series of evocative "mappings" or visual "bewritings" of the Sinitic idea of *Li*.

The etymology of the *Li* character is explained in the ancient Chinese dictionary *Shuōwén Jiězì* (說文解字) simply as "to treat jade", using such carving craft as a metaphor for the unfolding of reality along the lines of power.[223] It is also a metaphor for the work of functional differentiation or — from the perspective of the active human subject — for analysis, that is preparatory for the arrangement of matter in a shape that is appropriate for a given context (e.g., a style of jade carving that complies with market standards).[224] As such, it may be rendered by the terms "principle", "order", "pattern" of development, or "organism". Ziporyn considers the following to be the best renditions: "organisation", "pattern of coherence", or even "focus" or "field" of intelligibility. The Hellenic concept of *Logos* is frequently used in specialistic Sinological literature as a legitimate translation of *Li*.[225]

2.1.1.1. CORRELATIVE PATTERN AND HIERARCHIC RHIZOME-ARBORESCENCE

The *Li* is not an order imposed from the outside by a separate agent but an intrinsic movement of organisation. It is the spontaneous unfolding of things and their harmonious interaction with the other things in the world. As such, it has been described as a "correlative pattern".[226] The scholar A.C. Graham defines the *Li* as the pattern generated by the supreme

---

222 Ziporyn (2008), pp. 1-5, note 4.

223 Ibidem, p. 8.

224 Ibidem, pp. 9-10.

225 Ibidem, p. 6.

226 Ziporyn (2008), pp. 11-13.

One, which proceeds by branching by division.[227] Graham's visualisation may be described as a hierarchic arborescence or, even more evocatively, as a rhizome that grows out of the highest or central One, thus a hierarchic rhizome.

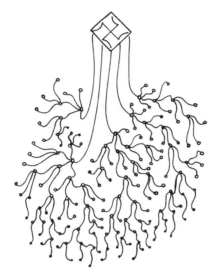

Figure 6: The one *Li* and its many *li*(s) visualised as a rhizomatic-arborescent architecture, endowed with verticality as the multiplicity of centres of irradiation which are begotten by the supreme source represent its order and relink back to it. The concept of the rhizome is Deleuze-Guattarian; Aleksandr Dugin defines postmodern philosophies like that of Deleuze and Guattari as a "demonic texture" that offers new capabilities for the interpretation of reality but upholds a "horizontal" perspective that allows for "multiple, non-hierarchical" ingoing and outgoing "points of representation and interpretation". Such philosophies may prove to be efficacious for the destruction of stagnant Western thought and even for the construction of the Fourth Political Theory if endowed with "verticality", which is what the Fourth Political Theory seeks and wants to establish.[228] Such verticality might be found in some of the Sinitic cosmologies deepened throughout the following parts of the essay, especially as the nature and the cosmogenic working of the centres of irradiation that proceed from the supreme source will become clearer.

227 Ibidem, p. 13. Ziporyn relies upon: Graham, A.C. (1986). "The Ch'eng-Chu Theory of Human Nature". *Studies in Chinese Philosophy and Philosophical Literature*. Singapore: Institute of East Asian Philosophies. p. 421.

228 Dugin (2012), pp. 25, 40, 171 & 183.

The image of the arborescence is a good description of the *Li* as a projection or continuum of reality, avoiding a separation between a metaphysical and a physical realm. Indeed, *li*(s) differ from the Christian reading of the Western conception of the Platonic forms or ideas, conceived as perfectly pristine in the *Hyperuranion* ("over the top of the sky", what we have discussed as the transcendent pre-Heaven or hyper-Heaven in the last section of the foregoing chapter[229]), which is their metaphysical, immaterial and immutable realm, but intermingling and changing, thus becoming impure, through their acts of giving shape to physical things in matter.[230] In fact, such distinction between the *Hyperuranion* and the experienced reality is part of the same corruption of thought brought about by the errors of Christianity, thoroughly discussed in the foregoing chapter. Plato is clear in identifying the "ideas" or "forms" (singular ἰδέᾱ *idéā*, Koine Greek εἰδέα *eidéa*, feminine of εἶδος *eîdos*, a term which beyond "form" may mean "style", "type", "image", and even "arrow", figuratively describing the coming into being of things, the emanation from a source which is their "cause" and "reason", αἰτία *aitía*[231]) as the "essences" (οὐσία *ousíā*; i.e. the "way of being", cf. the Doric variation ἐσσία *essía*, more conservative and similar to Latin) of things, and in saying that the entities are constituent parts (by "participation", μέθεξις *méthexis*) of them.

According to Sinitic thinking, the *Li* is malleable in itself. There are coarser and easier *li*(s), lines of reality in which things are generated in accordance with their own character. Yet, things' positions within the arborescence of the *Li* may be altered, by entities themselves, through the cultivation and expansion of awareness.[232] This conception of the *Li* as a tree or hierarchic rhizomatic structure may be easily analogised with the Gnostic

---

229 The *Hyperuranion* is the same as *Hyperborea* ("beyond the northern top of the sky").

230 Ziporyn (2008), p. 4.

231 Both *idea* and *eidos* come from the Indo-European root **ueid-* ("to see/to know"). Cf. Pokorny (1959), pp. 1123-1127: **uei-, *ueiə-, *ui-, *ueid-*.

232 Ziporyn (2008), p. 14.

Logos as *Ktisma*. The Sinitic concept, however, is more dynamic and gives a pivotal role to humanity.[233]

According to what hitherto described, the *Li* is at the same time what makes things the guise they are and what prompts things to be what they might and ought to be. Being the *Li* malleable, an entity may penetrate ever-finer lines of being by means of appropriate techniques and by adopting appropriate styles in order to reach higher states of consciousness and sublimate one's energy-body (*qi*).[234] "Sages"/"wisemen" (*shèngrén* 圣人, also "holy man", "saint")[235] are those who are able to ascend into the heights of the arborescence of the *Li*, and by doing or having done so, they establish a vertical hierarchy in the human realm. They emerge amongst humanity as archetypes of excellence and perfection, symbols of the struggle to become similar to the One.[236]

When it is conceived as a synonym or factor of "coherence" or "harmony" (和 *hé*), as done by the scholar Willard Peterson, the Li is presented through another concept that highlights its correlativeness and contextuality. It is the "sticking together" of the parts of an entity that makes such an entity

---

233 Ibidem, pp. 15-16 for Graham's description of Zhu Xi's *Li*.

234 Ibidem, pp. 14-15.

235 "Sage" and "wise" come, respectively, from the Indo-European roots **sek-* ("to see/to show/to speak"; cf. also "to seek") and **ueid-* ("to see/to know"; cf. Latin *vídeo*, *vidēre* and all its cognates). The latter stems in turn from **uei-*, which is the root of "wise" in the sense of "mode/form", "way", "wit", Latin *vīs* ("force" and "craft"), Sanskrit वेद *véda* ("knowledge"). Cf. "wizard". Cf. also the other derivative root **ueik-* ("to turn/bend/spellbind/sacrifice"), of Latin *vincō*, *vincere* ("to win") and *vinciō*, *vincīre* ("to bend"), from which also come the Germanic words "witch(er)" (the Latin equivalent *strix* being a reference to the "owl", a creature related to vision, knowledge, philosophy) and "wicked". Cf. Pokorny (1959), pp. 896-898: **sek-*, **sekw-*; pp. 1123-1127: **uei-*, **ueiə-*, **ui-*, **ueid-*; pp. 1128-1131: **ueik-*, **ueig-*.

236 Ziporyn (2008), pp. 14-15. Within Christianity (yet, not justifying what to the author of the present essay is a mass ideology levelling humanity towards lower states of being) a similar view may be found only in Eastern Orthodox traditions. According to the Slovenian philosopher Slavoj Žižek, who, by the way, integrates Confucianism and Chinese philosophy in his discourses, only Eastern Orthodoxy provides the way for true *imitatio Christi*. In Eastern Orthodoxy, the Christ does not have an exceptional status but is rather a model to be imitated: all men may strive to become God. See: Žižek (2006), p. 187.

a whole entity. At the same time, the *Li* is also the sticking together of the entity with the other beings and the broader context surrounding it. This gradual process of correlation unfolds itself both towards the microcosm and towards the macrocosm.[237] The concept of coherence may also represent an individual entity's tenacious effort of realisation, including both the entity's potentiality and actuality, without setting a separation between causes and effects.[238]

2.1.1.2. ARS OPERANDI, *FIELD-FOCUS, AND* ARS CONTEXTUALIS

When conceived as an individual entity's mode of self-unfolding, the effort to realise its own potentiality, *li* is analogous to the Hellenic concept of *thymos*, the soul that strives for recognition. It may also be compared to François Jullien's conception of entity as "propensity".

Jullien himself discusses the *Li*, defining it as a pattern (紋 *wén*) of "configuration" (形 *xíng*, a word which means simultaneously "nature", "shape", "body" and "that which appears"),[239] and especially as *Ars Operandi*. He uses the metaphor of jade carving to give prominence to the techno-practical essence of the *Li*. The multiple *li*(s) constitute a "branching grid", which is the great *Li*. Jullien betones the role of the individual who may grasp the various branches and work in and by means of them to move within the great grid of the *Li*.

David Hall and Roger Ames propose yet another evocative Western-terminology rendition and visualisation of the *Li*. They define it as a "field-focus" of correlation, approached by means of analogical and metaphorical modalities of thinking,

---

237 Ibidem, p. 18. Ziporyn relies upon: Peterson, Willard (1986). "Another Look at Li". *Bulletin of Sung-Yuan Studies*, 18. Berkeley, California: Society for Song, Yuan, and Conquest Dynasty Studies. p. 14.

238 Ibidem, pp. 20-22.

239 Jullien (2016), pp. 98-99.

as opposed to analytical, causal, and metonymic modalities. Remarkably, the analogical modality has the capacity to understand analytical thinking, while the opposite is not possible. The *Li* manifests itself in what Hall and Ames define as "correlative groupings" or "image clusters" of "complex semantic associations", within which individuals "reflect into one another" (are reciprocally intelligible) in a rich network of aesthetic significance. Conceived as a correlative logic, the *Li* is definable as a logic of process and flux, in which relations are not definitively fixed since "they are only a matter of empirical experience and conventional interpretation". Relations organise themselves according to the here and now, the current this and that.[240] Correlative thinking is otherwise understandable by means of the concept of symbol, so that the *Li* may be regarded as a "symbolic field".

Ziporyn also propounds the rendition of *Li* through the concept of *Ars Contextualis*. Ruist philosophy emphasises that civil reasoning (*wénlǐ* 文理) is the manifestation on the human plane of the universal *Li*. There is no separation between the two; the *Li* is neither subjective nor objective and is never independent of contextual reality. Amongst humanity, the *Li* is what gathers individuals into communities, an "ongoing process of correlation and negotiation" through congeniality, sympathy, and productivity, which at the same time shapes the individuals' characters. The *Li* establishes continuity among entities, constituting groups as broader organisms. Like the jade carver, the *Li* "brings into coherence the preëxisting raw material" according to both individual potentials and the demands of the context.[241]

---

240 Ziporyn (2008), pp. 22-24. The author relies upon: Hall, David; Ames, Roger (1995). *Anticipating China: Thinking Through the Narratives of Chinese and Western Culture*. Albany, New York: State University of New York Press. pp. 136-141.

241 Ibidem, pp. 25-30.

2.1.1.3. PENDULUM, VORTEX-VERTEX, AND MORALITY AS SUCH

Ziporyn further deepens the analysis of the *Li* by highlighting that the Chinese term conveys the meaning of a togetherness that is marked by value. This conception entails that there are types of togetherness that, contrariwise, are immoral and do not qualify as *Li* since they alienate individuals from the world.[242] What qualifies as *Li* is a coherence that enables the partaking individuals to sublimate their desires in the creation of values, establishing a morality. It is important to highlight that the word "morality" (Latin *mos*, *mores*), meaning a measured and regulated quality of being, is a derivative of the Indo-European root **me-*, "to measure", a semantic field that also "man" (German *Mann* and *Mensch*), "mind" and "medium/middle" ultimately belong to.[243] The *Li* may therefore be regarded as measure and ability to measure, and ultimately morality as such, in itself.

Ziporyn represents the *Li* through the evocative images of the "pendulum", and the "vortex-vertex", a symbolism, the latter one, which will recur a few sections onwards in the present chapter.[244] In his theory, the *Li* is the centre of gravity towards which individuals tend. They swing between extreme poles of reality (*yin* and *yang*) but have an orienting focus, which is their own particular *li* and the universal *Li*. Those entities who wander too far away from the focus may no longer swing back towards the opposite pole and lose their own reason of being or their moral value within a context.[245]

---

242 Ibidem, pp. 30-31.

243 Pokorny (1959), pp. 703-706 ff: **me-*, **mo-*, **met-*, **med-*; pp. 726-728: **men-*; Watkins (2000), p. 51: **me-1*, **me-2*. We have seen, in the section 1.3.3 of the essay, how the Mesopotamian *me*, the "measures" of things, may be related to the same Indo-European root and are comparable to the Sinitic *li* within the structure of religious cosmology.

244 Section 2.2.2 of the present essay, about the leftward vortex of *yin* and the rightward vertex of *yang*.

245 Ziporyn (2008), p. 32.

When things are part of a moralised togetherness appropriate for them, they are satisfied, prosperous, and reproduce. In moralised groups, the single parts functionally coalesce, their selves are united in a higher consciousness, and they work together to the same ends. Such an integrated group, in turn, spontaneously seeks coherence — or inherence — into a wider context, and this process of moral expansion replicates itself into both the microcosm and the macrocosm.[246]

In groups that hinge upon the *Li*, individuals gather by reciprocal intelligibility; that is to say, they reciprocally recognise each other because they share ends, cognitive faculties, and style of interaction. The *Li* is, therefore, at one time the principle and the consequences of the constitution of integrated groups. Reciprocal intelligibility among individuals within coherent groups is expressed in Sinitic thinking by the concept of *gǎnyìng* (感应 "resonance", "feeling-response").[247]

In the *Odyssey*, Homer says, "God brings like and like together". Analogously, the *Lüshi chunqiu* (c. 239 BCE) says that:[248]

> Things of the same kind summon each other, those with the same vital energy join together, sounds that match resonate. Thus if you strum a *gong* note, other *gong* will resonate; if you strum a *jue* note, other *jue* will vibrate. Use a dragon to bring rain; use the form to move the shadow. The masses of people think that fortune and misfortune come from fate [*ming*]. How could they know from where they truly come!

246 Ibidem, pp. 34-35.

247 Ibidem, pp. 40-41.

248 Perkins (2016), § 5 – "Correlative Cosmology". Quotes: Chen, Qiyou (1984). *Lüshi Chunqiu Xinshi*. Shanghai, China: Shanghai Guji Chubanshe.

Figure 7: Representation of the *Li* as vortex-vertex and pendulum, as rendered in Western terminology by the scholar of Chinese philosophy Brook Ziporyn. The European tradition of the Christmas tree, or *Tannenbaum* ("fir tree") in its German denomination — being a representation originally belonging to Germanic cultures — symbolises the same structure of the being of things, of reality, or space-time, in its self-production, and also the same bell-shaped vault of Heaven hinged at the north celestial pole. In the Germanic cultures from which it derives, the Christmas tree symbolised the cosmic tree *Yggdrasill*.

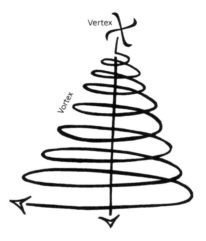

2.1.2. *LI* 礼: RITE AND RITUALISING AS MORALISING SPACE-TIME

Now the Rites necessarily have their origin in the Supreme One, which divides to become Heaven and Earth, revolves to become *yin* and *yang*, and changes to become the four seasons.

"Record of Rites" (Liji)[249]

Sigurdsson defines *lǐ* 礼 (classical character: 禮), with the meaning of "ritual", as a device for the regular invocation/ evocation and cultivation of spirit(s), which is flexible and adaptable to the continuously changing reality. Confucius and his close disciples theorised the implementation of *li* as instruments

---

249 *Liji zhengyi, Shisanjing zhushu* 22.1426. As quoted in: Pankenier (2013), p. 88.

for their project of reviving Zhou culture. Rituals consist in the "active and personalised participation" of individuals in a "tradition's sustention and evolution".[250] When looked at from a merely sociological perspective, *li* may appear as efficacious tools for the education and the cultivation of individuals and societies.[251] In the following sections, I illustrate the *li* as an axiological instrument for appropriately moving in space, thriving in time, and — summarising these two perspectives — ceremonially centring and verticalising space-time, in sight of Heaven. In De Martino's terminology, the rite (which, as the practical counterpart of myth, constitutes the symbol) is a technical device of *imitatio naturae*, for imitating the circle of the eternal return of nature to project the spiral of culture, shaping time into a history.[252] In the light of the idea of Heaven in Sinitic thinking, we may more clearly speak about rite as *imitatio Caeli*, imitation of Heaven, or, as it will be made clearer in the third chapter, of the stellar configurations of the circle of the north celestial pole.

2.1.2.1. RITUALISING FOR APPROPRIATELY INTERACTING IN SPACE

The purpose of rituals is to establish communication with the continuously changing reality. Within Sinitic tradition, Ruism prioritises the establishment and upholding of morality and thus civil society, which is seen in a continuum with the environment and the universal process of naturation. Taoism differs from the Ruist perspective by prioritising a mystical, personal, and localised understanding of the process of nature, conceiving human society as a distinct entity that depends on the former.[253]

The shared idea is that harmony never crystallises into a definitive and permanent code since the things in the world

---

250 Sigurdsson (2004), p. v.

251 Ibidem, p. vi.

252 De Martino (1977), p. 223.

253 Sigurdsson (2004), pp. 16-17.

"persist in a continuous process of emerging order", in a continuous reconfiguration. The universal *Li* is iridescent and constantly changing, and the incompleteness of creation is precisely what permits the movement and renewal of life. As part of the world, humans should "themselves participate in this process by configuring and reconfiguring their position within the whole".[254]

Humanity realises its true role within the world when ways of symbolic and decorous interaction with the latter and with the forces at play within it are established. Rituals and morality spontaneously arise in the process of negotiation with such forces, and simultaneously they permit the continuity in time of moralised humanity. Concisely, rituals (*li*) establish and transmit true humanity. Interaction is progressively autopersonal (directed towards oneself), interpersonal (directed towards others), and then directed towards the gods working in the umbegoing world.[255]

The etymological dictionary *Shuōwén Jiězì* explains that *li* means the "appropriate footsteps" to be followed "to serve the spirits". Sigurdsson adds that they are devices aimed at establishing morality, but also instruments that provide individuals with the skill to enter the moral sphere without injuring themselves.[256] Noteworthily, the Latinate word "appropriate/proper" comes from *proprius*, which means "one's own", or "congenial/congenital", "characteristic". The Sinitic equivalent of *proprius* is the cardinal Ruist concept of *yì* 义, usually rendered as "righteousness/correctness".[257] Sigurdsson defines it as a "heuristic model for acquiring the skill of successfully realising the values of the cultural tradition", for

---

254 Ibidem, p. 17. We have already illustrated, in the section 1.2.3 of the essay, the Sinitic conception of truth as not monolithic or monotonic, but as eternally operating in the present as a multiplicity of truths, of variations of the one truth. Cf. Pattberg (2009), pp. 17-18. We have also seen, in the section 1.3.3, the similarity of the Sinitic and Mesopotamian conceptions of the active, co-creating, role of humanity in the cosmos.

255 Sigurdsson (2004), pp. 17-18.

256 Ibidem, p. 20. Sigurdsson relies upon: Vandermeersch, Léon (1994). *Etudes sinologiques*. Paris, France: Presse Universitaire de France. pp. 144-145.

257 Ibidem, p. 52, note 39.

education and socialisation, and therefore humanisation and identification, within the cultural tradition. This is the meaning of being ritualised.[258]

Rituals (*li*) are the concrescence of various orders of being (*li*) within the universal *Li*. As such, they may be conceived as devices that give individuals the ability to traverse the various orders — or the spheres of the Gnostic *Ktisma* cosmology, or the branches of the *Li* intended as an arborescent structure. It is by means of acquired ritual styles that an individual may move across the cosmos, enter various groups, and establish relations with other individuals. Ultimately, rituals may be regarded not only as means of contextual coherence but also as practical tools for the self-transformation and emancipation of individuals, tools to create and switch reality.

2.1.2.2. RITUALISING FOR THRIVING IN TIME

The Chinese word for "tradition" is *chuántǒng* 传统. The literal meaning of the compound is "to transmit the main threads", and expresses the notion in the same way as it is intended in the West. However, this word is a relatively modern loan from the Japanese language, which coined it as a translation of the Western concept.[259]

Sigurdsson describes the classical Chinese notion of tradition as a way "through which the present arrives from the past", expressed by the word *dao*. So, tradition is identified with the process of life itself or the "course of things"; Jullien's description of *Dao*. According to Sigurdsson, the graphical etymology of 道 *Dao* expresses the "leading forth of the essential", since it is made up of 辵 *pi*, meaning "to lead through" (literally "foot") and 首 *shou*, meaning "head" or "foremost/gist".[260] René Guénon similarly describes the grapheme *Dao* as formed "from the signs

---

258 Ibidem, pp. 21-25.

259 Ibidem, p. 44.

260 Ibidem, pp. 49-50. Sigurdsson relies upon: Jullien (1995), p. 260.

of the head and the feet, being thus equivalent to the *alpha* and the *omega*" (of Western traditions).[261]

In the *Zhongyong* ("Doctrine of the Mean"[262]), Confucius says that the true teacher is "one who realises the new by reviewing the old". The praxis of *li* is always a means for reconfiguring inherited tradition. It is neither theoretically dogmatic nor practically stagnant. Being conceived as a response to the present context, ritual is a thoughtful and creative action that reckons relevant values from the past and interprets them to fit the demands of the forces at play in the given context. Tradition is an ever-living transmission of *li*; its shape is never fixed, and it has to be regarded as a potentiality always in the making.[263]

Ritual action is inseparable from time since it unfolds in time with a rhythm and directionality.[264] The intrinsic temporality of ritual action shows its cosmological implications, especially considering its function in establishing individuality as a centring and creating, or co-creating, entity.

Sigurdsson, relying upon Tang Junyi (1909-1978), who has been an influential modern Chinese philosopher and exponent of New Confucianism, says that in Sinitic thinking, space and time are not conceived as separate beings. Together, they make up the cosmos as a dynamic propensity or duration. The Sinitic word for "cosmos" is the same as that for "space-time", *yǔzhòu* 宇宙. The extended literal meaning of the graphemes is, respectively, "up and down and in the four directions" and "tracing back to the past and arriving in the present". Or, "what is above, below and in the four directions" and "what is past, present and future", of which

---

261 Guénon (1962), p. 124, note 12.

262 *Zhongyong* is usually translated as "Doctrine of the Mean", but, relying upon Sigurdsson's (2004, p. 79) etymological analyses, "Practice of the Centre" is proposable as an alternative.

263 Sigurdsson (2004), pp. 51-52.

264 Ibidem, pp. 55-56. Sigurdsson relies upon: Bourdieu, Pierre (1990). *The Logic of Practice*. Richard Nice (Trans.). Redwood City, California: Stanford University Press. p. 81.

yu is *yin* and *zhou* is *yang*, as enunciated by Feng Yulan.[265] Tang underlines that the perspective of humanity is always located at the centre (*zhōng* 中) of such cosmology.[266]

As explained hereinabove, mankind works to uphold the harmony of the cosmos through a ritual praxis that Sigurdsson considers the very *telos* of Ruism. The purpose of such praxis does not consist in attaining an objective truth but rather in steadily and appropriately harmonising oneself with the forces at play within a given spatiotemporal configuration of reality in order to prosper by exploiting the latter's potentiality. Jullien describes such ability as a craft/artistic wisdom.[267]

2.1.2.3. RITUALISING AS PRAGMATIC HABITUALITY

Sigurdsson proffers a further explanation of *li* through the concept of *habitus* (which is the perfect participle of the Latin verb *habeō*, *habēre*, "to have/own", and is considered as synonymous with the already treated *mos*, "morality"), described by Pierre Bourdieu as a "system of structured, structuring dispositions" that is "constituted in practice and is always oriented towards practical functions". Habituality synthesises in one single concept the preëminent pragmatism and contextuality of the *li*. The *habitus* is a historically and culturally pertinent practice, forged by the experience of a given configuration of reality as the best way to interact with the latter, and it is as well "the active presence of the whole past of which it is the product".[268] The *habitus* is, in other words, contextually and temporally legitimised and able to adapt itself to the shifting conditions and to individual actors' peculiar experiences; at the same time, it is traditional, i.e., transmittable between

---

265 Feng (1948), p. 307.

266 Sigurdsson (2004), pp. 56-58.

267 Ibidem, p. 59. Sigurdsson quotes: Jullien (1995), p. 15.

268 Ibidem, p. 121. The quotes are from: Bourdieu (1990), op. cit., pp. 52-56.

individuals, in the present and towards the future. Every context and contextualised entity has what Bourdieu calls its own "logic of practice" of space-time.[269] The *li* as *habitus* is interpretable as a "spatiotemporal pragmatism".

Conceived as *habitus*, ritual wholly overlaps with "reasoning", in the latter's definition given by John Dewey in *Democracy and Education* (1916), later conflated with that of "intelligence":[270]

> Reason is just the ability to bring the subject matter of prior experience to bear the significance of the subject matter of a new experience. A person is reasonable in the degree in which he is habitually open to seeing an event which immediately strikes his senses not as an isolated thing but in its connection with the common experience of mankind.

2.1.2.4. RITUALISING FOR CEREMONIALLY CENTRING AND VERTICALISING SPACE-TIME

As explained hitherto, rite is a heuristic device for interacting with the ever-shifting *yuzhou*, and for persisting and prospering within it. Classical Sinitic thinking, anteceding both Confucianism and Taoism developed the floating theoretical system of the *Yijing* ("Book of Changes") to deal with the flowing reality. Sigurdsson says that fluidity has the "heuristic function of unblocking the mind to possibilities". According to A.C. Graham, fluidity in an ever-shifting context is "indispensable for creative thinking", since it is the ability to "respond to new and complex situations", and to "wake up to new correlations of similarities and connexions".[271] According to Tu Weiming, Sinitic cosmology is neither cyclical nor spiral

269 Ibidem, pp. 121-122.

270 Ibidem, pp. 115-116. Sigurdsson relies upon: Dewey, John (1944). *Democracy and Education: An Introduction to the Philosophy of Education*. New York City, New York: Free Press. p. 343.

271 Ibidem, pp. 62-64. Sigurdsson relies upon: Graham, A.C. (1989). *Disputers of the Tao: Philosophical Argument in Ancient China*. Chicago, Illinois: Open Court Publishing. p. 368.

but "transformational", and "numerous human and nonhuman factors are involved in shaping its form and direction".[272]

According to Sigurdsson, watchful awareness is needed to grasp the ever-emerging order within the "processual and transformational" cosmos. The *li* requires the subject's individuality within the context and confirms the individual with centrality. The individual has to be disposed to perform appropriate actions to get a response from the other forces at play in the context; that is to say, it has to act ceremonially (cf. Sanskrit कर्मन् *kárman*, equivalent and coming from the same Indo-European root).[273] This is the meaning of the Sinitic concept of "efficacy" and the purpose of the rituals within the cosmos.[274] Centrality permits the individual to relate with others, instituting a "communal humanity" (仁 *rén*) which is characterised by a centre and harmonised with the environment.[275] Xunzi explicitly describes *li* as a device for establishing and maintaining the centre:[276]

> The way of the ancient kings consisted in exalting communal humanity (*ren*) whereby they followed centrality (*zhong*) in enacting it. What is meant with centrality? I say that it consists in ritual (*li*) and appropriateness (*yi*). The way that I am speaking of is not the Way of Heaven, nor the Way of Earth, but the Way of Man embodied in the conduct of the sages (*junzi*).

---

272 Ibidem, p. 65. Sigurdsson relies upon: Tu, Weiming (1985). *Confucian Thought: Selfhood as Creative Transformation.* Albany, New York: State University of New York Press. p. 39. In China, there is a long-standing tradition of systematisation of the ancient pre-Confucian and pre-Taoist heritage, and synthesis of all its posterior formulations (Confucian, Taoist and other), amongst whose most recent manifestations there is the 21st-century movement of Weixinism (唯心教 *Wéixīnjiào*; literally, "Heart-Mind Only").

273 Ibidem. The root is *kr-*, meaning "concretion". Cf. Pokorny (1959), pp. 530-532: *kar-*; p. 567 ff: *ker-*, *kor-*, *kr-*; p. 574 ff: *ker-*, *kerə-*, *kra-*, *kerei-*, *kereu-*.

274 Jullien (1995), p. 15.

275 Sigurdsson (2004), p. 82.

276 Ibidem, pp. 83-84. Sigurdsson quotes the section "Teachings of the Confucians" of the *Xunzi*, from: Huang, William (1966). *A Concordance to Hsun Tzu.* Harvard-Yenching Institute Sinological Index Series, Index no. 22. Taibei, China: Chinese Materials and Research Center. I have slightly modified the quote.

Yuzhou, like all Chinese nouns in general, may be interpreted as either singular or plural depending on the context. The universe/cosmos is not a single, static space that contains everything but a configuration or structure that manifests itself in the multiplicity of microcosms and macrocosms. In this sense, any entity is itself a *yuzhou*, and rite is its own way of manifestation within matter.

The *yuzhou*, space-time, may therefore be interpreted as the *Li* itself, as the processual structure, or intrinsically temporal modality, of generation shared by all entities.[277] It is worthwhile to highlight again, since in this chapter it has remained hithertofore an unspoken premise, that in Sinitic thinking creation is not *ex nihilo* but *Ordo ab Chao*, as we have already discussed in the foregoing chapter in comparison with Mesopotamian thought.[278] Order ongoingly emerges from a "muddled confusion", "turbid waters" (混沌 *Hùndùn*), which is nevertheless a "nothingness", a "void" (无 *wú*) of infinite potentiality.

The *jūnzǐ* 君子, literally the "lord's son", is the Sinitic equivalent of the Hellenic concept of *aristos*, or the etheling.[279] Historically it defined the aristocratic class, but its meaning is more complex. They are the leaders of communal humanity, those who can grasp the ever-emerging and ever-shifting orders (*li*) of the *yuzhou*, organising such potentialities by instituting ceremonial centrality (*zhong*). Otherwise said, they are the equivalent of the sages in other terminological systems, and,

---

277 *Yuzhou* may be regarded as synthesising in one single concept the Heideggerian phenomenology of Being as intrinsically temporal (cf. *Sein und Zeit*).

278 Section 1.3.3 of the present essay.

279 Hereinafter, I consistently translate *junzi* as etheling in most occurrences. "Etheling", otherwise spelled "ætheling" or "atheling", is an archaic English word (cf. Old English *æþeling*) meaning a person "of noble/ethel, gentile birth", variously used in the Anglo-Saxon literary tradition to mean "chief", "prince", "hero", "saint", "deity", "Christ". Cf. Proto-Germanic *aþalingaz*, German *Adel* ("nobility", "gentility"), Old High German *Attila, Ezzilo*. Cf. Germanic rune *othala/ethel* ᛟ, "ight/lineage/heritage/patrimony". "Ethel" is ultimately traced back to the Indo-European *átta, "parent/progenitor/ancestor" (cf. Pokorny [1959], p. 71: *atos, *atta). There is evidence that the term was present among most continental Germanic peoples, and that it referred to the sacerdotal class, to the holders of a sacral power. Cf. Balbo (1836), p. 34. Therefore, "etheling" conveys the same meanings as *junzi*, with semantic nuances expressing a spiritual and divine quality, virtue, and generative power.

as I further explain in forthcoming sections, they function as centralisers of space-time, and institutors of vertical civilisation. The ever-emerging order of the world (*Li*) and the centralising and verticalising ritual (*li*) action of those who represent it is, as we will see even more clearly further onwards, anchored in Heaven and is the attuning with the rhythms of the God of Heaven, not being, therefore, a haphazard waggling like the meaningless productions of the pseudo-"reason" of Western modernity, which has lost Heaven and bereft humanity of its co-creating role, after the failure of the wait for the action of the abstract, non-existent God of Christianity.[280]

Figure 8: Attempted artistic representation of the *yuzhou*, space-time intended as 宇 "up and down and in the four directions" and 宙 "tracing back to the past and arriving in the present", in other words, space-time as "propensity/procession" or "duration". As a particular contextual expression of such pattern, any spatiotemporal entity is a propensity, a *thymos*, in the Hellenic terminology used hereinbefore. Each *yuzhou* contains micro-*yuzhou*(s) and is itself contained in macro-*yuzhou*(s).

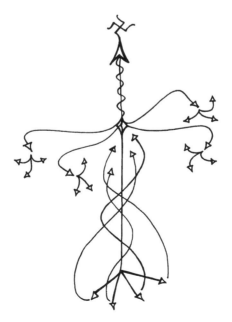

---

280 As discussed in the section 1.2.2 of the essay.

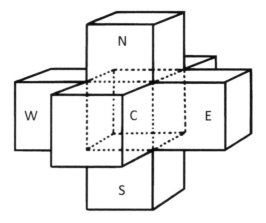

The *yuzhou* has also been represented as in the figure above as the "tesseract" or quadridimensional hypercube (the fourth dimension being time), a term coined by Charles Howard Hinton in his 1888 essay *A New Era of Thought*. It is an axonometry, a "corridor of space", in terms of Jan Krikke, that institutionalises time. The centre and the four directions, as we will also see further onwards in the present essay, have the following associations: the centre is yellow, earth, the year and man (intended as super-animal, able to mediate *yin* and *yang*); south is red, fire, the phoenix, summer, and is major *yang*; north is black, water, the tortoise, winter, and is major *yin*; east is blue-green, wood, the dragon, spring, and is minor *yang*; west is white, metal, the tiger, autumn, and is minor *yin*.[281]

2.2. *ZU* 祖: LACANIAN READING OF SINITIC PATRIARCHAL AXIOLOGY

In this section, I outline an interpretation of the foremost importance of patriarchal ancestrality in Sinitic thinking through the lens of Lacanian psychoanalytical aesthetics. I axiologically study the concept of *zǔ* 祖 ("ancestor/progenitor" or "patriarch/ forefather") as a means for addressing, steering and sublimating the unreasoned primordial reality. The latter, in Lacanianism, corresponds to *Das Ding* (the "Thing"), which, through a further conceptual distinction, I reinterpret as the *Yin*-Thing and as the phase of withdrawal of the *li*(s), the formless chthonic female

---

281 Krikke (1998), figure 2-13.

matrix, the primordial *hūlē* (ὕλη, the dark "forest") of Hellenic thought, which receives form (μορφή *morphē̃*) from God.

I argue that the *zu* corresponds precisely to the Lacanian concept of the Name of the Father, which defines whatever principle has the power to make the subject into an individual entity. The Name of the Father includes: names that identify human beings, the cultural tradition to which they pertain, and the power of this system to project individuals from the past towards the future. Under such acceptation, the "name" overlaps completely with the concepts of *li* as *nomos* (with which "name" is even etymologically related, by the Indo-European root **nem-*[282]) and *habitus*, as well as with "morality", "measure", "means", "meter" and their root *me*, also shared by the Mesopotamian tradition as shown in the previous chapter.[283] Nonetheless, "name" may also be interpreted as denoting the principle which embodies a particular *li* and institutionalises it as *nomos/habitus* among men, that is to say, the factor (in the literal sense of "maker/doer") of the *li*.

2.2.1. *MING* 名 AND *MING* 命: NAME AND POWER

Significantly, the Chinese language expresses the notions of "name" and "destiny" or "order" with two near-homophonous words appertaining to the same semantic range, respectively 名 *míng* and 命 *mìng*. Similar analogies may be found in Western languages by highlighting the etymological relation between "name" (Latin *nomen*, Germanic **namô*), the Greek *nomos* and the Latin *numen* (i.e. respectively, "law" and "spirit"), as well as *norma* ("norm", "carpenter's square"). Names, whenever they are appropriate names, identify entities in accordance with their very gist, by outlining their edges (i.e. boundaries or "terms"). Befitting names "draw out things", and, in doing so, they support their development.

---

282 Pokorny (1959), pp. 763-764: **nem-*. From the same root derive the Latin *nomen*, *numen*, and *numerus*.

283 Sections 1.3.3 and 2.1.1.3 of the present essay.

In Sinitic thinking, any entity or group of entities, conceived as a genetic lineage, has a *zu*, a source and founding normative principle; a patriarch. The concept of the patriarch overlaps with that of "deity" (*di*), which is somehow different from that of "god/spirit" (*shen*); this last defines entities in their propensity or spontaneous tendency, the living flows, whether belonging to the great gods of the macrocosmic phenomena or to the forefathers of whatsoever human phenomenon. In other words, spirit is the perpetuation of an originating act and, at the same time, is the memory of the act's initiator, who continues to live in the offspring, while a deity is the initiator itself, an incarnated numinous potency. The grapheme *zu* is composed of the character meaning "to manifest/to show" but also "to worship", 示 *shì*, as the left radical, and by the character for "altar tablet", 且 *zŭ*, which is also the original form of the grapheme zu, a tangible record of the "name", as the right radical. Another Chinese word indicating ancestrality is 宗 *zōng*, which is wider in scope since it conveys both the concept of patriarch and that of the spiritual tradition which originates from that patriarch (i.e. the ancestry).

The etymology of the word "father" evokes a meaning that pertains to what hitherto explained: it comes from the Indo-European root **phter*, which also gives origin to the Latin verb *pātrō*, *pātrāre*, which means "begetting", in the sense of "onsetting", "bringing about", thus implying an agent who "does", founds and leads a thing forward, similarly to the notion of factor (i.e. doer, as aforesaid, but also speaker/sayer/teller; cf. also the Latin *parēns*, "progenitor").[284]

A *zu* is one who sets the norm of an entity, tracing the edges and the trajectories of the phenomenon. In other words, it morally sets the *numen* in motion, according to a certain style and towards a certain direction, acting as an educator of being.

---

284 Note that the root of the Latin *pater* and of the Germanic "father", as well as of "factor", is the same, and also produces the Sanskrit पितृ *pitṛ* amongst others. The P switched to F in many words, especially in Germanic, due to the phenomena of consonantic rotation which happened within these languages. Also related, in Latin, are the noun *fas* ("expression", "word") and the verb *faciō, facere* ("to do").

By swapping the terms of the Lacanian concept of the "Name of the Father", the progenitor of a phenomenon may be defined as the "Father/Factor of the Name". Once its ontological role is clarified, the concept of *zu* may be easily overlapped with those of the sage/etheling previously described, as the crafter of a particularised *li* and centraliser of a spatiotemporal coalescence.

2.2.2. THE *YANG*-THING THAT SQUARES THE *YIN*-THING

By means of Lacanian theory, I conceptualise the *zu* as a wherewithal for the sublimation of human thinking, a structuring framework for dealing with the Thing, informing this last as a cosmos, a decorated reality.[285] Said otherwise, the *zu* works as the principle begetting what I have previously defined a *Yang*-Thing, and as the *Yang*-Thing itself. It exploits the potentiality of the *Yin*-Thing, which is the primordial state of undifferentiation. My implementation of the Sinitic binary dynamism in Lacanianism, that is to say my formulation of the conceptual distinction between the *Yin*-Thing and the *Yang*-Thing, is intended to untangle the general *Das Ding* from its connotations, whether *yang*-positive or *yin*-negative, approximating it to the Sinitic *Dao*. Jacques Lacan himself, in his latter years, was inspired by Sinitic philosophy.[286] The negative interpretation of the Thing prevails in the Lacanian conception (Lacan may be identified as one of those postmodern philosophers whom Aleksandr Dugin defines as the "demonic texture" of postmodern postliberalism), while the positive one prevails in Heidegger's conception, which in the following chapter I disambiguate as the *Yang*-Thing.

---

285 Recalcati (2007), pp. 4-5.

286 Ruina (2014), pp. 7-8.

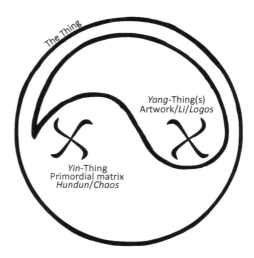

The Thing

Yang-Thing(s)
Artwork/*Li/Logos*

Yin-Thing
Primordial matrix
Hundun/Chaos

Figure 9: Diagram showing the superior, unitary Thing as composed by the dynamic interplay between the *Yin*-Thing and the *Yang*-Thing, in the guise of the traditional Sinitic symbol of the "diagram of the Supreme Polarity" (太极图 *Tàijítú*) → ☯. The *Yin*-Thing is the destructive Thing whose description prevails in Lacan, which is nothing else than returning *Chaos*, ultimate fragmentation later to be reabsorbed into undifferentiated material oneness. The *Yang*-Thing is, on the contrary, the created and creative Thing, whose description is contained in Heidegger's namesake essay; it is the self-emanating, functionally and differentially organising, normative pattern of the *Logos*. Given that the word "thing" has in itself a positive meaning, which will be explained later in the essay,[287] I suggest "Unthing" as another, more appropriate descriptor for the *Yin*-Thing, and for its activity, I suggest "unthinging".[288]

In Sinitic cosmology, the *yin* phase is that which precedes, and yet functions as the basis for, any ordering working coming from Heaven. The Lacanian *Yin*-Thing, which is the equivalent of the Freudian *Todestrieb*, is the opposite movement to that of creation, holding the individual back to primordial indistinction.

---

287 Section 3.2.2.2 of the present essay.

288 The sinister, ghastly *Yin*-Thing or "Unthing" is magistrally represented in the cinematographic series *The Thing*, in which a monstrous disorganic entity from the Antarctic reproduces itself by infecting, destroying and blending the bodies of a team of human explorers, and in the first movie everything begins with a dog, alluding to the symbolism of the constellations of the south celestial pole.

The *Yin*-Thing is not the rightward manifestation of the order of the God of Heaven, namely the functionally manifold *Yang*-Thing, but rather its leftward reabsorption into amorphous oneness. It may be identified with brute matter, the mother, or the matrix.[289] It may also be identified as psychotic stagnation and sclerotisation, ominous repetition hampering transformation, the consequential yearning for death and ultimately as death itself.[290] At the same time, it is also the potentiality out of which the particular *li*(s) draw their sustenance and the substance to which they give shape. The *Yin*-Thing is the indistinct oneness resurfacing when a given configuration of the *Li* dissolves, making space for a new configuration. It overlaps with the Sinitic concept of *Hundun* (literally the "muddled confusion" of "turbid waters"), out of which organised reality emerges by continuous creation (*creatio continua*), that is to say, by the continuously changing functional configuration of *Tian*'s *Li*. Ultimately, the *Yin*-Thing and the *Yang*-Thing may be identified as the *Chaos* and the *Logos* of Western thought.

Neutrally conceived as distinguished from both the *yin* phase of reabsorption and the *yang* phase of functional organisation, as superior to both *Chaos* and *Logos*, the Thing may be defined, in the wake of Isabelle Robinet's definition of *Hundun*, as the inchoate state of things and yet a receptacle for whatsoever possibility.[291] The Italian philosopher Francesca

---

289 Noteworthily, the words "mother" and "matter" (Latin *māter* and *māteria*) have the same etymological origin. A similar process of derivation gives "pattern" starting from *pater*. Even more evocatively, "female", Latin *fēmina*, and cognate words including *fētus* ("pregnant", "impregnated", "soaked"), all go back to the Indo-European root **dheh(y)-* which means "to suck", from which also comes the Latin verb *fellō, fellāre* ("to suck") and the noun *fellō, fellōnis* ("felon", "sucker"). The Thing, conceived as matrix and female, is wholly identifiable as the *yin*, black phase of reality, which even in Sinitic symbolism is feminine (and associated to the great goddesses of the underworld, of the terrestrial surface, and of the western direction). As everything is material, the feminine is quantitatively prevalent in reality; the masculine functions as the principle for the differentiation and sublimation of feminine undifferentiation. For the etymology of "female" see: De Vaan (2008), p. 210, entry: *fēmina*.

290 Recalcati (2007), pp. 4-5.

291 Robinet (2007), pp. 523-525.

Ruina describes it as a void of infinite potentiality that outlines entities' edges and therefore is, at one time, both damnation and possibility of defined existence.[292] The Italian psychoanalyst Massimo Recalcati defines the Thing as a "causative void".[293]

The *zu*, or the Father of the Name, or the *Yang*-Thing, functions as a framework for shaping the molten *Yin*-Thing, regulating and exploiting its whirling potentiality. Drawing upon the leftwards rotating power of the *Yin*-Thing vortex, the Father of the Name artistically sublimates it generating a rightward *Yang*-Thing vertex, distinguished from primordial oneness and therefore bequeathed with identity and personality.[294] The *Yang*-Thing's action is symbolic since it opens a gap between the individual and the primordial oneness, a distance wherein thinking may move and by means of which the individual may deal with the *Yin*-Thing and elaborate it. Recalcati defines sublimation as a "symbolic operation" for treating the "inauspicious passion for the deadly, incestuous unity which reabsorbs the subject's being".[295] Ruina compares fatherly action and creation to an artwork, which develops in the tension generated by the separation from the Thing, which alludes to this last and simultaneously provides the ability to deal with reality's traumatic infinity.[296] Fatherly influence enables the individual to see the *Yin*-Thing as an infinite potentiality for creation, highlighting its plasticity and simultaneously offering tools for its elaboration.[297] The artwork verges on the Thing but distances itself from the Thing enough so as not to be swallowed by the Thing's maelstrom.[298] Yet, the *Yang*-Thing, inasmuch as it is a "work",[299] is not definitively fixed and codified but is rather

292 Ruina (2014), p. 2.

293 Recalcati (2007), p. 42.

294 Ibidem, p. 11.

295 Ibidem, p. 5.

296 Ruina (2014), p. 2.

297 Recalcati (2007), p. 24.

298 Ibidem, p. 30; Ruina (2014), p. 2.

299 Cf. Heidegger's discussion of *Werk* and *wirken*, and *Wirklichkeit* ("reality" as

a continuous moulding and functional organisation of the *Yin*-Thing's haziness.[300] Ultimately, Recalcati sees fatherly action as not merely ideal but principally aesthetical and ethical since it creates a moralised individual endowed with value and the ability to act valuably.[301]

The concept of fatherly action as *Yang*-Thing discussed hitherto overlaps with that of the *li*(s) which build reality, with that of the *zu*, or the names which govern the phenomena, and ultimately with that of the sages/ethelings, the masters of the *li*(s) and centralisers/verticalisers, or, in a word, polarisers, of space-time. I argue that such activity of the *Yang*-Thing may be regarded as a squaring operation, linking my integration of Lacanian terminology and *yinyang* cosmology to Sinitic theory and theurgy, which hinge upon the concept of the square as a tool for connecting with Heaven, as it will be thoroughly discussed in the third chapter.

"elaboration") as — etymologically — the whirl of the self-unfolding of things, which is the same as Greek *érgon* (ἔργον, "work", "urging", "rising"; Doric preserving the more philological form ἔργον, *wérgon*) and *physis* (φύσις, "nature", "birth"), in "The Question Concerning Technology" (*Die Frage nach der Technik*). Cf. Pokorny (1959), pp. 168-169: **uerg-, *ureg-*.

300 Recalcati (2007), p. 44.

301 Ibidem, pp. 8 & 18.

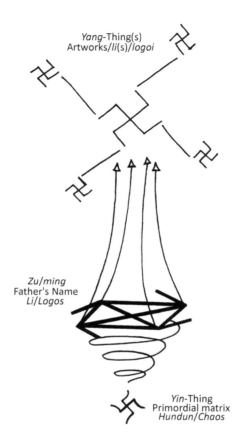

Yang-Thing(s)
Artworks/*li*(s)/*logoi*

Zu/ming
Father's Name
Li/Logos

Yin-Thing
Primordial matrix
Hundun/Chaos

Figure 10: Attempted visual representation of the squaring action of the *zu*, or the name, which masks and moulds the *Yin*-Thing (leftwise-spinning hooked cross), i.e. primordial reality full of infinite potentiality (*Hundun*), projecting its movement toward a sublime end which is, in turn, further productive, thus making the *Yang*-Thing (rightwise-spinning hooked cross), the artwork.

2.2.3. *ZU* AS MULTIPLE CENTRALISERS OF HEAVEN

The Chinese scholar Yao Xinzhong highlights that the *zu* are mediators of Heaven. Like the previously discussed figure of the sage, they function as establishers and archetypes of an order of being. They embody and reproduce Heaven's power in a particular space-time localisation. According to the American Sinologist Benjamin I. Schwartz, "the human intellect which brings order to chaos is itself an incarnation of the powers of Heaven [...]. Once the normative human culture is realized, man is aligned with the harmonies of the universe".[302] In other words, human intelligence itself, which produces normative culture (i.e. *nomos*), is the *Nous* of Heaven (i.e. *Li*) coming in the flesh (i.e. concreting in the *zu*). The lineage established by a *zu* is the bond between humanity and the supreme God of Heaven, the way which relinks back to the height of God and permits communication with it. Ceremonies of ancestral worship are aimed at steadily renewing a phenomenon's foundation act and, therefore, the bond with God.[303]

The *zu*/sages may be regarded as a manifold alternative to the objectified Christ that worked as the pole of rotation of the medieval European civilisation and which obdurately persists, emptied of its original significance, after the latter's dissolution. Unlike the objectified *Logos* of Christianity, reduced to a specific spatiotemporal entity (Jesus, had he existed or not), the *zu* and sages function as multiple "christs" warping space-time as a polycentric weft, a multiplicity of spatiotemporal configurations of Heaven.

In this regard, it is worthwhile to reconstruct the etymology of the word "christ". It is undisputed that it derives from the Greek *khristós* (χριστός, the ritually "anointed one"), itself coming from the verb *khríō* (χρίω, "to anoint"), evoking an image of the *Logos* as pervading the world like a fluid. However, I advance an auxiliary etymology connecting the word to the Indo-European root **kr-/*kar-/*ker-/*kor-*, which means "to grow/wax/concrete", but also "to top/garnish", and is at the base of concepts like the Latin *carō*, *carnis* ("flesh"), *creō*, *creāre* ("to create"), and *crēscō*, *crēscere* ("to grow/to rise"; n.b. that "grow" comes from the same root), and of further derivative words

302 Schwartz (1973), p. 38.

303 Yao (2010), p. 116.

such as "creation", "concretion", *caerimōnia* ("ceremony"), *carmen* ("ceremonial prayer"; cf. Sanskrit *karman*), and also *corpus* ("body"). In Germanic, the words "hard" (Proto-Germanic **harduz*), verbally "to harden", and "green" (Proto-Germanic **grōniz*; whereas the Latin *viridis, viride* belongs to the semantic field of *vērus*, "true"), ultimately derive from the same root.[304] The Germanic word "heart" (Proto-Germanic **hertô*), as well as the Latin *cor, cordis* ("heart", "mind") and the Greek καρδιά *kardiá*, and the Latin verb *crēdō, crēdere* ("to believe"), come from the alteration **krd-*.[305] Such etymology provides the way to interpret "christ" directly as "concretion", that is to say at one time both centralisation and centraliser of Heaven.

Similarly, Germanic words like "body" (cf. also German *Bottech*, Proto-Germanic **budagą*) and "bud" (Proto-Germanic **buddǫ*) have the same root of the Sanskrit *buddha* (the "awoken" being), the Indo-European **bheudh*, which means "to be awake/aware", like the Sanskrit verb *bodhati*, and related to other roots like **bha* ("to shine" or "to speak") and **bheu* ("to be/exist/grow"); cf. the verb to be itself, coming from Proto-Germanic **beuną*).[306] The 卍 *swastika*, which, as we have already mentioned, is a pan-Eurasian symbol of the pole of Heaven,[307] in the Buddhist tradition symbolises the mind-heart of being, of the *buddha(s)* characterised by the *buddhi* ("awakening/ awareness/enlightenment"), anchored in Heaven.

The *zu* — intended not only as the patriarch of a kin but also as the founding father, or god, of a category of entities — and its creative production represent what Ernesto de Martino defines, in his reading of the Heideggerian *Dasein*, the world-building (*Weltbildend*) presentification. It is a movement which

---

304 Pokorny (1959), pp. 530-532: **kar-*; p. 567 ff: **ker-*, **kor-*, **kr-*; p. 574 ff: **ker-*, **kerə-*, **kra-*, **kerei-*, **kereu-*; Watkins (2000), p. 40: **ker-3*.

305 Ibidem, pp. 579-580: **kerd-*, **krd-*. **kred-*.

306 Pokorny (1959), pp. 104-105: **bha-*, **bho-*, **bhə-*; p. 146 ff: **bheu-*, **bhou-*, **bhu-*, **bheudh-*; Watkins (2000), pp. 7-11: **bheu-*, **bha-1*, **bheudh-*. For the etymological relation of "body", "buddha", but also "build", see: Young (2007), p. 89.

307 Section 1.3.3 of the present essay.

always proceeds from the private towards the public, as an anastrophic movement, an ascension, because what is private "has a physiological sense when it enshrines a promise of publicisation, when it is introduced as a moment in an intersubjective dynamic of valorisation, when it becomes sooner or later communicative word and gesture"[308] — that is, when it is inserted into a world of intersubjective morality, a hodology, a templated and ritualised world. The *Dasein*, therefore, that is man as a presentification which is bequeathed with value and thus with power, is possible only in a "world of the fathers",[309] in a world which is "its own" (appropriated; *suus*),[310] where it is inlaid in a history and a memory, since it is always called to be a "producer of new value" and a "creative agent of new history", and only the inspiration to "retrospective memories of efficacious behaviours" of the ancestors allows to modify reality to produce new value,[311] so that "the past, which is always marching, embodies and ekes itself in an absolutely new present".[312] Where there are no longer history and memory, the presentification wanes in a catastrophic privatisation, and the civilisation of the fathers withers in angst in the chaotic whirlpool of the forces of the Earth, of the amorphous matrix, of the South Pole (the subterranean Hell; the Latin *Infernus*, the Indian *Naraka*, the Mesopotamian *Irkalla*), the "spirit of heaviness and darkness".[313]

---

308 De Martino (1977), p. 50.

309 Dumézil (1974), p. 42. I consulted the Italian translation of Georges Dumézil's *Les dieux des Germains* (1959), which is based on the second edition of the French original. At the cited page the author gives the etymology of the Germanic notion of *weraldiz*, "world", as the "togetherness of men" (*weraz*, "were" in its seldom used English derivative, especially in compounds) "generation after generation" (*aldiz*, "old"). The Latin *mundus*, instead, comes from the Indo-European root *mand-* which means "to adorn" and "to clean" (cf. Sanskrit *mandati*), thus a world is a "cleansed and ordered space" (cf. Sanskrit *mandala*). See: Pianigiani (1907), entry: *mondo*. From specialisations of the same root *mand-*, itself going back to *man-*, the root pertaining to anything related to the "mind", also derives the noun "mandarin", referring to the Confucian state scholars in imperial China.

310 De Martino (1977), pp. 51 & 107.

311 Ibidem, pp. 96, 142-144.

312 Ibidem, p. 567. Here De Martino cites Paul Bergson.

313 Ibidem, p. 203.

2.3. *REN* 仁: HUMAN TELEOLOGY AND ANTHROPOGOGY

As explained hithertofore, rites are: ① spatially, cosmic/cosmetic devices, that is to say devices aimed at establishing orderly contexts in harmony with the universal *Li*; ② temporally, traditional/ancestral devices, that is to say, *habiti* for transmitting configurations of space from the past towards the future; and ultimately they are ③ spatiotemporally and historically religious, in the sense that they relink (Latin *religō*, *religāre*), in the here and now, various types of men among themselves, to their own god, and back to the highest God of Heaven.

In this third section of the second chapter, I treat the Ruist concept of *rén* 仁, usually translated as "humanisation", but which I render as "anthropogogy", the education of human essence with the aim of sagehood, and heavenliness. Sigurdsson directly renders *ren*, based on the word's etymology, as "communal humanity", that is to say, constituted humanity, in groupings of commonly owned spiritual sense.[314] Anthropogogy is engrafted onto the theory of *Li*; it is a teleology of the human being in the sense that it is both the spontaneous process of birth, growth and maturation of human essence and the active concern for its cultivation with the purpose of becoming heavenlier. As such, anthropogogy is in itself a flexible and floating process that adapts to the various *li*(s), the ever-shifting configurations of reality, rather than a fixed set of rules.

2.3.1. *TIANXING* AND *TIANMING*: HEAVENLY GIST AND HEAVENLY MANDATE

According to the *Zhongyong* and Mencius, the tendency to morally organise is intrinsic to humanity's innermost gist, *xìng* 性. This grapheme means "nature/character" or "gist/essence" and is not limited to "humanity" as it is conceived in modern

---

314 Sigurdsson (2004), p. 125.

Western thought, that is to say, mankind only, but to all "human beings" in the sense of earthen beings, earthlings, beings which grow out of the earth (*humus*).[315] *Xing* is bestowed by Heaven, and it is therefore a spark of Heaven within humanity (it is even connected to the near-homophonous 星 *xīng*, meaning "star"). Indeed, in Song-dynasty Neo-Confucian interpretations, it is described as the "heavenly gist" (天性 *tiānxìng*) that foregoes and begets any particularised human manifestation.[316] The incarnated centre of irradiation of this heavenly gist is the heart/mind, *xīn* 心. It functions as the source of appropriate spontaneous behaviours, which coalesce into rituals performed by the entity as it grows and interacts with the umbegoing world. Regarded from this perspective, rituals appear as spontaneous ways of articulation of an entity's gist and, at the same time, as models for its further cultivation. Sages/ethelings are those men whose *xing* is properly realised as *tianxing*, that is, those men whose *xing* is heavenlier.[317]

Within reality, *xing* interplays with *tiānmìng* 天命 or *mìng* 命, literally "destiny", though not intended in a strongly deterministic sense. Sigurdsson opts for the translation "forces of circumstance".[318] I consider it comparable to Heidegger's concept of *Geworfenheit*, on the basis of the fact that *ming*, which is semantically related to the near-homophonous word for "name" (名 *míng*), is usually translated as "mandate", and implies a sorting and allotment of circumstances (the Heideggerian *Grundstimmungen*), determined by Heaven.

According to Mencius, *xing* is good (*shàn* 善): humanity has the innate tendency to grow by means of appropriate (*yi*) behaviours and rituals, ultimately attaining the wisdom (*zhì* 智) which allows distinguishing between right and wrong. In

---

315 Pokorny (1959), p. 414 ff: *ghdhem-, *ghdhom-. A root meaning "earth", "soil", "ground", and which has also been articulated in the forms (e.g. in Greek) Δη/Δα *De/Da* and Γῆ *Ge*, the latter properly meaning "Earth" (cf. Latin *Gaia*).

316 Makeham (2010), p. 50.

317 Sigurdsson (2004), p. 126.

318 Ibidem, pp. 134-135.

other words, good nature means the ability to regulate one's spontaneous emotions (*qíng* 情), transforming them into contextually functional thoughtful actions, that is, the power of moralising. Anyone has the potential to become a sage, and learning from those who have already attained sagehood is considered the cornerstone for building a moralised society where the cultivation of *xing* is possible. As Mencius states, sages of the past who are still worshipped in the present were outstanding individuals who wholly developed their heart-mind, becoming heavenly. According to Mencius, it is unquestionable that one's own *ming*, or position within the cosmos, influences a superior or inferior development of one's own *xing*. However, he remarks that what distinguishes a sage is his capacity and tenacity to steadfastly verticalise his heart-mind in any circumstances, even unfavourable ones.[319]

Interestingly, the Chinese word for "tenacity" is *rènxìng* 韧性, nearly homophonous of *rénxìng* 人性, literally "human gist". We have seen in the first chapter[320] how "truth" is a "tree", the tenacity of "duration", thus the temporalisation, of being which comes to light and extends itself. The Latin words "cult", "culture", and "cultivation" (all related to the verb *colō, colere, cultum*, from an earlier **quelō*, which means "to till/abide/protect" and by extension "to worship"; the earliest Indo-European root is **kel*, meaning to be "high/aloft/excelled") do not refer to the worshipping of some transcendent pseudo-"God" (like that of Christianity), but to the ordering and favouring of entities in this world. As seen, the Sinitic concepts 神 *shén*, 礼 *lǐ*, and 祖 *zǔ*, referring to modalities of being in the world, all contain the radical 礻 *shì*, meaning "to worship", thus channelling the ideas of "cultivating what shows itself/what rightens (towards Heaven)/the nominalisation of phenomena".

Xunzi provides a view of *xing* as not exactly good, but rather *è* 恶. This term means "fickle", "erratic", "inconstant", but is otherwise translatable as "ferocious". This concept appears

319 Ibidem, pp. 127-136.

320 Section 1.1.3 of the present essay.

evocatively analogous to the Hellenic *thymos* interpreted as "wrath", the neutral red impulse that in Plato's *Phaedrus'* Chariot Allegory, which gives a representation of the soul's tripartition, is the charioteer who may be driven either by the "white horse" towards higher dimensions of reason or by the "black horse" towards lower dimensions of concupiscence. Sigurdsson translates *è* as "problematic nature".[321] Xunzi says that *xing* is good in the sense of being transformable through rituals through praiseworthy effort/action (*wéi* 爲). Such plastic nature of humanity, and of other entities as well, is openness to constant cultivation and improvement. Xunzi says that what distinguishes a man from brute matter is the ability of appropriate patterning and ritualising (*li*). Sages, by virtue of their heavenlier essence, are those who appropriately (*yi*) connect natural patterns and cultural patterns, thus, sages are the most appropriate human beings.[322] Such acceptation establishes a noteworthy analogy with the etymological meaning of *Ar*-words, "properly joining/moving/acting", in orthopraxy with Heaven, the supreme model of the sages.[323]

Sigurdsson defines the somehow different teleologies of Mencius and Xunzi as, respectively, anthropogogical optimism and activism. Mencius emphasises innate improvability, whereas Xunzi gives preëminence to individual conscious will and work in the effort to become heavenlier. These perspectives are not reciprocally exclusive but are rather complementary, forming an integrated Ruist teleology.[324]

---

321 Sigurdsson (2004), pp. 137-138. Regarding the Platonic Chariot Allegory, a similar symbolism is found in Siberian Tengrism, in which Genghis Khan, the incarnation of the supreme God of Heaven (*Tengri*, related to the Sumerian *Dingir*) as cosmic sovereign, is conceived as having a "black spirit" symbolising his incarnated and martial nature, and a "white spirit" symbolising his divine investiture and anchorage to the transcendent principle of reality. The two spirits are represented by white and black *tugs* (banners made of horse hair) in the temples dedicated to Genghis Khan. Cf. Dugin (1992), p. 136, where such duality is cursorily treated.

322 Ibidem, pp. 138-143.

323 See the section 1.3.1 of the present essay regarding the *Ar* root.

324 Sigurdsson (2004), p. 144.

2.3.2. ANTHROPOGOGY AS TWOFOLD-FOURFOLD BUILDING

Suppose the *telos* of humanity is to bring *xing* to its heavenlier states. In that case, the *telos* of Ruism is to institute auspicious conditions and practices for such purposes as self-cultivation/refinement or self-building (修身 *xiūshēn*).[325] Sigurdsson compares the *xiushen* to the German notion of *Bildung* ("building", "edification"), and to the Latin *ēdūcō*, *ēdūcere* ("to lead forth/to draw out") and *ēducāre* ("to raise/ bring up/educate").[326] Sigurdsson also outlines a parallel between *xiushen* and the Icelandic notion — Icelandic language being the most archaic form of Germanic still spoken — of *menntun*, which wholly preserves the continuity between education and culture. *Menntun* is translated as "education", but literally means "becoming a man", and it is related to "menning", which means "culture" as, literally, the process of "man-making", humanisation.[327]

The English language provides an endogenous cognate of the Icelandic term, manning, which nevertheless has acquired different meanings. Alternatively to "anthropogogy", translating *ren* and *xiushen* with derivatives of the word "man" would be a worthy choice in a Germanic context since the Germanic word "man" (Proto-Germanic **mann*, basically unvaried from earlier Proto-Indo-European) precisely distinguishes "mankind" from "humanity", the latter meaning "being from the earth/made up of earth" (Latin *homō*, Germanic **gumô*),[328] thus being as not necessarily shaped by Heaven, possibly still in the state of brute matter. Furthermore, "man" is etymologically related to "mind", and even to "hand" (cf. Latin *manu*, thus to the concept of dexterity) and "male"

---

325 Ibidem, p. 147.

326 Ibidem, pp. 149-150.

327 Ibidem, p. 150.

328 Pokorny (1959), p. 414 ff: **ghdhem-, *ghdhom-*.

(cf. Latin *mās*), in addition to being related, as previously seen, also to "morality" and "measure".[329]

In Germanic mythology, there is even the theonym *Mannus*, the progenitor of mankind and founder of civilisation (related to the Vedic *Manu*). Relevantly, the Chinese grapheme *ren* is a compound of the homophone 人 *rén*, which means "man", and 二 *èr*, which means "two". Anthropogogy is, therefore, a fourfold praxis realising as a dynamism between two elements within a master-disciple relationship in the pedagogical reading made by Sigurdsson,[330] male-female, or past-future relationship, patriarch-genealogical offspring. It is a fourfold praxis because the dynamism, the working in the present, takes place in the four directions of space. The anthropogogical process and its outcome, mankind, is the third element that arises from that dynamism.

In early Germanic thinking, the father of *Mannus* is *Tuisto*, also spelled *Tuisco*.[331] The name, attested as such in Tacitus' *Germania*, is a Latinised form of an ancient Germanic theonym which may be rendered in modern English as "Two", or more accurately "Twice" or "Twist", or "Tween/Twixt" (the root of "two", Proto-Germanic **twai*, with the adjectival suffix **-iskaz*; cf. Old High German *zwisk/twisk*, the modern *Zwischen*).[332] Therefore, Germanic thinking offers an analogous conception of mankind as generated by the dynamism of a duality. Furthermore, *Tuisto*'s Sanskrit equivalent is *Tvastar*,[333] and it is described in Vedic literature as the visible creativity emanated

---

329 Pokorny (1959), p. 700 ff: **manus*, **monus*; Watkins (2000), p. 51: **man-1*, **man-2*; p. 54: **men-1*, **men-2*. N.b. that despite having instituted such distinction between the words "humanity" and "mankind", so that the former ("earthly" humanity) appears as somewhat inferior to the latter (heavenly "mankind", the offspring of *Mannus*) — a distinction which is even more relevant given the contemporary globalised meaning of "humanity" —, throughout the essay I continue to use predominantly "humanity", reserving "mankind" to the few cases in which the narrower meaning is pertinent.

330 Sigurdsson (2004), pp. 184-189.

331 Frawley (2001), p. 236.

332 Pokorny (1959), pp. 228-232: **duo(u)*. Also see: Latham (1851), pp. 24-26.

333 Frawley (2001), p. 236.

by the absolute God, *Vishvakarman* (the "All-Doer"). An analogy may be made between this conception and the Sinitic vision of the *Tian/Di/Dao* begetting the 太极 *Tàijí* ("Supreme Polarity") of *yinyang*, that in turn begets all things.

Figure 11: Germanic rune of *Tius* (**Tīwaz* ↑), another name for *Tuisto*.[334] The theonym *Tiwaz* (Proto-Germanic; attested as Latinised *Tius*, archaic/modern English *Tiw/Tue*, Nordic *Tyr*, German *Ziu* or *Cyo*, Gothic *Teiws*), originates from the generic Indo-European term for "deity" (**deywos*), was identified as the supreme God of Heaven (*Dyeus*), but in later times as the god of war, and further defined in Latin inscriptions as *Mars/Tius Thinxsus/Thincsus/Thingsus* (Proto-Germanic **Þingsaz*), that is to say, "God of the Thing". The word "thing" comes from the root **tenk-*, meaning "to extend/stretch" but also "to thicken", which in turn is related to the root **teng-/*tong-*, of "thought", explained in the preface of the present essay.[335] It is important to keep in mind the semantic web connecting divinity, duality, war and thing, as well as the etymologies of such words; they will prove relevant in the next chapter of the essay, where they are further deepened.

Sigurdsson further analogises the Ruist concept of self-cultivation and education to H.G. Gadamer's idea of "edification", consisting of an aesthetical and historical experience, a constant extension of the self beyond its own limits, towards one's group's common self, and then further beyond towards other groups' selves. Other analogies are made with Wilhelm

---

334 Latham (1851), pp. 24-26: *Tuisto, Tuisco, Tiusco, Tiu*. N.b. Latham considers *Tuisco* or, better, *Tiusco*, to be the original, adjectival form of the theonym, and *Tuisto* a corruption.

335 Pokorny (1959), pp. 1067-1068: **tenk-*.

Dilthey's *Erlebnis* ("lived experience"), as opposed to the *Erfahrung* of modern sciences, and with John Dewey's education as a "continuum of interrelated experiences" which progressively endows the individual with normative instruments needed for the further integration of new data. According to Dewey's definition, reasoning means to meaningfully interweave such an experiential continuum, arranging the collected data into a meaningful coherence.[336]

A representation similar to the German "edification", especially the image given by Gadamer, is contained in the "Great Learning" (大学 *Dàxué*), where self-cultivation is explained as an ordering activity which extends from the individual self to all things of creation, all proceeding from Heaven (*tiānxià* 天下, literally "under-Heaven") — we are still within the *Li*, acting through the *li*(s). One of the most quoted excerpts of the Great Learning is the following one, proposed here in the translation of James Legge:[337]

> [In order to realise peace of everything *tianxia* (everything coming from Heaven)] Wishing to order well their states, they [the ancients] first regulated their families. Wishing to regulate their families, they first cultivated their persons. Wishing to cultivate their persons, they first rectified their hearts. Wishing to rectify their hearts, they first sought to be sincere in their thoughts. Wishing to be sincere in their thoughts, they first extended to the utmost their knowledge. The extension of knowledge is by the investigation of things.

Sigurdsson says that Legge's translation may be misinterpreted as portraying a "step-to-step linear teleology" of learning. In the original text of the Great Learning, indeed, the stages are consecutive yet not separated, and it is possible to move across them and simultaneously undertake more than one of them.[338]

The common denominator of these analogical interpretations is that anthropogogy is neither solipsistic nor an unsystematic accumulation of notions but is rather a communicative and

336 Sigurdsson (2004), pp. 151-163.

337 Ibidem, pp. 201-202.

338 Ibidem, pp. 202-203.

projective building, contextualised in space (working in the present of the four directions) and ongoing in time (double dynamism of past and future). The heavenly gist of humanity comes to fruition in moralised communities which reproduce Heaven on Earth, wherein the individual is bequeathed with meaning, consisting in cultivating, through the presencing of consciousness, the coherence between the experience inherited from the past and the projects for the future.

2.3.3. ANTHROPOGOGY AS HEAVENLY VIRTUE

Sigurdsson, in the footsteps of Ron G. Williams and James W. Boyd, describes the anthropogogical function of ritual as artwork. Rite is the craft of simultaneously learning and practising activities for developing the *xing*, that is to say, the heavenly gist of humanity, and for moralising instincts; at the same time, it is the craft of instituting and ongoingly renewing a favourable environment for such cultivation, that is to say, a morally organised world aligned with Heaven.[339]

The quality of the sage/etheling who properly and celestially realises *xing* is *dé* 德, "virtue", but also translated as "excellence" and "efficacy". *De*, in Sinitic philosophy, is described as the quality of being one with the *Dao* of Heaven. The attainment of the *de* is the purpose of anthropogogy, and in turn, the *de* is the ability to educate others; it is the heavenly power "to initiate things and bring them to completion", to appropriately change, improve and set things in space and time. The scholar Peter Boodberg translated *de* as "indarrect" (his coinage meaning "innerly upright") power, which is a power exerting itself without coercion; Boodberg notes that its graphic etymology indicates that it is composed of *xīn* 心, "heart", and *zhí* 直, "(up)right", indicating an ascending movement, and that in its most ancient acceptation it indicated a sort of "electric charge", waxing and

---

339 Ibidem, pp. 169-174 & 191. Sigurdsson relies upon: Williams, Ron G.; Boyd, James W. (1993). *Ritual Art and Knowledge: Aesthetic Theory and Zoroastrian Ritual*. Columbia, South Carolina: University of South Carolina Press. p. 93.

waning according to mysterious laws and capable of being transmitted.[340] The Sinologist Victor H. Mair propounds an Indo-European phonetic etymology of the Chinese word, tracing it back to the Indo-European root *dugh* and later Germanic *dugan*, which is the base of a series of words including the English "doughty" (worthy, stouthearted) and "douth" (virtue).[341] Interestingly, Mair proposes an Indo-European derivation also for *Dao*: the Old Chinese pronunciation of such word was *Drog* or *Dorg*, which he links to Proto-Indo-European *dergh-/*dheragh-/*dhreg-* ("to take/to grasp", "to pull/to drag", "to slide/ to slither", "to strike", and "way/movement"), from which spurt the English "track" and "trek", the Russian дорога *doroga* ("way/ road") and its Slavic cognates, the Latin *trahō*, *trahere* and many other cognates,[342] indicating the flow of reality gushing from the supreme transcendent source of Heaven to be rectified again towards the supreme source of Heaven.

Remarkably, even the Greek word *arete*, "virtue", the quality of the *aristoi*, as shown in the foregoing chapter, is connected to the root *Ar*,[343] indicating the principle and Reason of the universe in Heaven, and the movement to conform to it. Not randomly, the Latin word "virtue" itself may also mean a correct "movement" and "reason" of being (Latin *virtūs*, from *vir*, "man" as "male"; cf. "were" in archaic English; cf. also the aforediscussed *viridis* and *vērus*). The Sinitic *de* as an "electric charge" descending from Heaven and corroborated by correct movement of alignment with Heaven, by "divine orientation" towards the North Pole and imitation of its spinning asterisms, which gives order to the physical structure of the entity which receives it, and which is irradiable to the surrounding matter giving order to it, is comparable to the Mesopotamian *melam*, the Iranian *khvarenah* (both meaning a "divine radiance/

---

340 Boodberg (1953), pp. 323-325.

341 Mair (1990a), p. 134.

342 Ibidem, p. 132. For the roots see: Pokorny (1959), pp. 212-213, 257 & 273: *dergh-, *dheragh-, *dhreg-*.

343 Section 1.3.1 of the present essay.

splendour"), as well as the Sanskrit *ojas* and the Latin *augus* (both meaning a "spiritual force/vigour" to develop things), which Dugin describes as the "energy of condensed light which equates men to gods", and which is symbolised by fire (the element characterised by ascending movement) and by the raptor bird (especially the eagle or hawk).[344]

It is worthwhile noting that, even in the light of the absence of soul-body or in-out dualisms in Sinitic thinking, *xiushen* is a cultivation of both the mind and of the body. Etymologically analysed, the concept of *xiushen* is a compound of *shēn* 身, which means "body" and "character" and is phonetically cognate to the word for "god/spirit", and *xiū* 修, which is explained in the *Shuowen Jiezi* as meaning "to decorate/to ornament". Thus, *xiushen* may be exhaustively rendered as "ornamenting one's body and character", one's own nature.[345]

2.3.4. OURANOGEOANTHROPISM: TELEOLOGICAL VERTICALITY

Besides the hereinbefore bespoken conception of the *zu* as particularised and localised incarnations and centralisers/polarisers of Heaven, it is worthwhile highlighting that Sinitic thinking provides the devices for conceiving the human figure itself as a symbol of Heaven. The grapheme *Tiān* 天 — as already enunciated, usually translated as "Heaven" or "Sky", but meaning as well the universal highest "God", "Day", the spring of *Li* and of all things — is the sketch of a human figure. Lillian Tseng says that the grapheme is a derivative of 大 *dà*, "a person standing with legs apart and arms stretched out", denoting "adulthood", "magnificence", and "full growth", with the addition of a big head, which originally (11th-10th century BCE) was a circle and afterwards was simplified (by the 9th century BCE) as a horizontal line.[346]

---

344 Dugin (1992), pp. 11-12, where the author discusses the Iranian concept of *khvarenah*, spelled *hvareno* in his book.

345 Sigurdsson (2004), p. 199.

346 Tseng (2011), pp. 1-2.

As demonstrated hereinabove, the heavenly gist (*tianxing*) and its virtue (*de*) are bijectively related and come from Heaven. They may otherwise be defined as the potentiality and activity of Heaven itself in the flesh. Shirley Chan, in her study of Heaven as explained in the Guodian texts, which were rediscovered in 1993, says that the *xing* is bestowed by Heaven to "follow and be guided by the heavenly principle" (i.e. *Li*).[347] Relying upon the basic graphic etymology provided by Chan, Heaven may be conceived as the virtual potentiality intrinsic to all creation. All things, in their own way, contain Heaven and unfold it according to their own *li*. Yet, it is in mankind that Heaven comes to the awareness of itself and comes to its highest maturity in the sages/ethelings who can reproduce the heavenly power in civilisation in a civilising action. Chan describes the etheling as the intermediary between Heaven and other entities.[348]

The relational axis between Heaven and humanity may be analogised to Heidegger's idea of "ontological difference" (*Ontologische Differenz*) between *Seyn* and the various entities (*Seyn* means "Being"; Heidegger recovers an archaic spelling of *sein* to portray the whole spatiotemporal universe as an unfolding process, and the universe itself as the supreme "Being" — it is sometimes rendered in English as "Beyng", a 14th-century spelling of "being"). The etheling may be compared to Heidegger's concept of *Dasein*, which is always *mit-ein-Ander-in-der-Welt-Sein* ("being-in-the-world-with-another"), likewise the Sinitic idea of *ren*, which realises itself in the fourdimensional space-time springing from a twofold dynamism. Because of such ontological difference between the creature and the creator, which is the same as Jullien's concept of "gap" (*écart*) between entities, human life and thinking is possible. Since it is ever-unfinished, human reality is ever-cultivable and ever-improvable; it is an ongoing anthropogogy and ongoing harmonisation with the ever-shifting conditions of Heaven through the continuous invention and practice of appropriate rituals.

---

347 Chan (2012), p. 106.

348 Ibidem, p. 117.

Ruist thinkers have discussed such a relationship in various terms. The underlying idea of all their conceptions is that there is a "harmonious unity of Heaven and mankind" (天人合一 *tiānrén héyī*), which together with Earth form the 天地人 *tiāndìrén* vertical relational scheme, which I translate here as "ouranogeoanthropism" — a Greek-language rendition of such ontological system, which, starting from Heaven (Οὐρανός *Ouranós*) comes on Earth (Γεω *Geō*) through mankind (*anthropos*)[349] —, also defined as the Threefold Potentiality (三才 *Sāncái*).[350]

Figure 12: The diagram above shows the ouranogeoanthropic relational scheme or the Threefold Potentiality, that is to say the vertical shaft of the cosmos, with humanity as the intermediary between Heaven and Earth. Shown below are versions of the grapheme *cái* (才), "power" and "wealth", "well-standing", respectively in ① Shang oracular script, ② Zhou bronze script, ③ Zhou large seal script (attested in the Ming *Liushutong*) and ④ Han *Shuowen Jiezi* script, the latter two of which give the idea of a rotating cross. Interestingly, the scheme mirrors the grapheme 王 *wáng* ("king"), which I explain later in the essay.

---

349 My coinage "ouranogeoanthropism" is inspired by similar Hellenising compounds coined by Aleksandr Dugin to define similar relational tensions in Heidegger's phenomenology, mentioned in the section 3.3.2 of the present essay.

350 *Tiandiren* and *Sancai* are cursorily explained in: Cua (2013), p. 376.

The Han-dynasty scholar Dong Zhongshu (董仲舒 179-104 BCE) formulated a doctrine of *tiānrén gǎnyìng* (天人感应), literally the "interaction between Heaven and humanity", in which the mind-body continuum of the human being is considered as a micro-Heaven, as reproducing Heaven itself. Mencius speaks of *tiānrén hédé* (天人和德), literally the "harmonised virtue of Heaven and humanity".

Xunzi instead discusses umbe *tiānrén zhīfēn* (天人之分), the "division between Heaven and humanity", which, like Heidegger's "ontological difference" and Jullien's "gap", does not imply a separation between the two, but rather a dynamic tension. Xunzi says that Heaven's creativity is auspiciously constant (常 *cháng*), and mankind has to be consonant with Heaven's constancy, which offers the proper spatiotemporal conjunctures for the development of human *tianxing*.

Chan corroborates a non-dualistic interpretation of the "interaction of Heaven and humanity". The ideas of "unity of Heaven and humanity" and "division between Heaven and humanity" do not exclude each other; rather, it is humanity's awareness of Heaven that institutes at one time both the ontological differentiation between the two and the differential dynamism. Awareness of Heaven also infuses such dynamism with teleological worth: since "Heaven generates and man completes" (天生人成 *tiānshēng rénchéng*) things, mankind has the intrinsic role of fostering, or cultivating, creation,[351] just like in ancient Mesopotamian culture.

Elsewise said, Sinitic thinking explains the division between Heaven and humanity as a dynamic duality rather than as a radical dichotomy. Human agency acquires a central, possibly vertical, role within such duality. It is entrusted with the responsibility to be the intermediary between Heaven and Earth, cooperating with Heaven for the wellbeing of all entities, within a celestially-ordered civilisation, by attuning the productivity of the Earth with the celestial rhythms/spirits, by harmonising the human *xing* with Heaven.

---

351 Chan (2011), pp. 64-67.

Such teleology sharply contrasts with Western ideas of humanity as either impotent or destined to succumb to circumstances, even unlucky ones (represented by the figure of the Christ interpreted as a renunciation of agency), or as what Dugin describes as the illusory omnipotence of the pseudo-free anomic individual-object of the post-Christian postliberal machination of a global market society of Westernising postmodernity. Sino-Ruist thinking provides an alternative conception of humanity as an ever-unfinished and therefore ever-transformable and ever-improvable embodiment of Heaven itself, of the God which is in the heights of the Heavens, thus in the heights of all beings. *Altus* in Latin ("high"), like *uls*, *ulter* ("further", "yond", "beyond"), *alius* and *alter* ("other"), and the Germanic **aldaz* (from which come *alt* in German and "old" in English) and **allaz* (all both in English and German) which have preserved more archaic meanings, derive from the same Indo-European root **al-/*ol-/*el-*, which indicated the "yond", "beyond": [352] the heights of the Heavens indicate ontological anteriority, not merely dimensional stature, thus the generative source of all Heavens, of all entities, the Wholly Other (*Ganz Anderes*) of Rudolf Otto; the patriarchs of beings and before/above them the supreme forefather of all the forms of the universe (曾祖父 *zēngzǔfù*, another definition of the supreme God in Chinese[353]). Man is a micro-Heaven harboured within macro-Heavens, all called to be reflections of the supreme Heaven.

---

352 Pokorny (1959), p. 24 ff: **al-*, **ol-*.

353 Zhong (2014), p. 84, note 282.

CHAPTER 3

SINO-RUIST COSMOTHEANTHROPISM

The Fourth Political Theory may easily turn toward everything that preceded modernity in order to draw its inspiration. The acknowledgement of "God's death" ceases to be the mandatory imperative for those who want to stay relevant. [...] When it [theology] returns, postmodernity (globalisation, postliberalism and the post-industrial society) is easily recognised as the "kingdom of the Antichrist"[354] (or its counterpart in other religions [...]). This is not simply a metaphor capable of mobilising the masses, but a religious fact — the fact of the Apocalypse. [...] If atheism, in the New Era, ceases to be something mandatory for the Fourth Political Theory, then the theology of monotheistic religions, which at one time displaced other sacred cultures, will not be the ultimate truth, either [...]. Theoretically, nothing limits the possibilities for an in-depth readdressing of the ancient archaic values, which can take their place in the new ideological construction, upon being adequately recognised and understood. [...] Not only the highest supra-mental symbols of faith can be taken on board once again as a new shield [...]. If we reject the idea of progress that is inherent in modernity [...], then all that is ancient gains value and credibility for us simply by virtue of the fact that it is ancient. [...] "Ancient" means good, and the more ancient — the better. Of all creations, Heaven is the most ancient one. The carriers of the Fourth Political Theory must strive toward rediscovering it in the near future.

Aleksandr Dugin[355]

The sky itself as a religious institution, before even gods are spoken of as inhabiting the sky, reveals transcendence. In this sense it is a symbol of orientation. Its height and its vault place the human within a proper

---

354 If we assume, as proposed in the section 2.2.3 of the present essay, that "Christ" derives from the Indo-European root *kr-, which indicates "coalescence", "aggregation", on the other hand "Antichrist" is whatsoever force of disgregation, decomposition, discordance, which breaks up things in parts, societies in anomic individuals, and which separates entities from their patriarchal spirits, and thence from the God of Heaven. It is whatsoever force contrary to the *Logos*, which is not religious but areligious, which does not relink but unlink, which is not patriarchic but anarchic, which unleashes *Chaos* and dissolves entities into the primordial formless abyss of the matrix: egalitarianism, liberalism, feminism (i.e. suckism), materialism (i.e. motherism), Christianity (which we may now redefine "sclerotism"; note that the word "cretin" comes from the same root, via the Franco-Provençal form of "Christian", *crétin*).

355 Dugin (2012), pp. 27-28.

realm — the situation of finitude in the face of the exaltation of the transcendent starry and shining vault of heaven. Consciousness itself is the most specific correlate of this grandeur of the sky; we are situated as humans in this manner.

Charles Long, referring to Mircea Eliade's
Patterns in Comparative Religions, 1958.[356]

— PROLEGOMENON: RETURNING TO HEAVEN

In this chapter, I examine Sinitic "cosmotheanthropism", that is, the conception of cosmos, divinity and humanity as a synergic continuum. I focus on two fundamental notions of this "religio-political vision", namely *Di* or *Tian* — i.e. the notion of supreme God of Heaven — and the figure of the Yellow Deity, god of the humano-cosmic axial centre. I analyse the symbolic meaning of the graphemes expressing *Di* and *Tian* through phonetic and graphic etymologies, simultaneously showing their relation to the early Indo-European *Deus* and *Dies* to reactivate these last concepts and reweave an old and yet always new fundamental theological symbolic web. Tersely said, the purpose is to "return to Heaven", or to redirect the gaze of humanity towards what divinity actually is; to rectify the forces of the Earth towards Heaven.

The intuition of *Di* or *Tian*, that is, Heaven — the experience of the blue starry sky as the primary symbol of a metaphysical order permeating all the physical dimensions, and metonymically the notion of the highest God — is the birth momentum of human consciousness. As Norman Giradot says in his foreword to David W. Pankenier's *Astrology and Cosmology in Early China* (2013), the astral patterns showing themselves in the sky, and their movements, were a powerful inspiration for early stargazers. There is an "archaic and fundamental human ability to see the sky as a sign with a message of existential meaning that calls for a cultural response", to see the sky as an "inexhaustible

---

356 The same quote, which I reproduce here verbatim, introduces Norman Giradot's foreword to David W. Pankenier's 2013 work *Astrology and Cosmology in Early China: Conforming Earth to Heaven.* p. xvii.

hierophany". I argue that such sight and consequent awareness left an indelible impression, or rather an inextinguishable influx, in the whirls of the minds of early star-gazers, indeed triggering the development of self-consciousness and the *superego*. All aspects of culture, from architecture to social organisation, originated as ritual actions aimed at reproducing the patterns of Heaven to model humanity after Heaven. Ultimately, the evolution of humanity proceeds in response to the heavenly movements. The "awesome vision of the sky" was originally "a revelation of the human participation in the celestial patterns that define the entire cosmos".[357] Being is time; Heaven is time. Evolution is dragged by the participation of the many times of humans, or of entities in a wider sense, to the great time of Heaven (the God-Year; *annus*, the Latin word for "year", is related to the Mesopotamian ✳ *An*).

I agree with Giradot that understanding Sinitic thinking "is simultaneously to know the wellspring of human nature".[358] Pankenier notes that this knowledge of the sky and intuition of divinity was not unique to China.[359] John C. Didier, throughout his *In and Outside the Square* (2009), discusses other Eurasian cultures' symbolism pertaining to the same vision.[360] However, I think that due to its ideographic writing system and its emphasis on a contextual and ancestral anthropogogy conceived as the very religion that binds humanity to the utmost God, Sinitic thinking has preserved this divine wisdom in an exceptionally coherent way. In the first chapter of the present essay, we have analysed the Mesopotamian tradition as a common denominator between Sinitic and Indo-European cultures;[361] what distinguishes Sinitic culture among them, and strengthens its role as a platform wherefrom to start for a re-understanding of the other two and the renovation of Europe and Eurasia, is

---

357 Pankenier (2013), p. xix.

358 Ibidem.

359 Ibidem, p. xviii.

360 Dider (2009), vol. I, passim.

361 Section 1.3.3 of the present essay.

also the fact that it is alive and lively. Sinitic thinking underlines the flexibility and adaptability of the divine principles to the ever-changing configurations of the world for a continuous renewal of order, avoiding the stiffening of the latter into conclusive codes. This is exactly the why of Chinese culture's millenary longevity, of its capability of tenaciously rejuvenating itself, just like a tree, just like what is true.[362]

The Sinitic glyphs pertaining to the experience of divinity may be regarded as instruments of both theory (θεωρία *theōría*, "divine visualisation") and theurgy (θεουργία *theourgía*, "divine work"), of cosmogenic/cosmetic (i.e. order-making) praxis within a quadridimensional cosmotheanthropic architecture. As for what concerns sight and vision, it is worthwhile to indicate now that it is a quality not only of the symbolism of raptor birds (the diurnal eagle or the nocturnal owl),[363] but also of another being which is a symbol of wisdom, the snake, "dragon" according to its Greek-rooted name, δράκων *drákōn* linked to the verb δρακεῖν *drakeîn* ("to see" sharply, "to gaze", "to stare", "to observe", but also "to live"). It is दृश् *dṛś* ("to see") in Sanskrit, and the derived term (amongst others) दर्शन *dárśana* means "sight", "vision", and also systematic "philosophy". The common Indo-European root is **derk-*, "to see".[364] The Dragon, devalued in the West, is a particularly significant being in Sinitic culture, and its symbolism is explained further in the present chapter. Like in the Nietzschean *Zarathustra*, the eagle is a symbol of human reason (pride). When well used, it does not fly away in

---

362 We have seen in the section 1.1.3 the etymological relationship between "truth" and "tree", in Indo-European languages, and especially Germanic, these terms representing the procession, or propensity, of being. In the section 1.2.3 we have seen the difference between the Sinitic and the Western conception of truth.

363 As seen in a note (235) in the section 2.1.1.1, in which I discussed the owl. Note that in ancient Germanic the name of the "owl" (**uwwalǭ*, diminutive of **uwwǭ*, from which also comes the German *Eule* for instance) indicates the eagle-owl of Eurasia (German: *Uhu*), and its same root is that of the "howl" (German: *Heulen*) of the wolf. Cf. Orel (2003), p. 436. The eagle is another raptor bird associated with wisdom; already in Mesopotamia it represented the men of wisdom (𒍪 *zu*), the court scholars, *apkallu*, who, like eagles, are able to gaze directly at the Sun. Cf. Parpola (1993), p. 167, note 31 & p. 198, note 143.

364 Pokorny (1959), p. 213: **derk-*.

meaningless abstraction but plays with the potentiality of the eternal return of the snake (wisdom), projecting it into the spiral of time. Thus, philosophy is intended as the "science of the serpent", of the development, of generation, and thus of time; keep in mind this symbolism.

In the last section, I discuss the Yellow Deity as a palingenesis of the *Logos*, of its rebirth as *Dasein/Zwischen, Ort* and *Ereignis*, relying upon Heideggerian and Duginian philosophy, and likening it to the "cosmic Christ" of Bonaventuran theology, also with the purpose of unfixing the latter and identifying it with the figure of the Eurasian cosmic sovereign. Lastly, I investigate some instances of what I define *interpretatio sinica*, that is, the functional and etymological equation of the Yellow Deity and other deities of Sinitic religio-cosmology with those of Mesopotamian and Indo-European religio-cosmologies. As already affirmed in the first chapter,[365] the four-dimensional cosmology — or seven-dimensional, as we will see — that is illustrated in these pages may be compared to ancient Mesopotamian conceptions but also to the Jewish mysticism of the *Merkabah*, the *Hayyoth* and the *Heikhaloth*, and to subsequent Christian and angelological rehashes in Late Antiquity (cf. *Corpus Dionysianum*).

3.1. THEORETICAL DEVICES FOR CONTEMPLATING HEAVEN: ETYMOLOGIES OF SINITIC SIGNIFIERS OF DIVINITY AND THEIR CONNECTION TO INDO-EUROPEAN

3.1.1. *BEIJI*: THE NORTHERN HEIGHTH

Shàngdì (上帝 "Supreme/Highest Deity") or simply *Dì* (帝 "Deity") is the olden conception of the utmost God of Heaven and its universe that continues in modern-day Sino-Ruist theology. Historical evidence of the primacy of this notion in

---

365 Section 1.3.3 of the present essay.

Sinitic religion dates back to the Shang (17th-11th centuries BCE) and Zhou (11th-3rd centuries BCE) dynasties. By the early Zhou, the concept was conveyed by a new semantic field pertaining to *Tiān* 天, "Heaven".[366] During the Warring States period in the latter Zhou epoch, as well as during the subsequent Han dynasty (3rd century BCE to 3rd century CE), the supernal God became known as the *Tàiyī* (太一 "Supreme One")[367] and its *Dao* (or the *Dao* as a single concept in Taoism, which instituted itself just in this period),[368] which is to say the *Li*. What is important for the present etymological study is that the *Di* or *Tian* was identified with the north celestial pole (北极 *Běijí*, "Northern Pole/Heighth"), and with the Big Dipper (北斗 *Běidǒu*, "Northern Dipper", as defined in Chinese) and the Little Dipper constellations (or Great and Small Chariot) which turn around it.[369] More detailedly, as already said in the first chapter with regards to pan-Eurasian religio-cosmological knowledge,[370] the ecliptic North Pole, fixed and coiled by the constellation of the Dragon (天龙 *Tiānlóng*, "Dragon of Heaven"), represented the quiescent, and also unknown, aspect of the God, whereas the precessional North Pole, which moves, and its wheeling Chariots, represented its active, and more immediately visible, aspect. The Chariots form the bodies, respectively, of the Great She-bear (*Ursa Major*) and the Little She-bear (*Ursa Minor*), whence the association of polar symbolism to such animals — otherwise, raptor birds, wolves, or other free animals such as the eight-legged horse of Odin, *Sleipnir* — and the meaning of the Greek name "Arctic" (αρκτικός *arktikós*, "of the north/she-bear"; of the ἀρκτος *árktos*), and in medieval Germanic culture were also called, respectively, the Chariot of the Man/of Charles/of Odin and the Chariot of the Woman, representing the male and female aspects, or the phase of begetting (*yang*) and that of reabsorption (*yin*),

---

366 Pankenier (1995), p. 172.

367 Pankenier (2013), pp. 8-9.

368 Pankenier (2004), pp. 214-218.

369 Ibidem.

370 Section 1.3.3 of the present essay.

of the God.[371] The feminine principle of reabsorption into the chaotic amorphous matrix is also associated with the Antarctic, with the south celestial pole and its constellations, the Southern Cross (*Crux*), the Great Dog (*Canis Major*) and the Little Dog (*Canis Minor*), the dog being the chthonic hybrid animal symbol of death and thralldom *par exellence*.[372] The seven stars of the Big Dipper (cf. Latin *septemtriones*, "seven bulls" or forthwith "seven stars"), in the Sinitic and in the broader pan-Eurasian tradition as well, are considered the active powers of the God, personified as seven deities, and reflected in the seven planets (including the two luminaries, the Sun and the Moon), and in the Sinitic tradition are also bewritten as *Di*'s celestial vehicle, as reported, for instance, in Sima Qian's *Treatise on the Celestial Officers* (in the first half of the Han epoch):[373]

> The Dipper is the Deity's carriage. It revolves about the centre, visiting and regulating each of the four regions. It divides *yin* from *yang*, establishes the four seasons, equalises the five elemental phases, deploys the seasonal junctures and angular measures, and determines the various periodicities: all these are tied to the Dipper.

Even before the foundation of the centralised Chinese empire, in the late Warring States period, Confucius likened the virtue (*de*) of the sages to the north celestial pole; as the *Analects* report:[374]

> The Master said: To conduct government by virtue may be compared to the North Star: it occupies its place, while the myriad stars revolve around it.

David W. Pankenier provides insightful studies about the origin of the graphemes for *Di* and *Tian*, drawn by connecting the

---

371 See the note 179 of the present essay for further details, where I also explain that "Charles", *karl* in Norse and *churl* as an English alternative, is an ancient Germanic concept of free man.

372 Allen (1963), pp. 184-191 & 437, where *Crux* is identified as the "southern celestial horologe" and as the "Southern Chariot"; pp. 117-135 for *Canis Major* and *Canis Minor*.

373 As quoted in: Pankenier (2013), p. 9.

374 Pankenier (2004). Quotes the *Analects* 2:1.

Dippers in order to locate the true North.[375] Although the active power of the centre of the universe that produces and regulates everything was conveniently identified, in different epochs, with one or another pole star (currently α *Ursae Minoris*) due to the axial precession, the *Zhuangzi* — one of the founding texts of early Taoism — says that "the virtue of the Supreme One is emptiness", or 無 *wú* in Chinese, which literally means "no-thing" or "non-presence" (opposite to 有 *yǒu*, "presence"),[376] which is the starless ecliptic North Pole coiled by the Dragon. There was an awareness that the true north is empty of stars, that the supreme power is protean, and that its identification with the given contemporary pole star was an expedient which hinted at the quiescent supreme unity.[377] Indeed, while Taoism, with its doctrine of the *wuwei* (effortless activity), emphasises the shapelessness of the original source (the *Dao* as 无极 *Wújí*, "Without Pole", the ecliptic centre, which at a second time becomes the *Taiji*, the celestial centre) — and at the same time its formidable potency and indispensability, which is like that of the void hub of a wheel — and only alludes to its astral connections, the Confucian tradition explicitly espouses both the astral identification of the spring of the universe and its natural order with the Northern Heighth, and the identification of its incarnate power, the third aspect — the earthly one — of the God of Heaven described in the first chapter, with the authority of the sage and king, in such function defined as the "One-Man".[378]

As represented in the *Heguanzi*, the rotation of the Big Dipper around the hub of the skies was conceived as the supreme horologe (i.e. "order-saying", given the etymology), the foremost symbol of the divine order, as the ladle by means of which the God of Heaven pours its power into the world:[379]

375 Pankenier (2013), pp. 83-117: Chapter 3 – "Looking to the Supernal Lord".

376 *Zhuangzi jijie* 32.453. *Wu*, which also means simply "not", refers to a lack of differentiated beings, not to the *nil* (*nihil*). Also see: Perkins (2016), § 3.1 – "Monism".

377 Pankenier (2013), p. 90.

378 Pankenier (2004), pp. 219-220.

379 Ibidem, p. 220. Quotes the *Heguanzi* 5:21/1-4; also see note 24.

When the handle of the Dipper points to the east at dawn, it is spring to all the world. When the handle of the Dipper points to the south, it is summer to all the world. When the handle of the Dipper points to the west, it is autumn to all the world. When the handle of the Dipper points to the north, it is winter to all the world. As the handle of the Dipper rotates above, so affairs are set below.

Pankenier argues that for the entire pre-imperial period of China, the precessional North Pole's track was not close to a bright object that might serve as the pole star. He proffers that the Sinitic character *Di* was developed as a template to locate the true north, drawn by connecting the "bowl" of the Little Dipper (γ and β, plus 5 *Ursae Minoris*) and the "handle" of the Big Dipper (ζ, ε, and δ *Ursae Majoris*). As Pankenier says, the grapheme's origin may be traced to long before the early Shang script of the thirteenth century BCE.[380]

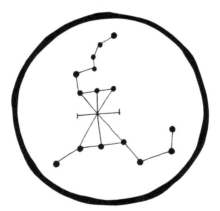

Figure 13: Shang inscriptions' version of the character *Di* is outlined by connecting the stars γ, β, and 5 of the Little She-bear (of which the former two are part of the "bowl" of the Little Dipper) and ζ, ε, and δ of the Big Dipper/Great Chariot. The centre of the asterisk-like shape approximates the precessional North Pole of around 2000 BCE. The uppermost dot in the drawing is α *Ursae Minoris*, the current pole star close to the contemporary precessional pole.[381]

---

380 Ibidem, pp. 226-236.

381 Ibidem.

Regarding linguistic evidence, Pankenier, based on Bernhard Karlgren's *Grammata Serica Recensa*, illustrates how *Di* belongs to a semantic field that conveys the meaning of "conforming with/conjoining appropriately" and "to do/form" (cf. 締 *dì*).[382] The *Shuowen Jiezi* explains *Di* metonymically through its derivative homophone 諦 *dì*, which means "careful/ attentive", or verbally "to look into/to examine", which already weaves connections with the previous discourses about *Ar* and *Li*: the former implies rectification, alignment with Heaven, and the latter may mean "natural science" by itself.[383] Moreover, the other derivative homophone 谛 *dì* is "meaning", "significance". Later texts explain the grapheme for "deity" through yet another homophone, 蒂 *dì*, meaning "calyx" or the "footstalk" which holds a fruit or an inflorescence, which falls and produces other life, thus giving a poetic idea of "deity" as a generative principle of a category of beings,[384] the same figurative explanation given for the Mesopotamian grapheme ✳ *An* ("Heaven") or *dingir* ("divinity") by the Assyriologist Pietro Mander, as we have seen.[385] The Sinologist Victor H. Mair establishes an analogy, drawn by both graphic and phonetic means, between the Sinitic *Di* and the Mesopotamian *dingir*, both centres of irradiation of reality.[386]

Pankenier further explicates the meaning of the crossbar element in the grapheme *Di*. According to him, it depicts one of the earliest forms of the square of carpentry used to make right angles. Indeed, it is present clearly in the Shang version of the glyph *jǔ* 矩, → 𢀜, meaning the "carpenter's square" itself or "rule", and even in the Shang grapheme *fāng* 方, → 𠂤, meaning "square", but also "phase", "direction", "way" and "power", all pertaining to fourfold reality. We have seen that in Latin, the carpenter's

---

382 Ibidem, p. 234.

383 See the sections 1.1.3 and 1.3.1.

384 Pankenier (2004), p. 231, note 46; Didier (2009), vol. II, p. 111.

385 Section 1.3.3 of the present essay.

386 Mair (2011), pp. 97-98, note 26.

square is the *norma*, highlighting its connection with "name" and *numen*.[387] The Shang alternative glyph for the concept of *fang* was a cross potent → 卄,[388] also indicated by Mair as the archaic form of 巫 *wū*, meaning "shaman" and semantically connected with the aforementioned concept of non-presence/vacuity. Mair reconstructs the phonetic etymology of *wu*, tracing it back, through the Old Chinese pronunciation **myag* (the first syllable vocalised *mu* and later changed to *wu*, is still vocalised *mu* in Korean and Japanese), to the Old Persian **maguš*, Latinised *magus, magi*, that is to say, "mage" (from which also comes the modern vulgarised Western concept of "magician").[389] According to his studies, based on recent archaeological discoveries, the *wu* — who strongly influenced the royal courts of early pre-imperial China — were Indo-European priests (cf. the later Zoroastrian *magi*). "Mage", from the Indo-European root **magh*, originally meant one who is "powerful" or "skilful" by virtue of his knowledge of astro-cosmological religion.[390] Interestingly, Pankenier finds that even the Shang grapheme for the concept of *yāng* 央, → 大 , meaning "centre", depicts a man with a head shaped like a carpenter's square (which is also the case of the Zhou grapheme for *Tian*, as demonstrated hereinunder).[391] It is worth highlighting that the Shang-Zhou glyph is also glaringly similar to other ancient symbols of divinity, including the Egyptian *ankh* ☥ and the paleo-Christian Chi-Rho, which, as enunciated by Guénon, convey the same meanings.[392]

Tian is explained in the *Shuowen Jiezi*, through a phonetic and graphic etymology, as meaning the "Great One", as follows:[393]

---

387 Section 2.2.1 of the present essay.

388 All the graphemes are examined in: Pankenier (2013), pp. 112-113.

389 For the cross potent as the archaic grapheme *wu* see: Mair (2012), pp. 265-279.

390 Mair (2011), pp. 93-97: Part 4 – "Magi from the West".

391 Pankenier (2013), pp. 112-113.

392 Guénon (1962), pp. 63-65 ff, note 9 & 309, note 2. Note that the glyph also resembles a bird, a winged man, the traditional icon of an angel; other symbols of the North Pole.

393 As quoted in: Didier (2009), vol. III, p. 1.

> Tian is diān 顛 ("top"), the highest and unexceeded. It derives from the characters yī 一, "one", and dà 大, "big".

As Didier says, this etymology is specious, as it merely witnesses the phonetic connection of *Tian* and *dian* (at the time when the dictionary was written, the 2nd century CE) but does not elucidate how the former was derived from the latter. Our knowledge of the archaic, Shang-Zhou versions of the character provides us with the basis for a deeper etymological study.[394]

Didier notes that the Shang-Zhou versions of the glyph show, instead of the top horizontal line, two parallel horizontal lines, often connected to form a square (Zhou variants) which in other cases is rendered as a circle. The Chinese scholar Wang Guowei (1877-1927) interprets *Tian* as representing a person's silhouette with an emphasised head.[395] The scholar Gao Hongjin argues that the emphasised head is 口 *Dīng*, "square" (archaic grapheme for the modern 丁).[396] Didier, throughout his work, identifies *Ding* as the polar square, that is, the Northern Heighth itself, drawn in the same way as *Di* between the two Dippers.[397] Differently, as explicated a few paragraphs onwards, Pankenier does not identify *Ding* with the Northern Heighth but rather with the square of the constellation Pegasus which was used as a template for the projection of the true north. Didier affirms that the character *Tian* is derived phonetically from the Shang pronunciation of *Ding*, that is *Teeŋ, but graphically from the same source of *Di*, that is *Ding*, that is to say, the asterisms of the Northern Heighth.[398]

---

394 Ibidem, pp. 1-2.

395 Ibidem, p. 2.

396 Ibidem, pp. 3-4.

397 Ibidem, vol. I, p. 216.

398 Ibidem, vol. III, pp. 5-6.

Figure 14: The graphs above are the Zhou versions of *Tian* (天), showing a humanoid shape with a squared (囗 *ding*) head or two horizontal bars.[399] The row below shows versions of *Di* (帝). The bar on top of some of them is 上 *shàng*, to signify "highest" when the grapheme refers to the supreme God of Heaven.[400] The leftmost one is the modern standard character; the others to its right are the most common Shang versions. Amongst these, the fourth and sixth (fifth and seventh if we consider the whole row) are the verbal homophone 禘 *dì* ("to divine", "to sacrifice"), whose modern standard is distinguished by the prefixing of the signifier for altar or cult (礻 *shì*).[401] According to Didier, the fourth may represent a fish entering the squared north celestial pole,[402] or rather, according to Pankenier, the Square of Pegasus or Celestial Temple at the moment when it aligns with the north celestial pole. Pankenier finds that also 鼎 *dǐng*, ritual "cauldron", "thurible", might have derived from the verbal *di*.[403] The rightmost grapheme of the row is 上甲 *Shàngjiǎ*, "Supreme Ancestor" of the universe, an alternative appellation of the supreme God of the Northern Heighth in Shang times.[404]

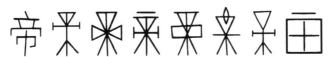

I notice that among the Sinitic graphemes that have been identified as the nominal and verbal forms of *Di* by Pankenier and Didier alike,[405] the verbal forms are similar to the Zhou version of *Tian*, in that both are composed of the quadrangular element intersecting or adjoining the anthropoid element. Pankenier's

399 Ibidem, pp. 3-4.

400 Ibidem, vol. II, p. 133.

401 Didier (2009), vol. II, p. 107 ff; Pankenier (2013), p. 103.

402 Didier (2009), vol. III, p. 6.

403 Pankenier (2013), pp. 136-148.

404 Didier (2009), vol. II, pp. 227-228.

405 Didier (2009), vol. II, p. 107 ff; Pankenier (2013), p. 103.

identification of the square element as Pegasus might offer the basis for identifying *Tian* as the verbal form of *Di*, graphically representing Pegasus' square at the moment when it aligns with the Northern Heighth. Assuming that *Tian* originated as verbal, its meaning would be "to sacrifice", "to divine" (to harmonise with the order of Heaven and to put it into practice), that is to say theurgy, or demiurgy (if intended as "working in the middle" between Heaven and Earth). In my interpretation, the grapheme represents a man with the head informed/instructed by the polar God of Heaven, i.e., a man psychically haunted by the sight of God, in awe of God, and thenceforth invested with the ability to work with the divine norm.

The foremost concern for the present study is the identification of God as the "potency of the pivot of the skies".[406] I want to emphasise the significance of fourfold symbolism as a template of the Northern Heighth both in its precessional configuration — currently with α *Ursae Minoris* as the pole star — and intended as the ecliptic pivot in the Dragon. The rotation of the Great Chariot and of the Little Dipper, or Great and Little She-bear, umbe the Northern Heighth, draws a well-known symbol of both quiescent centrality and whirling unfolding of ordered action: the hooked cross, also known by its Sanskrit appellation स्वस्तिक *swastika*, 卍/萬 *wàn* in the Chinese language, which, as we have seen in the first chapter, means "myriad", "all things" and "universe".[407] The Sanskrit word means either "it is the good" or "self-being", and the symbol is still widely used throughout Asia for religious purposes.[408]

Didier himself links the *swastika* and other cruciform and fourfold signs to polar symbolism.[409] Historical representations of the hooked cross are indubitably intertwined with the movements of the Indo-Europeans throughout Eurasia and

---

406 Pankenier (2004), p. 236.

407 Section 1.3.3 of the present essay.

408 Guénon (1962), pp. 63-65 ff.

409 Didier (2009), vol. III, p. 256.

the cultures they founded.[410] The Danish historian Ludvig Müller (1809-1891) outspokenly identifies the hooked cross as a symbol expressing "figuratively the word *theos*", much like the Mesopotamian glyph *dingir* and the Chinese *di*, and, in its highest signification, he identifies it as being the "emblem of the divinity who comprehended all the gods [...] of the omnipotent God of the universe",[411] the Chinese *Ding*, *Di* or *Tian*, the Mesopotamian *An* or utmost *Dingir* of Heaven. Walter H. Medhurst shows affinities in the usage of "deity", Chinese *di*, Greek *theos* and Latin *deus*, for incarnate powers imitating the supreme Godhead.[412]

---

410 Goblet d'Alviella (1894), pp. 73-82.

411 Müller (1877), p. 107.

412 Medhurst (1847), p. 260.

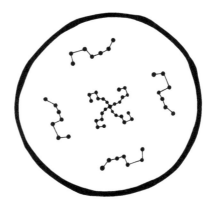

Figure 15: The *swastika* pattern is drawn by the rotation of the Dippers/She-bears umbe the precessional north celestial pivot during the four phases of the year (exact positions at midnight respectively in Spring [east], Summer [south], Autumn [west], and Winter [north]); the contemporary pole star, that is α *Ursae Minoris*, is the first star of the "handle" of the Little Dipper (or "rudder" of the Small Chariot), at the centre of the drawing.

Noteworthily, with the change of pole stars throughout the millennia due to axial procession, the configuration alters and yet maintains *swastika*-like shapes; the same applies if we consider the turning of the same asterisms around the ecliptic pole. Indeed, according to Reza Assasi, the *swastika* apodeictically represents the ecliptic pole centred in ζ *Draconis*, with the Dragon as one of the beams; it is the *Zurvan* ("Time") of Zoroastrianism, generator of both *Ahura Mazda* and *Angra Mainyu*, and of *Mithra* their mediator.[413]

Hooked crosses may be regarded as either gyrating leftwise or rightwise. Guénon illustrates the symbolism of the left and the right as representing the twofold power of the supreme God, of *yin* and *yang*, death and life, destruction and production, absorption/inhalation and emanation/exhalation, dissipation/dissolution and condensation/coagulation, also symbolised at once by the thunderbolt (cf. the Vedic वज्र *vájra*, also meaning "diamond").[414] It is ultimately the 奥丁 *Àodīng* (Odin), the "Arcane Square"; it is not haphazard that one of the other names of the hooked cross (or of one of its variants, the circled cross ⊕) is "Odin's Cross".[415]

413 Assasi (2013), pp. 411-414.

414 Guénon (1962), pp. 176-177.

415 Koch (1955), p. 94.

3.1.2. *DI* AND *DEUS*, *TIAN* AND *DIES*, *KUNLUN* AND *CAELUM*

The scholar Zhou Jixu, on the basis of historical documentation, argues that the supreme God that is central to Sinitic religion and philosophy inherited from the Xia, Shang and Zhou dynasties, that is *Di* or *Tian*, comes from the same root of the Indo-European concept of God, i.e. **Dyeus*.[416] It is noteworthy that even the latter's Etruscan equivalent, *Tin* or *Tinh*, sounds strikingly similar to the Sinitic name.

From *Dyeus* derive the Sanskrit *Dyáuḥ*; the Proto-Italic **Djous* and later Latin *Deus* (also shortened as *Ius*, which in the nominative case came to mean "right", "justice" and therefore as a theonym was replaced by the compound *Iu-piter*, i.e. *Deus Pater*, cf. Sanskrit द्यौष्पति *Dyauṣ Pitṛ*) and the Hellenic Ζεύς *Zeús* (cf. conservative Laconian Δεύς *Deús*, cf. Ζεῦ Πάτερ *Zeû Páter*). The Latin *diuus*, later spelled *dīvus*, Greek *dîos* (δῖος), Sanskrit देव *devá*, and possibly also the Germanic **Tīwaz* (cf. English *Tiw/Tue*, Nordic *Tyr*, German *Ziu/Cyo*, Gothic *Teiws*; which differ from the other forms became the theonym of the god of war), all mean "divine/godlike", and come from the alternate root **deywos*. All the Indo-European variations share the root **dei-*, which means "to shine". Therefore, "deity" pertains to the semantic field of "light", and something that qualifies as "divine" is "shining", "luminous", and "enlightening". Pokorny says that the primary meaning of words derived from **dei-* is the shining Heaven and anything that is shining and therefore celestial.[417] **Dyeus Phter*, based on this etymological study, is the "Heavenly Father" or "Shining Factor".

According to Zhou, ancient Sinitic and Indo-European religions focused on the same conception of the supreme God, and this, together with the proposed cognation of words referring to such a concept, may harken back to Indo-European settlers in

---

416 Cf. Zhou (2005), passim.

417 Ibidem, pp. 12-13. For further detail see: Pokorny (1959), pp. 183-187: **dei-*, **deiə-*, **di-*, **dia-*.

the valley of the Yellow River, who would have exerted a strong influence on the early stages of Sinitic civilisation.[418] As seen in the first chapter of the present essay, Sino-Babylonianism holds that these settlers came from Mesopotamia.[419]

One of the names of the Northern Heighth, as we have said, is 天樞 *Tiānshū*, "Pivot of Heaven". This compound contains 樞 *shū*, which is the "centre of power", constituted by the radical for "cult" or "worship" on the left and by 區 *qū*, "area", "location", on the right, which is in its turn constituted by 品 *pǐn* in 匸 *xì*, an "enclosure". *Pin* may mean "three men", but Didier informs that anciently it also meant "stars", "stellar light". The same term 星 *xīng*, "stars", but also "deities/ancestors" (and phonetically related to the term for "essence" discussed in the previous chapter[420]), in Shang script and up to the Han dynasty was represented as three or more squares, which Didier identifies as a tripled 口 *Dīng*, a use which continues in the modern 晶 *jīng*, meaning "crystal", "shining", "perfect/celestial light". While *Shangdi* was the hinge and the celestial vault, all the other gods were its stars, 下帝 *xiàdì*, "minor gods/ancestors" part of the supernal God.[421] As seen, even in Mesopotamia, they used to represent the concept of "star" doubling or tripling the grapheme ✳ *dingir*. The "three men" represented by *pin* in the Pivot of Heaven are unmistakeably the three aspects of the God of Heaven and the three circles of constellations associated with them spinning umbe the north ecliptic pole, about which we have discussed in the first chapter, common to the Sinitic tradition, to the Mesopotamian one as well, and to the broader pan-Eurasian religio-cosmology.[422]

Zhou reconstructs the Old Chinese phonetic transcriptions of *Di*, *Tian* and *di* (divine sacrifice) respectively as *Tees, *Thiim and *dees.[423] He then affirms that *Tian* has the same origin as the

---

418 Ibidem, p. 13 ff.

419 Section 1.3.3 of the present essay.

420 Section 2.3.1 of the present essay.

421 Didier (2009), vol. II, pp. 213-219.

422 Section 1.3.3 of the present essay.

423 Zhou (2005), pp. 1-3.

Germanic word "day" (German *Tag*, Proto-Germanic **dagaz*) and the Latin *dies* ("day"; cf. Italian *dì*). The Latin *dies* came from the declension of **Djous*, through the accusative *Diem* (cf. Sanskrit द्याम् *dyām*, Greek Ζῆν *Zēn* [declension of *Zeus*] and Russian день *den'*). Zhou asserts that the same process gave rise to the Old Chinese **Thiim* or **Thiin*, modern *Tian*.[424]

Victor H. Mair propounds a further comparison between Sinitic and Indo-European words pertaining to godhead. Another Chinese word for the sky is 祁连 *Qílián*, which is also the name of a group of mountains in northwest China. Zhou etymologically relates it to **Qhl'iin*, which he says to be an Old Chinese pronunciation of **Thiim*.[425] Mair puts forward that *Qilian* is rather a variant of 崑崙 *Kūnlún*, the name of the broader mountain range of which the same *Qilian* are part, but primarily a mythological concept of the *axis mundi* of which the physical mountains are themselves a symbol. He etymologically traces *Kunlun* back to the Tocharian *Kaelum*, itself a cognate of Latin *Caelum*.[426] The Tocharians were an Indo-European population who inhabited the Tarim valley in modern Xinjiang (and were present also in other regions of what is today China) until the late 1st millennium CE.

The scholar Serge Papillon, who has studied the close relation of early Sinitic and Tocharian religion, associates, relying upon Chinese sources, the same concept of *Kunlun* to the north polar asterisms and reports that it is mythologically described as the abode of the Yellow Deity, the god of centrality (*zhōng* 中):[427]

> […] Mount Kunlun was supposed to be situated at the centre of the world. It was under the Pole Star. It was also called "Bell Mountain", but the word *zhong*, "bell", is pronounced the same way as the word "centre, midst". It could therefore be

---

424 Ibidem, pp. 13-14.

425 Ibidem, p. 13.

426 Mair (2011), pp. 97-98, note 26. The author relies upon: Lin, Meicun (1998). "Qilian and Kunlun – The Earliest Tokharian Loan-words in Ancient Chinese". Victor H. Mair (Ed.). *The Bronze Age and Early Iron Age Peoples of Eastern Central Asia*, 2 vols. Washington, D.C.: Institute for the Study of Man. vol. 1, pp. 476-482.

427 Papillon (2005), pp. 18-19. Corroborating the translation of *Huangdi* as "Yellow Deity", p. 18 says: "[…] ils ont appelé *Huangdi* le Dieu (*di*) Jaune (*huang*)".

"Central Mountain", whence the Chinese considered *Huangdi* [the Yellow Deity] as the god of the centre.

Figure 16: Variants of 星 *xīng*, "star(s)", "god(s)", "ancestor(s)" in the Shang-dynasty script, made up of three or more squares (口 *dīng*).

Represented below are the Shang versions of the graphemes 子 *zi* (the two uppermost ones, meaning "son" and "male offspring", which were also used as the surname of the Shang royal kin[428]), the Shang version of 字 *zì* (the lowermost one, meaning "word" and "symbol", representing a son protected within a household), and the Qin and Han versions of 中 *zhōng* (the two on the right, meaning "centrality", "middle", "inside", "within"). Didier connects all of them to the same semantic group. They share the graphic element of the God of the Northern Height (口 *Ding*). The graphemes for "son" represent a child who has in mind the north celestial pole or the ritual vessel or space used to mimic the latter's power on Earth, instituting spiritual and political centrality. The grapheme for *zhong*, which is the term denoting a celestial civilisation and even part of the Chinese name of "China" itself, 中国 *Zhōngguó*, the "Centred Nation" or "Middle Land", represents a spirit ascending to and crossing the north celestial pole, or the *axis mundi* piercing the polar *Ding*. It represents the celestial civilisation inside the square, the civilisation which is spatiotemporally attuned, through its religio-political centre, with the great time of Heaven, thus working as a gateway for the sublimation of all spirits, as a "Gate of Heaven" (天门 *Tiānmén*).[429]

---

428 Didier (2009), vol. II, p. 226.

429 Ibidem, pp. 190-191.

3.1.3. *DING*: THE DETERMINER

As seen, Didier holds that 口 *Dīng* ("Square") is the oldest grapheme representing the God of the Northern Heighth, underlying both *Di* and *Tian*.[430] Pankenier gives a slightly different interpretation. He connects the aforementioned *Ding* to the function of the near-homophonous grapheme 定 *Dìng* ("Determiner", or "Classifier", or "Stabiliser"; cf. also 顶 *dǐng*, "top/apex"), which stands for an asterism later in history known as the "Celestial Temple"[431] — in the West known as the Great Square of Pegasus. Pankenier sustains that it was used as a device for aligning earthly activities with the Northern Heighth, determining the right time of the year for performing seminal deeds, when "the soil's *materia vitalis* (*qi*) emerges in pulsation", to "construct inner and outer walls and build capitals and cities", that is to say, to institute centrality (*zhong*) and dispose of the cardinal four quarters of the space.[432] This appropriate time was "when *Ding* was centred" on the astronomical meridian, that is to say when *Ding* culminated in aligning with the Northern Pivot, which in the Mesopotamian religious tradition is the "Celestial City", the *Nibiru* ("Polar Station/Crossing") of the seven *Anunnaki*.[433] I think that Didier's and Pankenier's interpretations are not mutually exclusive and that the square may be regarded as a symbol with multiple meanings like the *swastika*, representing both the current northern precessional pole, the ecliptic pole, and the virtue of Heaven at work in every creature of space-time, and space-time itself. Ultimately, any fourfold symbol represents the *yuzhou* as a quadridimensional structure, as the Heideggerian "Fouring" will be discussed in a few paragraphs.

---

430 Ibidem, vol. I, p. 216.

431 The "Celestial Temple" in the Western religious tradition and beyond is either the reflection of the "Celestial City" or "City of God", or else is the Celestial City itself.

432 Pankenier (2013), pp. 118-148: Chapter 4 – "Bringing Heaven down to Earth". Quotes are taken from pp. 136-138. Also see: Pankenier (2009), passim.

433 Ibidem, p. 128.

Figure 17: The constellation below is Pegasus, which contains *Ding*, that is to say the Great Square of Pegasus. The constellations above are represented to give an idea of Pegasus' position in relation to the Northern Heighth. They are simplifications of the Small Chariot, shown on the left with an accentuated α *Ursae Minoris* (which is the current pole star), and the Dragon, shown on the right, which encompasses the starless ecliptic pole, itself indicated by a fictional dot. It is worth heeding that the distance between *Ding* and the Northern Heighth is here considerably shrunk for the manoeuvrability of the drawing.

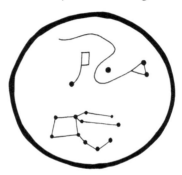

Pankenier provides an etymology of *Ding*, intended as the Celestial Temple, linking it to the semantic nexus which comprehends *zhèng* (正 "right/straight/correct") and *zhēn* (真 "true"), all sharing the common Old Chinese phonetic root: **deŋ* (Middle Chinese **deeŋs*) which means "to fix", "to rectify", to bring into congruence with the supernal force of *Di*.[434]

Pankenier also bespeaks the effects on the human psyche that such star-gazing methods would have triggered. Psychological intentionality in the magical use of language and logic of orientation would have arisen out of the effort to align humanity with the astral revelation of the order of Heaven.[435] He also underscores that it was in the second millennium BCE that a radical transition to quadrangular architectural models took place, testifying to the development of theoretical reasoning and spatial planning informed by cosmological thinking.[436]

---

434 Ibidem, pp. 140-142. Also see the section 1.1.3 of the present essay, where I already discussed *zheng*.

435 Ibidem, p. 143.

436 Ibidem, p. 146.

Taking one further step, I argue that the sight of the spinning constellations of the Northern Heighth marked at the same time the moment of the birth of human self-consciousness and the awareness of the supreme God of the universe, the two being ultimately the same insight, upon which witfulness and wistfulness grew and progressively evolved (intended as the capacity to grasp and reuse the celestial norms). The sight of the supreme God of the Northern Heighth marked the birth of the *superego*, which is the awareness of the "divine human shape", the model of human evolution. The struggle to emulate the order of Heaven, the "ancient ritual preoccupation with taking divine direction from the spirit of the celestial pole", which entailed "bringing a normative aspect of the mysterious Heaven down to Earth",[437] inspired the development of ritual cultures and of wheel, pin and wedge technologies.

As seen hithertofore, the olden Sinitic glyphs representing both the supreme God of the universe and the devices to communicate with it and bring its order (*Li*) into fruition depict a man with a head in the shape of a square — "informed" by the square, the divine measure. Such graphemes depict the moment of the "creation of man", of the birth of human self-consciousness and the *superego*, or — using an ancient poetic figure — of God "fulgurating" man, whereafter the latter becomes invested with the ability of appropriate ritualising (*li*). It was at one time the origin of science (the awareness of the celestial norm), self-awareness, and craft (τέχνη *tékhnē*; technology), the power to reproduce the celestial norm in the furrow dug between creator and creature, working with the former and within the tension of the latter.[438] It was the origin of civilisation.

It is worth noting that in Indo-European cultures, the symbol of the wheel merges with that of the thunderbolt, the scythe, the hammer and the axe, and other tools of war and art. For instance, the "hammer of thunder" (*mjǫllnir*, literally the "miller",

---

437 Ibidem, p. 114.

438 Mander (2011), p. 14. The author discusses the symbolism of the furrow wherefrom the principle or "head" (*sag*) of man was drawn, in the Mesopotamian myth of creation.

which is *Thor*, "Thunder", Odin's son) of early Germanic culture is the same as the Vedic वज्र *vájra* ("thunderbolt/diamond") of Indian culture, the cross-like symbol of divine power, of the *Logos*, as Georges Dumézil and René Guénon point out,[439] and a hammer and chisel or an axe are also the weapons of the eagle-faced Thunder God (雷公 *Léigōng* or 雷神 *Léishén*) of Chinese tradition, who is an attribute of the Yellow Deity.

The "rectification of names" (*zhengming*) thus takes the meaning of the verticalisation of human spirits towards Heaven, their heightening towards a supreme end, and the participation of their many times, through appropriate conjunctions, in the great time of Heaven, the ultimate driver of human evolution, and in the public institution of the great time into a celestial civilisation. It is tacit that, enantiodromically, by "inversion of sign" — speaking in the wake of Ernesto de Martino — the loss of the awareness of the universal God and of its order manifesting itself in the vault of the skies, the falling out of the great time or spirit of Heaven, and the active denial of the hierarchy of the divine generation that follows such rupture (degeneration), result in the horizontal collapse of all forces, their psychopathological privatisation, the maddening of human reason and its enslavement by the forces of death — of the Earth, of the Matrix —, in the misuse of technology for the establishment of nonsensical theories and structures channelling such forces, and in the consequential involution of humanity into an unconscious state, into egoism, and then the fall of the *ego* into the mere animalism of the *id*.

Sinitic thinking, by virtue of its strong betoning of visuality and ancestrality, has preserved in a consistent manner cosmotheanthropism, offering an understanding of God, man and the ordered world of the generations as a synergic continuum — or, more detailedly, an understanding of the world as ordered by the interaction between humanity and divinity — rather than as separate entities as they are conceived in modern Western thought. This is reflected in a continuity of theory and praxis: from such

---

439 Dumézil (1974), p. 121. Also see: Guénon (1962), p. 167 ff: Chapter 25 – "Thunderbolts", p. 173 ff: Chapter 26 – "Symbolic Weapons".

a perspective, divinity and humanity, theoretical/theological and theurgical/demiurgical methods, may be regarded as two facets of the same experience of reality. The 口 *Dīng*, or — transposing it into the Germanic world — the 奥丁 *Àodīng*, the "Mysterious Square", Odin the Wanderer, is not merely the supreme God coming to light as the Northern Heighth and its starry order, and not merely the square of carpentry (or demiurgy) as a utensil; it is human consciousness itself and its power to craft the world in rightwise accordance (or leftwise discordance) with the order of Heaven. It is the same human demiurge (also understandable as "shaper of people"), nomothete or legislator (law-giver), onomaturge (name-worker) or denominator, or determiner.

Figure 18: On the left is my own rendition, in a simplified fashion, of one of the most spellbinding petroglyphs of Val Camonica, found at the Rock Art Natural Reserve of Ceto, Cimbergo and Paspardo (Foppe, R. 24), in Lombardy. It depicts someone who in all likelihood is a warrior shaman, with a dagger or chisel in the right hand, and a carpenter's square in the left hand. He is stricken and awoken (whence the crown of rays around his head, five to the left and three to the right) while gazing at the "Camunian Rose", which is unmistakeably another version of the cruciform patterns of the north celestial pole. On the right is another stylised rendition of the iconography of the *Leigong* ("Lord of Thunder") of Chinese culture, complete with all the traditional iconographic elements associated with the god, including the hammer and chisel and the face of an eagle. It is worthwhile noting the similarity of this figure with that of the god of thunder in Indo-European cultures, for instance, the Vedic *Indra* and the Germanic *Thor*.

3.2. THEURGICAL DEVICES FOR TEMPLATING EARTH: ARCHITECTURES OF SPACE-TIME

3.2.1. INSIDE AND OUTSIDE FOURFOLD BIOASTRALITY

As formulated by Mircea Eliade: "Reality is a function of the imitation of a celestial archetype", which reflects itself in the microcosm and the macrocosm, and is attained through "the practice of ritual ceremonies to maintain harmony between the world of the gods and the world of men"; reality consists in the "participation in the symbolism of the centre, as expressed by some form of *axis mundi*". The consecrated space that whirls around this pivot is oriented in a fourfold directionality.[440]

> Heaven suspends images to manifest the propitious and the inauspicious, and the sage makes of himself their semblance [...]. Anciently, in ruling all-under-Heaven [the emanated creation], *Paoxi* [i.e. *Fuxi*, the male component of a pair of gods, the female of whom is *Nuwa*, who hold respectively the square (tool of his wife *Nuwa*/Earth) and the compass (tool of her husband *Fuxi*/Heaven) personifying the *yang* holding the virtue of *yin* and *yin* holding the virtue of *yang*] looked up to observe the images in Heaven and looked down to observe the patterns on Earth.
>
> *Xici zhuan ("Appended Phrases"),*
> *commentary to the Yijing.[441]*

According to my hypothesis, the sight of *Di*, of the skyborne divine revelation, was for early star-gazers the impulse to the sublimation of thought; it was the moment of the "creation of mankind", that is to say, the spark that triggered the development of both inward individual consciousness and outward collective consciousnesses, of the *superego* and of the very shape of "man". Civilisation, with this term meaning the divine or celestial city or civilisation, consisted in setting the time of oneself and

---

440 Pankenier (2004), p. 224.

441 Pankenier (2013), p. 149. I have slightly modified the quote.

one's group in accordance with the higher rhythms of Heaven, with the great time of Heaven, through appropriate ritualising, that is to say, through the reproduction of celestial luminous configurations and of their movements (*tianxian* and *tianwei*), triggering a movement of spiral evolution towards Heaven.[442]

Such evolution was more than merely social (intended in the perspective of modern, disconnected "sociological sciences") and architectural; it was first of all psychical and thereby physical (intended in the original sense of *physis*); in one word, it was psychophysical. Accepting the continuity of mind and body, I borrow René Berthelot's term "bioastrality"[443] to define my idea that the early star-gazers' psychophysical constitution was impacted in the very moment when they beheld the divine revelation of the circumpolar asterisms, beginning to harmonise themselves through then instituting civilisation, the 国 *guó* ("country", "state"; represented by the grapheme for "jade", 玉 *yù*, which is an alteration of 王 *wáng*, the "king", within the square): think about the Seven Hills and Kings of Rome, another terrestrial representation of the seven stars of the Northern Heighth; or think about the quadrangular *mundus Cereris* at the centre of the four directions of Rome as a representation of the polar quadrangle, the *Ding* of Didier.[444] Bioastrality means that the imitation of the celestial patterns led and potentially continues to lead the development of the human gist, which originally came to a heavenlier realisation in the early star-gazers — the first ones who lifted their eyes from the ground and looked up to the sky — (the sages/ethelings) who theurgically/demiurgically acted as civilisers, drawing the patterns of Heaven down to the Earth and instituting them into centres of religio-political power, temporal power. Thus, bioastrality is definable not only as psychophysical on the individual level but also as socio-political on the level of collectivity. Human evolution should thus not be intended as a continuous, linear and irreversible process: as we have seen, the

---

442 Pankenier (1995), p. 131.

443 Didier (2009), vol. I, p. 203. Berthelot's theory is cursorily mentioned.

444 De Martino (1977), p. 212 ff.

fall outside the time of Heaven entails involution, the horizontal collapse of spiritual forces, the "spirit of heaviness and darkness" which drags towards the Earth, which overruns dying civilisations, as defined by De Martino.[445]

The Sinitic grapheme *Tian*, which as previously seen likely originated as the verb "to divine", is also apt to represent the verticality of human evolution, which emerges from the Earth and grows towards Heaven, and is modelled after the measure of Heaven. Noteworthily, the Dragon and other serpentine creatures symbolise such a process — the process of temporalisation which may be spirally projected in harmonisation with the great time of Heaven. The Dragon is at one time chthonic inchoate potentiality and impulse to ascension; it is a chthonic-watery force, the localised spirit (much like the Roman *genius*, itself represented by a snake in Roman kinship altars) which, when spirally projected and sublimated, rectified, becomes the necessary upsurge for rising towards Heaven.[446] Thus, the Dragon represents the unity of *yin* and *yang*,[447] the modality of manifestation of the *Li/Dao*, and the *Li/Dao* itself.

---

445 Ibidem, p. 203.

446 The constellation of the Dragon encircles the ecliptic North Pole. As such, it is the "Far Eastern symbol of the Word", i.e. of the Logos. Guénon (1962), pp. 91 & 139.

447 Pankenier (2013), p. 55: "[...] The dragon is protean. It is unique in embodying both *yin* and *yang* principles".

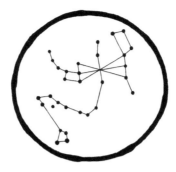

Figure 19: The constellation of the Dragon (*Draco*; 天龙 *Tiānlóng*) winding the ecliptic North Pole (represented by a fictional dot in its first bight), slithering between the Little Dipper (and the current precessional pole star, represented by the outermost dot of the Little Dipper's "handle") and the Big Dipper/Great Chariot.

As already explained in the caption of figure 15, Assasi connects the Dragon asterism itself to the *swastika* pattern if centred in ζ *Draconis*, close to the ecliptic North Pole. In Assasi's configuration, the body of the Dragon constitutes one of the beams of the *swastika*.[448] In Sinitic representations, the Dragon is the curved line in-between *yin* and *yang* (respectively, the Little Dipper and the Big Dipper) together forming the "diagram of the Supreme Polarity" (太极图 *Tàijítú*) → ☯. In Han-dynasty descriptions, the Dragon is also identified as the spear/sceptre of the supreme God, *Taiyi*.[449] Take heed that, drawing the glyph *Di* (帝) according to the method shown hereinbefore (figure 13), it precisely intersects the "tail" of the Dragon, and this might convey further meanings associated to the mythological theme of deities as vanquishers and tamers of dragons, i.e. moulders of the primordial potentiality.

It is also worthwhile to note that the Big Dipper in relation to the north celestial pole (either ecliptic or precessional) corresponds to the bird in the Ordos cross that I show in the frontispiece of the present essay. In other cultures, too, the Big Dipper is represented as a raptor bird atop the *axis mundi* tree (cf. the *Anzu* and *Ziz* in Mesopotamian and Jewish cultures, *Vedhrfolnir* atop the *Yggdrasill* in Germanic culture, and even the Mesoamerican *Itzam Yeh*, the "Serpent Bird"), while the Little Dipper is conceived as representing the supreme power as the awesome, both creative and destructive, humanising (i.e. man-making) factor (cf. the seven-stars Celestial Bull of the Epic of Gilgamesh[450]).

---

448 Assasi (2013), passim.

449 Didier (2009), vol. I, pp. 170-171.

450 Ibidem, p. 119.

According to Didier, the interpretation of Heaven as a force abiding within everything and no longer chiefly identified as the pivot of the vault of the sky emerged during the late Zhou dynasty (6th-5th century BCE).[451] According to him, it was not before the first millennium BCE (the transition from the Bronze Age to the Iron Age) that the precessional culmen became vacant of bodies that might serve as the pole star. Such hypothesis contrasts with that advocated by Pankenier, described hereinabove, according to which the pole had been vacant for the prior two millennia,[452] and it was known that pole stars were expedients meant to allude to the ecliptic pole, which is always empty of astral bodies. Pankenier says that a paradigmatic change in conceiving Heaven was stimulated by the long-time contemplation of the starless Northern Heighth, while according to Didier, it was the gradual religio-political collapse of the late Zhou dynasty and the fragmentation of sacral power into multiple potentates which fought for supremacy, that induced the intellectual quest for a new centre.[453] Both the authors agree that in the Warring States period of the late Zhou, there was a philosophical efflorescence around the concepts of *wuwei* and *wu* ("effortlessness" and "non-presence/vacuity") regarded as the unmoving cosmogonic source residing in everything, that ultimately coagulated into Chinese classical metaphysics and especially the Confucian tradition, which completed the "interiorisation" of Heaven and betoned self-cultivation and ritual morality.[454] Confucius espoused the olden theology of the God of the Northern Heighth but remoulded it as a teaching of inner divinity cultivable and exercisable by anybody. Therefore, he conciliated the positions of both traditionalist and reformer intellectuals into a new system. Such dual conception persisted in the metaphysics of the late Warring States and Qin-Han dynasties, reflected in the blurry demarcation between the *Taiyi* intended as the polar god of the

451 Ibidem, vol. III, pp. 74-80.

452 Ibidem, p. 78.

453 Ibidem, pp. 74-80.

454 Ibidem, pp. 80-83.

physical sky and the more abstract — *Yī*, the "One" in a Platonic sense, which begets the polar god as well as the myriad creatures of the world.[455]

In this regard, it is worthwhile explaining the meaning of the title of Didier's work, *In and Outside the Square*. It means "in and outside" the established order of the contemporary civilisation that reproduced Heaven's holy square on Earth. During the last centuries of the Zhou dynasty, ① "inside the square" and ② "outside the square" referred, respectively: ① the former, to people and intellectuals who belonged to the established and yet waning order, the ritually initiated and therefore "empowered" ones who still participated in society and communed with its centre of power which reflected the pivot of the sky; and ② the latter, to those who were alienated and disaffected, who did not participate in political society, since they were born outside of it or had consciously left it because of its decadence, who were uninitiated and therefore unaware of the appropriate rituals to deal with the central power. They were the conservative and reforming forces at play at the twilight of the Zhou dynasty. With the disintegration of the Zhou religio-political system between the ninth and the sixth centuries BCE, the ancient theology that once was the exclusive prerogative of the royal centre was gradually disseminated "outside the square" among the various local powers. Confucius, who identified himself as an "insider" of the old tradition (by virtue of being a descendant of the erstwhile ruling Shang lineage), emerged with his reform aiming at the reconstitution of society.[456]

Such understanding of post-Zhou pre-imperial Sinitic history, which moreover reflects the occurrences of the twilight of the Roman Empire, may be useful for reading the crisis of the contemporary Western civilisation in terms of an order that, having disconnected from Heaven, is rapidly waning, and is represented on one side by "insiders", namely those well-born parts of the population which are still informed by the Christian

455 Ibidem, pp. 86-90.

456 Ibidem.

religion and the models inherited from the medieval Germanic civilisation, which have, however, become empty formality having lost their original meaning; and on the other side by exponentially growing masses of "outsiders", namely bad-born disenfranchised people and immigrants. The distinction may be compared to Alain De Benoist's paradigm of the "periphery against the centre", devised to overcome the left/right dichotomy, which has become useless for reading contemporary politics.[457]

In one of his earliest works, Pankenier treats the hitherto described cosmo-theological background in its relation to statecraft. Human society within the political state, as a "self-contained cosmological whole" — with the power of the ruling centrality emanating in the four directions (四方 *sìfāng*), forming a fourfold structure —, reflected the order of Heaven.[458] In Pankenier's words:[459]

> The goal implicit in this mode of thought was to achieve a universal order, a perfect congruence between the natural and human rhythms, for which the ideal paradigm was found in the heavens. The constancy and regularity of certain celestial motions and their phenomenal manifestation in the seasonal rhythms initially provided patterns of permanence and timeliness to contrast with the constant flux of more mundane events [...]. The ability to comprehend the celestial motions and to sustain a reciprocal conformity between their regular variations and human activity, that is the discernment necessary to "pattern oneself on heaven" (象天 *xiàngtiān*), was a fundamental qualification of kingship.

In early China, shamans (*wu*) were the intermediaries of Heaven; they were defined as individuals so "perspicacious, single-minded and reverential" that their "understanding enabled them to make meaningful collation of what lies above and below, and their insight to illuminate what is distant and profound".[460]

---

457 Dugin (2012), p. 11.

458 Pankenier (1995), pp. 140-141.

459 Ibidem, p. 146.

460 *Guoyu* 18.1a ff.

Shamans were those able to attune human behaviour to Heaven, assigning to the various types of people their appropriate roles in society and conducting the sacrifices for the gods of ordered society and the cosmos. According to the scholar K.C. Chang, the authority to rule was originally the same as shamanism, and, especially in China, the king was also the head shaman.[461] The later Ruist concept of the sage developed from the role of the shamans, who, in Victor H. Mair's terms, are men endowed with superior power (*magh*, from which, besides "magic", also come the words "might", "magnet" and "machine", and the verb "to make"[462]) to master and to embody the models of Heaven, translating them into civilising norms (i.e. theurgy/demiurgy). As previously seen, the symbol of the *wu*, as well as the Western *magi*, is the cross potent, also known as the Teutonic Cross. According to Didier, it originated from the much older *swastika*, representing the Dippers and the Northern Heighth, and was likely taught in China, as well as elsewhere, by the Indo-Europeans.[463]

Pankenier suggests that the periodical cooptation and bureaucratisation of shamanism, and calendrical standardisation of astral wisdom, at the hands of ruling elites, resulted in discordance between human society and Heaven[464] and in consequent disaster and degeneration since "the people and the spirits intermingled and interfered with each other [...], calamities arrived in concert, and none lived out his allotted span of years".[465] In such times, time conjunctures are disrupted, "cereals do not ripen, the administration is dark and unenlightened, talented men of the people are in petty positions", and houses are not at peace.[466]

---

461 Pankenier (1995), pp. 150-151. The author refers to: Chang, K.C. (1983). *Art, Myth and Ritual: The Path to Political Authority in Ancient China*. Cambridge, Massachusetts: Harvard University Press.

462 Cf. Mair (1990b), passim.

463 Didier (2009), vol. I, pp. 257-259.

464 Pankenier (1995), pp. 151-155.

465 Ibidem, p. 153. Quotes the *Shiji* ("Scribal Records"), "Lishu" 26.1257.

466 Ibidem, p. 155. Quotes the *Shujing* ("Book of Documents"), "Hongfan" 33/29.

As already defined in the foregoing section, I hold that the inherent virtue of man, the heavenly gist that is Heaven itself incarnated and also the fulgurating awareness of such identity and of the capacity of the human intellect to co-work with Heaven for the evolution of the cosmos, is ultimately a fourfolding/foursquaring theurgical/demiurgical potency, that is to say, a power to architect[467] space-time as the "Fouring" — i.e. Martin Heidegger's *Vierung* — fostering its intrinsic modality of self-showing.

3.2.2. THE FOURFOLD-SEVENFOLD SPATIOTEMPORAL GOD

Pankenier says that representations of *Tian*'s manifold articulation harken back at least to the second millennium BCE and possibly to the early Bronze Age. The five planets that move independently from the background of fixed stars, later associated with the five elements and five colours, became identified as the Fivefold Supreme Deity (五方上帝 *Wǔfāng Shàngdì*) or the Five Deities (五帝 *Wǔdì*): the Blue/Green Deity (青帝 *Qīngdì* or 蒼帝 *Cāngdì*), the Red Deity (赤帝 *Chìdì*), the White Deity (白帝 *Báidì*), the Black Deity (黑帝 *Hēidì*) and the Yellow Deity. They are "Heaven's five assistants" and "architects of the subcelestial world as it comes into being in its multiplicity of forms". Some Han-dynasty depictions show them in the form of five men, each of whom holds a different construction tool.[468] They are also described as the "five changeable faces of Heaven", five different "accesses" or ritual perspectives to serve Heaven, suitable for different situations.[469]

Four of them are the spirits of the four directions, the four seasons, and four types of human temperament that

---

467 This word intended as verbal is still mostly confined to the field of information technology. I borrow it returning it to its pristine Greek etymology which means "to craft the *Arche*", i.e. "to realise the Origin".

468 Pankenier (1995), pp. 171-172, note 101. The *Wufang Shangdi* are further deepened in the section 3.3.3 of the present essay.

469 Zhong (2014), pp. 72-75.

articulate umbe the centre. This fourfold structure represents the horizontal beams of the cosmotheanthropic architecture of space-time (*yuzhou*), of which the vertical dimension is represented by the mainmast of the Threefold Potentiality (Heaven, humanity as the mediating term, and the Earth as the hosting base) of ouranogeoanthropism explained in the last section of the previous chapter.[470]

The focus of convergence and irradiance of the fourfold horizontal plane — that is to say, of the ontologico-topographical centrally-structured squared Earth, 地方 *difāng*[471] —, and of the threefold vertical shaft, is the Yellow Deity, the fifth of the *Wudi*, a symbol of the theurgical/demiurgical and cosmogenic power of human thought, of the sage/etheling, and of the *Di* in the flesh. The *yuzhou* (that is to say, the "coming to the present from the past and towards the future — in the four directions") may therefore be seen as a structure which is twofold (past-future), thus threefold (past-present-future) as time, and fourfold (the four directions) as space. It is a tri-quadridimensional structure, that is to say, a sevendimensional space-time, that manifests the Fivefold God, the Yellow Deity, which is its centre.

As we have already seen, five planets of the Sun system, including the Sun itself and the Moon, reflecting the seven stars of the Chariots, and personified as seven gods, were

---

470 Section 2.3.4 of the present essay.

471 For the cosmo-ontological concept of Earth (地 *di*) as "squared", in the sense of "structured" by irradiation from the centre, and by "recognising the categories of things" and their appropriate allotment, which is the original meaning of 方 *fang*, see: Didier (2009), vol. III, p. 173 ff, esp. pp. 184-186 & 192 ff. It is worth noting that in this context, and in the Chinese theory of the elements, this squared *di*, which is about the same as *qi*, or a more condensed *qi*, corresponds to the aether of the Western theory of the elements, the pre-element or fifth element which under the Lunar Gate may take the form of any of the other four elements: wood (E), fire (S), metal (W), and water (N) in the Chinese system; fire (E), earth (S), water (W) and air (N) in the Western system. Another important remark is that the directional associations of the four elements, and thus of the four human temperaments, or the four races, differ in the two traditions as they are perceived from different perspectives. The Chinese scheme is akin to that of Turanian traditions, while the Western scheme is that developed within Indo-European traditions.

considered as the operative powers of the God of Heaven and the seven planes of ascension to its supreme pole already in the Mesopotamian tradition, and, in the Sinitic tradition, they are conceived as the wain of the utmost God and the ladle which dispenses the divine power in the changeful world.[472]

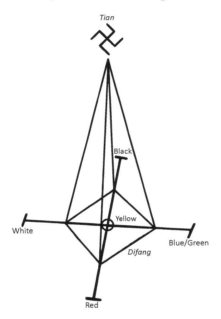

Figure 20: The *yuzhou* is represented as a sevenfold structure. *Tian* at the top generates the movements that manifest themselves as the five qualities of beings on a squarely ordered Earth (*difang*): the Blue/Green Deity, the Red Deity, the White Deity, the Black Deity and Yellow Deity, among which the former four are associated with the cardinal directions. The Yellow Deity corresponds to humanity and is the axle of convergence and irradiation of the whole structure, being the self-showing of *Tian* itself in physical reality.

3.2.2.1. YANG XIONG'S SQUARE AND COMPASS

The Confucian scholar and poet Yang Xiong (53 BCE-18 CE), in his *Taixuanjing* ("Book of the Supreme Mystery"), poetically

---

472 Sections 1.3.3 and 3.1.1 of the present essay, with further deepening in 3.3.3.

portrays the *yuzhou* as the Great Mystery (太玄 *Tàixuán*), as the immanent Way of Heaven, which is God constantly self-renewing itself, synergically manifesting itself through the threefold axle of ouranogeoanthropism to create and order things. The following text is Didier's translation of Yang's poetry:[473]

> The Mystery is that which abstrusely creates the myriad types [of things] but does not appear in physical form. It causes to be embodied [in thingness] vacuity and nothing and engenders the regulations [according to which the universe and all within it operate]. Encapsulated within the radiance of *numen* (*shenming*), it establishes the models. It conducts across and unifies past and present (i.e. all time), unfolding the types [of things]. It stimulates and causes to intermingle *yin* and *yang*, issuing pneuma (*qi*): [*yin* and *yang pneuma*] now separating, now conjoining, Heaven and Earth are [thereby] completed!

> Looking up to observe the [astral] images and looking down to view [earthly] circumstances, one investigates [the internal] nature to understand fate [as bestowed by the Mystery], to trace origins back to their beginnings, and to spy ends. [He finds that] the three measures (Heaven, Earth, and humanity) are of the same type and that [it is simply that] what is thick and what is thin rub against each other. What is cyclical (*yuan*) is unsettled (i.e. moves). What is sectioned (*fang*) retains conservatively. [When the unsettled] expectorates, then flows [*qi* into] embodiment. [When what retains] absorbs, then congeals [*qi* into] form. For this reason, what covers Heaven is called *yu*, and what effloresces *yu* is called *zhou*.

The *yuzhou* is at one time the forge and the artwork, the thing that is made by the activity of Heaven that incarnates and blooms in the wealthy receptacle of Earth. Yang writes:[474]

> Heaven is cyclical (*yuan*), and Earth is sectioning (*fang*). The heavenly pole is planted in the centre. In its (Heaven's) movement it produces the calendar. In its (the Earth's) quiescence [the calculation of] time depends on the twelve [months based on zodiacal heliacal risings] to produce the

---

473 Didier (2009), vol. III, pp. 193-194. He translates the *Taixuanjing* 7:6a.

474 Ibidem, pp. 194-195. *Taixuanjing* 7:8a & 9a.

seven governmental regulations. The active application (literally "art") of the Mystery illuminates it all.

The cyclical (*yuan*) and the compartmentalising (*fang*) grind against one another, and the hard and soft interfere with one another. When [one or the other of the contrasted pairs] has reached fruition, then its decline begins; when one is exhausted, then it is born again. Now full, now vacuous; now flowing, now stopped; all inconstant.

As understandable from what is enunciated hereinabove, *fang* means "to square" in the sense of "distributing/sectioning", that is to say, to give things their appropriate positioning according to their own quality. Things differentiate themselves in shapes and functions by contrast and reverberation with one another, as they are born "within the crucible of Heaven and Earth", and humanity is able to reproduce and complete such a model in the institution of political society.[475] Yang uses another poetic image, depicting Heaven as a "precipice" of forces and Earth as a "hole" that receives and harbours them.[476] Yang's conception of the *yuzhou* may be analogised to the Gnostic conception of the *Ktisma*, in which souls take various shapes as they condense and move across matter in accordance with their chosen directions.

In another passage, Yang gives a description of the *yuzhou* as an artwork, a production of the synergy of compass and square, respectively, the symbols of Heaven and Earth:[477]

Heaven cycles according to its (the Mystery's) way, and Earth, as a fence line, carries it (the way of the Mystery) to its end [in its production of things]. [Throughout this process] *yin* and *yang* intermingle haphazardly such that there is the male and there is the female. The Way of Heaven develops to form a compass. The Way of Earth develops to form a carpenter's square (*ju*). The compass moves, revolving through the encampments [of the twenty-eight celestial lodges]. The carpenter's square remains quiescent, settling all things. Revolving through the encampments

---

475 Ibidem, p. 195.

476 Ibidem, p. 196. Cf. *Taixuanjing* 10:4b.

477 Ibidem, pp. 196-199. *Taixuanjing* 10:1b-2a & 3b.

(Heaven) enables the *numen* to come to light. Settling things enables types to be coalesced. The coalescing of types enables fortune. The illumination of *numen* enables the establishment of the most exalted. The Mystery is all (what concerns) the Way of Heaven, the Way of Earth, and the Way of Humanity. When [spoken of] together, then we employ the term "Heaven" to name it. It is the way of ruler and subject, father and son, and husband and wife.

[…] The Mystery has one compass and one carpenter's square, one rope and one level, to traverse vertically and horizontally the ways of Heaven and Earth, to contain the numerological permutations of *yin* and *yang*.

Didier explicates that the Earth receives the cyclical life-giving movement started by Heaven, accretes and nurtures things in different ways, and allows things' various qualities to be apparent and delineable. In his own words: "The compass draws the circle, or the outlines of the cycle, in which all activity can take place; the carpenter's square measures and sections apart by type all things created within that cyclical process".[478]

Yang also explains "thinking" as equivalent to harbouring in one's mind the "compass" of the Mystery for gauging and measuring the *yuzhou*,[479] thus emphasising mankind's endowment of technical power to cooperate with Heaven and Earth in the ornamentation of space-time.

---

478 Ibidem, p. 199.

479 Ibidem, p. 198.

Figure 21: My own reproduction of ancient Chinese representations of *Fuxi* and *Nuwa*, gods of creation mythologically representing *yang* and *yin*, respectively, the first doubling in the manifestation of *Tian*. Each holds the technical tool belonging to the other, symbolising the complementarity of the polarity: *Nuwa* holds the compass of Heaven/ *Fuxi* and *Fuxi* holds the square of the Earth/*Nuwa*. Man is born as a child in-between the two, as the dynamic interaction of the two powers. They are comparable to *Lahmu* and *Lahamu*, and the two Leviathans, or the Leviathan and the Behemoth, in Mesopotamian and Jewish cultures, themselves represented as serpentine beings symbolising the fundamental duality of the cosmos.

3.2.2.2. HEIDEGGER'S FOURING

An analogy may be drawn between classical Sino-Ruist cosmotheanthropism, that is, the conception of a God-borne and man-crafted space-time, and Heideggerian phenomenology, specifically the concept of entities as "fourfold things". Such ontological vision is portrayed in Heidegger's speech *Das Ding* ("The Thing"), which was also the source of inspiration for Lacan's "Thing", discussed and redefined as *Yin*-Thing in the foregoing chapter.

In Heidegger's thought, the "Fouring" (*Vierung*) is the modality of the great "Fourfold" (*Geviert*), that is to say, the process of creation of the world and of the myriad things sojourning in it. It is the modality of Being itself (the *Seyn*) and of things coming into being. Elsewise said it is both the process of "worlding", of self-wielding of the world, and of "thinging" of things. The word "thing", as Heidegger elucidates making the etymology of the Old High German cognate *dinc* (the Proto-Germanic root is **thingą*), means "gathering", "aggregation".[480] Since the world itself is nothing but a "thing" greater than the things it contains, we may straightforwardly speak of such a process of continuous self-unfolding as the Thing. Exemplifying the Thing as a jug, Heidegger says that the potter who manufactures it circumscribes a central void making it a receptacle of being:[481]

> [...] The potter [...] shapes the void. For it, in it, and out of it, he forms the clay into the form. From start to finish the potter takes hold of the impalpable void and brings it forth as the container in the shape of a containing vessel. The jug's void determines all the handling in the process of making the vessel. The vessel's thingness does not lie at all in the material of which it consists, but in the void that holds.

---

480 Heidegger (1971), pp. 172-175. Although translated and published only in 1971, Heidegger first delivered his speech in 1950. About the etymology of "thing" also see the Indo-European root: Pokorny (1959), pp. 1067-1068: **tenk-*. The latter means "appointed/right timing"; it may be etymologically connected to the Chinese *Ding* semantic field.

481 Ibidem, p. 167.

The philosopher goes on with the depiction of his ontological vision, by describing the purpose of the power of the void, which is in its usability:[482]

> The twofold holding of the void rests on the outpouring. In the outpouring, the holding is authentically how it is. To pour from the jug is to give. The holding of the vessel occurs in the giving of the outpouring. Holding needs the void as that which holds. The nature of the holding void is gathered in the giving. [...] The giving, whereby the jug is a jug, gathers in the twofold holding — in the outpouring. We call the gathering of the twofold holding into the outpouring, which, as a being together, first constitutes the full presence of giving: the poured gift. The jug's jug-character consists in the poured gift of the pouring out.

The Thing is shown here as a dammed void[483] whose power is to hold, in its twofold aspect of taking and keeping, what is poured in, stabilising it. The Thing as a vessel receives, retains and contains what is poured in, and this twofold power acquires sense in outpouring the content as a gift.[484] Heidegger speaks of what I have previously defined as the *Yang*-Thing[485] — the edged and ornamented Thing, otherwise definable as the Squared Thing — the artwork that in turn has the power to create other artworks; it is the complementary opposite of the Lacanian *Yin*-Thing — the inchoate, undetermined and decomposing Thing, otherwise definable as the "Unthing" — which unveils the abysmal void that precedes creation and reabsorbs it when the boundaries, terms and norms dissolve.[486]

---

482 Ibidem, p. 169.

483 "Vase", "vessel", and also "vest" all come from the Indo-European root *wes-* which means "to dress/clothe", as the ordered, termed, named world, as the drape of the sky which covers the infinite of space, and in an extended sense, from the point of view of the entity, "to inhabit", to have moral habit, *habitus*, which in Latin also means "dress". See: Pokorny (1959), p. 1172 ff: *ues-*.

484 Heidegger (1971), pp. 169-170.

485 Section 2.2.2 of the present essay.

486 Heidegger (1971), p. 164: "The terrifying is [the] unsettling; it places everything outside its own nature".

Heidegger depicts creation as a watery outpouring from a twofold source, analogically to Sinitic representations like that of the *Taiyi Shengshui* ("The Great One Gives Birth to Water"), a cosmogonic text of the Warring States.[487] In Heidegger's vision, the outpouring either quenches the thirst of mortals or is a means of consecration, and further creation. As a libation or sacrifice, it is called a gush (German *Guss*) — a strong outflow — a word which etymologically stems from the Indo-European *ghu-*,[488] which has the same meaning and is also the root of the Germanic word "god" (German *Gott*, Proto-Germanic *gudą*).[489] God is a gush, and the Thing has the ability to convey the gush and pour it further. The taking and pouring in and from the jug is the twofold process of time, while the Fouring is the institution of time in space.

Heidegger continues by defining the terms of the Fouring:[490]

> In the gift of the outpouring earth and sky, divinities and mortals dwell together all at once. These four, at one because of what they themselves are, belong together. Preceding everything that is present, they are enfolded into a single fourfold. In the gift of the outpouring dwells the simple singlefoldness of the four. The gift of the outpouring is a gift because it stays earth and sky, divinities and mortals. [...] Staying appropriates. It brings the four into the light of their mutual belonging. From out of staying's simple onefoldness they are betrothed, entrusted to one another. At one in thus being entrusted to one another, they are unconcealed. The gift of the outpouring stays the onefold of the fourfold of the four, and in the poured gift the jug presences as jug. The gift gathers what belongs to giving: the twofold containing, the container, the void, and the outpouring as donation. What is gathered in the gift gathers itself in appropriately staying the fourfold. [...] The jug's presencing is the pure, giving gathering of the onefold fourfold into a single time-space, a single stay. The jug presences as a thing. [...] The thing things. [...] Appropriating the fourfold, it gathers

---

487 Didier (2019), vol. III, p. 120 ff. Contains excerpts from the *Taiyi Shengshui*.

488 Heidegger (1971), p. 170.

489 Pokorny (1959), p. 447 ff: *gheu-*.

490 Heidegger (1971), pp. 171-172.

the fourfold's stay, its while, into something that stays for a while: into this thing, that thing.

The gush is a process of continuous creation, consisting of the gathering of the four modalities of reality — Heaven, Earth, deities and mortals — in the guise of the Thing, in which they stay, that is to say, in which they are appropriately instituted. The Thing, in turn, has the power to pour the Fouring into establishing other things. The Thing has the power "to thing" other things and "to world" other worlds.

> Thinging, the thing stays the united four, earth and sky, divinities and mortals, in the simple onefold of their self-unified fourfold.

> Earth is the building bearer, nourishing with its fruits, tending water and rock, plant and animal. [...] The sky is the sun's path, the course of the moon, the glitter of the stars, the year's seasons, the light and dusk of day, the gloom and glow of night, the clemency and inclemency of the weather, the drifting clouds and blue depth of the ether. [...] The divinities are the beckoning messengers of the Godhead. Out of the hidden sway of the divinities the God emerges as what he is, which removes him from any comparison with beings that are present. [...] The mortals are human beings. They are called mortals because they can die. To die means to be capable of death as death. Only man dies. The animal perishes. It has death neither ahead of itself nor behind it. Death is the shrine of Nothing, that is, of that which in every respect is never something that merely exists, but which nevertheless presences, even as the mystery of Being itself. As the shrine of Nothing, death harbors within itself the presencing of Being. As the shrine of Nothing, death is the shelter of Being. We now call mortals mortals — not because their earthly life comes to an end, but because they are capable of death as death. Mortals are who they are, as mortals, present in the shelter of Being. They are the presencing relation to Being as Being.[491]

Like in the Sino-Ruist view and the Mesopotamian one, as explained in the first chapter of the present essay,[492] Heidegger

---

491 Ibidem, pp. 175-176.

492 Section 1.3.3 of the present essay.

recognises the special role of mankind in the ongoing process of creation. He says that men are mortal, in the sense that they "never merely exist" and are the only creatures capable of death, which is the "shrine of Nothing" and the "shelter of Being". Death is the shroud of the formidable void that is at the same time the infinite potentiality for creation starting from a twofoldness of tensional oppositions, like in the *Ginnungagap* ("genial/generative gap"), from which the gods emerge, of ancient Germanic thought. Death lurks within humanity, and man is the only being that may become aware of this, since the void is the interstice in which thought articulates, and man is the only being who may use the void's potentiality. Analogically, this void is the *wu* of Sinitic thinking, the hub of the wheel of the God of the Northern Heighth, the hollow of the *ding* cauldron which reproduces on Earth the *Ding* square of Heaven, and the "notself" which rests at the heart of things, and men may act as *wu* (in the word's other acceptation, shaman/sage), opening the void and making it operational. Heidegger means that men can grasp and enshrine, within their own notself, the Fouring/the Thing, which flows from the *Seyn* and is the *Seyn* itself. This is mankind's endowment and the technical power of fostering creation becoming vessels of Being. The presentifying men may act as caretakers of Being, making *Seyn* present to *Seyn* itself.

The Fouring, or Fourfolding, is not fixed: Heidegger says that the four facets of creation are engaged in a constant mirror-play, a play of reflection/speculation, wherethrough they compete with each other, appropriating and expropriating, interpreting one another; such reciprocal exchange is the unfolding of the oneness of *Seyn* into the *Geviert*:[493]

> Earth and sky, divinities and mortals — being at one with one another of their own accord — belong together by way of the simpleness of the united fourfold. Each of the four mirrors in its own way the presence of the others. Each therewith reflects itself in its own way into its own, within the simpleness of the four. This mirroring does not portray

493 Heidegger (1971), pp. 177-178.

a likeness. The mirroring, lightening each of the four, appropriates their own presencing into simple belonging to one another. Mirroring in this appropriating-lightening way, each of the four plays to each of the others. The appropriative mirroring sets each of the four free into its own, but it binds these free ones into the simplicity of their essential being toward one another. The mirroring that binds into freedom is the play that betroths each of the four to each through the enfolding clasp of their mutual appropriation. None of the four insists on its own separate particularity. Rather, each is expropriated, within their mutual appropriation, into its own being. This expropriative appropriating is the mirror-play of the fourfold. Out of the fourfold, the simple onefold of the four is ventured. […] The unity of the fourfold is the fouring. But the fouring does not come about in such a way that it encompasses the four and only afterward is added to them as that compass. Nor does the fouring exhaust itself in this, that the four, once they are there, stand side by side singly. The fouring, the unity of the four, presences as the appropriating mirror-play of the betrothed, each to the other in simple oneness.

In other words, the *Seyn* self-generates as the *Geviert*, in the process of the Fouring, and in turn, the four modes of being converge in the continuous reproduction and reconfiguration of the oneness of the *Seyn* in a swirling activity of mutual appropriation, that is interpretation. The Fouring is not an abstract rule that comes before the *Geviert*, but it is the coherence of the speculation play, it is the ringing dance of the four. Within this ring, the *Seyn* is present, the four coalesce, and the Thing is born. In this sense, the Thing gathers and institutes the four facets of creation; the Thing is a decorated coalescence of the four, and as such it enshrines the *Seyn*. According to Heidegger, the Fouring is what humanity may understand of the *Seyn*, the limit beyond which human thinking may not fathom.[494]

In the last parts of his speech, Heidegger defines things as particular condensations of Being.[495] In the ornamented Thing

---

494 Ibidem.

495 Ibidem, pp. 179-180.

(the *Yang*-Thing), the ringing of Heaven and Earth, deities and mortals, breaks free from the simple oneness by taking a certain configuration. Each entity, from trees to bridges, from deer to books, is a *Yang*-Thing, that is to say, a specific conformation of the four manifestations of Being, which depends on the context, on the already established relational tensions within the *Seyn*. The four faces of Heidegger's *Seyn* are the Sumerian-Mesopotamian *lamassu*, the Sinitic *Wufang Shangdi*, and the *Hayyoth* of Jewish mysticism.

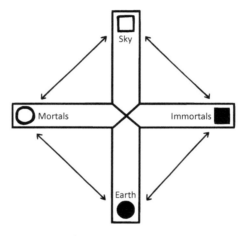

Figure 22: Attempted visual representation of the "thinging" and "worlding" interplay between Heaven, Earth, deities (immortals) and men (mortals); the process of *Seyn*. Heaven at the top is the immaterial source of the universal squaring order. Deities are placed between Heaven and Earth but are nearer to Heaven, wherefrom they come; they are immaterial "squaring" patterns, which nevertheless work through Earth, hide within it moulding things. The Earth at the bottom is the receptacle empty of shapes, and yet full of resources, in which heavenly principles may take root and articulate. Also men are placed between Heaven and Earth, and yet are more like the Earth, sharing, primordially, its "round" shapelessness and material ductility. Nevertheless, they have the ability of heightening themselves towards Heaven. They are *Dasein* once they become aware of the *Seyn*, become its vessels, *sacerdotes* ("endowed with the holy"), and act as its caretakers.

3.3. THE YELLOW DEITY AS PALINGENESIS OF THE *LOGOS*

[…] We may propose to consider Heidegger's *Dasein* as the subject of the Fourth Political Theory. *Dasein* is described in Heidegger's philosophy at length through its existential structure, which makes it possible to build a complex, holistic model based on it, the development of which will lead to, for instance, a new understanding of politics. […] If the subject is *Dasein*, then the Fourth Political Theory would constitute a fundamental ontological structure that is developed on the basis of existential anthropology. || The main idea of the Fourth Political Theory is to walk away from the dualism between the subject and the object, between intention and realisation, and from the dual topography which the philosophy of modernity, the science of modernity, and the politology of modernity are based on. […] *Dasein*, as proposed by Heidegger, is a way to overcome the subject-object duality, that is, an aspiration to find the root of ontology. Heidegger mentioned the *inzwischen*, or the "between", while talking about the existence of *Dasein*. The principal nature of *Dasein* is being "between".

Aleksandr Dugin[496]

3.3.1. *HUANGDI* AS COSMOGENIC CENTRING: ANALOGY WITH HEIDEGGER'S *DASEIN-ZWISCHEN-ORT*

The Yellow Deity (黄帝 *Huángdì*)[497] is the centre of the cosmotheanthropic architecture illustrated hereinbefore. It is the *Di* planted in the Earth's bosom, and arising as the vertical *axis mundi*, bridging the Earth and Heaven. It is the hub of emanation and convergence of Heaven's fourfold manifestation. As such, it

---

496 Dugin (2012), pp. 40-41 & 179.

497 Also translated as "Yellow Thearch" and "Yellow Emperor". Given the secularised meaning that the word "emperor" had acquired in the West, throughout my essay I use the translation "Yellow Deity" in most of the cases. I use "Yellow Emperor" when discussing euhemeristic accounts and hypotheses about the deity. Nevertheless, it is pertinent to mention the original synonymy of "emperor" and "interpreter" (cf. Latin *imperō*, *imperāre*, a variation of *in+parō*, *parāre*, meaning "to bring forth/arrange from within"; cf. also *interpretor*, *interpretārī*, "to father/make from within").

well represents Heidegger's Thing as the Fouring of *Seyn*, but also his conception of human gist as Therebeing (*Dasein*) and the Duginian "radical subject", shaped by the awareness of death in the short-circuit — in the collapse of the serpent of time in the present —, and the awareness of the creative dynamism begotten by the tensional void heart of *Seyn*. As Dugin says, the *Dasein* is the pre-dualistic Twice/Twist/Twixt (*Zwischen*), the *Dasein* is located "intween/intwixt" (*inzwischen*); it is the vertical gap and at the same time the tensional link between subject and object,[498] the common root from which all dualities emerge, providing a further identification with the olden Germanic conception of *Tuisto* explained in the foregoing chapter of the present essay.[499] It is the Dragon slithering in-between *yin* and *yang*. In Dugin's philosophy, the *Dasein* is a new conception of the *Logos* and of humanity that works as the central magnetic field of the Fourth Political Theory, whose actualisation will counterweight and win the postliberal wreckage to a new order. It is a fundamental ontological theory with at its core the awareness of the truth (the treeing[500]) of Being: "there" (*da*) and "being" (*sein*) is a gesture, an indication of where the fountain of Being is located.[501] Dugin analogises the *Zwischen* to Gilbert Durand's topographical *Traiectum*, the "trajectory" existing thwartwise subject and object, and the edge between interiority and exteriority. The *Traiectum* is the crossroads that "institutionalises time"; time is a function of the *Dasein* and becomes institutionalised in it.[502]

In Sinitic philosophy, as the middle of the crossing of the horizontal Earth and the vertical Heaven, the Yellow Deity coincides with humanity's position within the cosmotheanthropic structure of space-time: the intermediary between Heaven and Earth and the four directions. The Yellow Deity may be regarded as a representation of either

---

498 Dugin (2012), pp. 189-190.

499 Section 2.3.2 of the present essay.

500 Section 1.1.3 of the present essay.

501 Dugin (2012), p. 54.

502 Ibidem, p. 70.

mankind as the incarnation of Heaven or, in narrower terms, of the sage/etheling/*wu* who merges his own self with Heaven or who embodies Heaven in his notself, and therewith acts as theurge or demiurge.

Figure 23: Versions of the character 黄 *huáng* ("yellow/golden") respectively, from left to right, in ① Shang-Zhou bronze script, ② Shang oracular script, and ③ Zhou-Qin seal scripts.

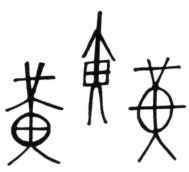

The etymology of the grapheme 黄 *huáng*, "yellow", but also "golden", corroborates such interpretation. In mythology, the Yellow Deity's personal name as a mortal is 轩辕 *Xuānyuán*, which means "Chariot Axle" or "Axial Shaft", clearly identifying him as the spindle of the Northern Heighth (and of the Chariots/Dippers). The graphic etymology of *huang* is ostensive: in both contemporary script, Shang oracular script, Shang-Zhou bronze script, and Zhou-Qin seal scripts, it is shown as an anthropoid figure that pierces/embodies a square or a cross. The two graphemes of which it is composed are 灮 *guāng*, which means "light" or "lightning/thunder", and 田 *tián*, which means "field/ploughed land" and belongs to the semantic series of "Heaven". In the oldest mythological accounts, it is also true that the Yellow Deity is identified as the eagle-faced Thunder God (*Leigong/Leishen*).[503] Therefore, the theonym *Huangdi* may be interpreted as "Lightning Deity who is instructed by Heaven

503 Eagle-faced like the men of wisdom (𣅈 *zu*) of ancient Mesopotamian culture, the eagle being able to gaze fixedly at the Sun, seeing the source of the world. See the note 363 of the present essay.

to edify[504] the Earth". Interestingly, the grapheme for "yellow" is also homophonous of 皇 *huáng* and near-homophonous of 王 *wáng*. The latter means "king" and the former "emperor" and was part of the title of the emperors of China since the country's unification at the hands of the Qin dynasty, whose first sovereign identified himself as 皇帝 *huángdì* ("divus emperor"). Both of them contain the element 工 *gōng*, "craft", which represents a *gnomon*, the carpenter's square, and according to Mark Edward Lewis is a synonym of *wu*.[505] According to the Chinese historian Qiu Xigui, the grapheme for "yellow" itself is a synonym of *wu*.[506]

The etymology hitherto enucleated provides the wherewithals to institute another analogy, this time with the Heideggerian concept of "location", *Ort* in German. The Yellow Deity, the incarnation of Heaven among humanity, functions as a cosmogenic centring of the four directions of space on Earth. In other words, it theurgically establishes a *locus*, which in Latin means an ordered, polished/political and thus clarified space, centre of gravitation and irradiation of civilising, "worlding" activity. Heidegger used the German word *Ort*, which originally meant the "tip of the spear", to express a similar concept in his essay *Georg Trakl. Eine Erörterung seines Gedichtes* (1953):[507]

> All the forces of the spear converge into its tip. The *Ort* gathers by attracting towards itself, as it is the highest and most extreme point. By bringing together, it transfixes and permeates everything. The *Ort*, as that which unites, draws to itself and keeps what it has drawn to itself. It does not keep what it has drawn to itself in the manner of a casket, but in order to integrate it within its own light, thereby giving it the ability to unfold according to its own true being.

504 In the original Latin acceptation of *aedificō, aedificāre* which means "to template", "to contemplate", "to term", "to make an ordered world".

505 Lewis (1999), pp. 205-206.

506 Wells (2014), p. 12, note 33.

507 The quote is from: Resta (2002), pp. 11-18. I have translated the excerpts in English from Italian language. Heidegger's original 1953 essay (in German) is: "Georg Trakl. Eine Erörterung seines Gedichtes". *Merkur*, 61(VII): 226-258.

The *Ort* is the centre of the cruciform of Heaven, Earth, deities and mortals, and as such, it is an actualisation of the Fouring wherein mankind may abide, a place of *habitus*. The *Ort* is a "cosmos", a decorated space, a templated world, an open space where things may appear in appropriate ways. It is a world wherein forces articulate appropriately in structures which reproduce the order of Heaven, and therefore things are not suffocated by an incoherent and undifferentiated totality. It is otherwise definable by means of other Heideggerian concepts: *Lichtung* ("glade/clearing"), which includes both the ideas of "lighting", "lightening", and "opening" and *Hut* (both "hut" and "hat", like the conical one of the mage, both reproducing the vault of Heaven), the fourfold shelter of the Fouring of Being.[508] *Erörterung*, the act of "indicating the locus" in the sense of "reminding the origin", is the theurgical role of the centring wiseman who makes himself *umbilicus* of the world, who makes a world.

In Han-dynasty sources, the Yellow Deity is conceived as well as the Solar God, with the other of the Five Deities representing his four seasonal and directional aspects, another analogy of cosmogenic centring and irradiation. In the 尸子 *Shīzi*, he is called the "Yellow Deity with Four Faces" (黄帝四面 *Huángdì Sìmiàn*).[509]

3.3.2. *HUANGDI* AS HEAVEN'S INCARNATION: DUGIN'S *EREIGNIS*, THE COSMIC CHRIST, AND THE EURASIAN EMPEROR

[...] Nothingness itself is the flip side of pure Being, which — in such a paradoxical way! — reminds mankind of its existence. If we correctly decipher the logic behind the unfurling of Being, then thinking mankind can save itself with lightning speed at the very moment of its greatest risk. "But where the danger lies, there also grows that which saves", Heidegger quotes from Hölderlin's poetry. Heidegger used a special term, *Ereignis* — the "event", to describe this sudden return of Being. It takes place exactly at midnight of the world's night — at the darkest moment in history. [...]

---

508 Ibidem. The concepts of *Ort*, *Lichtung*, *Hut* and also *Haus* are well synthesised in the first few paragraphs of the text.

509 Sun & Kistemaker (1997), p. 120.

At the heart of the Fourth Political Theory, as its magnetic centre, lies the trajectory of the approaching *Ereignis* [...].

Aleksandr Dugin[510]

> A great lightning encircled the pole star and lit up the countryside near the city; it aroused Fubao, who gave birth to Huangdi.[511]

In the above-cited excerpt from an apocryphal of the *Shijing* ("Book of Poetry"), as well as in other classical sources, the euhemerised Yellow Emperor — who in such contexts is identified as the historical founder of Chinese culture, the progenitor of all Chinese, or even straightaway as the progenitor of all humanity[512] — is explicitly identified as the incarnation of the supreme God of the Northern Heighth, in Han-dynasty sources also called the "Yellow God of the Northern Dipper" (黄神北斗 *Huángshén Běidǒu*) or "Supreme One of the Yellow/ Golden Centre" (中黄太乙 *Zhōnghuáng Tàiyǐ*). He is said to have been conceived by a virgin mother, who became pregnant by gazing at the rotating Great Chariot. He was the stepson of Shaodian, ruler of the state/ilk of the 有熊 *Yǒuxióng*, "Possessors of the She-bear", yet another evident link to the Northern Heighth (*Ursa Major*).[513] In an apocryphal text, it is said that the Yellow Emperor proceeds from "the essence of the Yellow God of the Northern Dipper", that he is born to "a daughter of a chthonic deity", and as such, he is "a cosmic product of the conflation of Heaven and Earth".[514] In the same

---

510 Dugin (2012), p. 29.

511 Excerpt from *Hanzhen wu*, an apocryphal of the Confucian *Shijing* ("Book of Poetry"). Quote taken from: Bonnefoy & Doniger (1993), p. 241.

512 Liu (1999), pp. 608-609.

513 Didier (2009), vol. I, pp. 153-154. Also Aleksandr Dugin, in his writings about Siberia, cursorily speaks about the birth of the blond-haired and blue-eyed sacerdotal kings of the Aryans (divided into Indo-Europeans and Turanians) from virgin mothers impregnated by the spirit of the North Pole, fecundated "without the intervention of a male", especially citing the story of Temüjin (Genghis Khan)'s birth from the lineage of the virgin Alan-Goa. Cf. Dugin (1992), pp. 133-136.

514 Espesset (2008), pp. 1061-1102. See pp. 26-27 and note 82 of the consulted version from the French archive HAL-SHS (Sciences de l'Homme et de la Société).

order of ideas, the Yellow God is defined as the "spiritual father and astral double of the Yellow Emperor".[515]

I assume that such a figure is a symbol of ① cosmogenic/ cosmetic (i.e. ordered world-making) centrality, of the notself/ emptied self (*kenosis*) of the sages who are aware of their identity with the universe — becoming theurgical vehicles of the God of the Northern Heighth[516] —, in other words, symbol of divine authority; ② of the axiality umbe which worlds articulate, of the diffuse *logoi* of the *Logos* (or *Li*), an ever-living and coherent web of patternings; and ③ of the *loci*, the *Orte* and *Lichtungen*, the templated worlds which expand around their own *li*. The Yellow Deity may ultimately be considered as a device for dissolving, unfixing from Christianity, and reconfiguring the concept of "Christ" merging it with that of the multiplex Eurasian saviour god-king, and for sparking a palingenesis of the *Logos* in the form of the Heideggerian and Duginian radical *Dasein* as *Zwischen*, in all its cosmogenic potentiality, for a new civilising configuration of Eurasia to be the gateway to the great time of Heaven.

Together with the theoretical tools of *Tian*, *Di* and *Ding*, the Yellow Deity might represent a model not merely for individual sages but first of all for the Eurasian cosmic sovereign, opening the space for channelling the order-making power of the God of the Northern Height on the Earth. The cosmic sovereign, a religio-political institution, utmost philosopher reconceptualiser of the world, might come not merely in the figure of a new Chinese sovereign (or a Great *Ru* in Jiang Qing's system, as we will see in the next chapter[517]), but in that of a pan-Eurasian emperor, overtopping local cosmic sovereigns, which might be that of China, that of Japan, a new tsar in Russia, and that of a reborn Greco-Romanity, or even a new *lugal* in the Celto-Germanic

---

515 Wells (2014), p. 42, note 25.

516 Lévi (2008), pp. 645-692. See p. 674 for the symbolism about asceticism.

517 Section 4.3 of the present essay.

north,[518] in Western Europe. A supreme pole overtopping a plural, multipolar world and capable of acknowledging the multiplicity of the poles.

As conjectured in the previous chapter, the word "christ" might derive from the same Indo-European root (*kr), which expresses "concretisation", "concrescence", "aggregation", but also "incorporation/embodiment" or "incarnation", and I have also instituted an analogy between this concept and that of the *buddha*.[519] An analogy between Sinitic cosmotheanthropism and the theology of Bonaventure (1221-1274), with his conception of "Christ the centre",[520] may be useful for the reconfiguration of the latter and its identification as the same as the Eurasian saviour god-king.

In the words of the Franciscan nun and philosopher Ilia Delio, Bonaventuran theology describes God as the "self-diffusive" principle of the universe, which continuously manifests itself as the Word in creation, as the axial Christ who centralises worlds:[521]

> God "speaks" Godself in all things. Creation bears a congruent relationship to the Word of God so that Christ is truly the center and goal of creation, and hence its metaphysical center.

Otherwise expressed:[522]

> The Son is that person eternally generated by the Father's self-diffusive goodness (*bonum diffusivum sui*), who is generated *per modum naturae* and, as such, is both the total personal expression of the Father as Word and the ultimate likeness to the Father as Image.

---

518 Within Zuism, Mesopotamian Neopaganism, there is figure of the *lugal* ("great man") as utmost sacerdotal king. As highlighted in a note of the first chapter (162 of the section 1.3.3), Zuism might work as a vehicle for triggering a rediscovery of the original meaning of all Indo-European traditions, and therefore as a vehicle for the resacralisation of entire Europe.

519 Section 2.2.3 of the present essay.

520 Delio (2007), p. 256.

521 Ibidem.

522 Ibidem, p. 259.

In his *Itinerarium Mentis in Deum*, Bonaventure says that the diffusion of God in temporal creation happens in the form of a centre or point of orientation within "the immensity of the divine goodness".[523]

In the following lines, Delio illustrates the Trinity as a process, as the enlivening Spirit, that is forebegotten by the continuous dynamic interaction between the Father and the Son. The Father (the Speaker) precedes the Son (the Spoken Word), and the Son proceeds from the Father and returns to the Father through the Spirit (the Speaking Word), itself proceeding from the Father.[524] Such depiction reflects the Sinitic conception of *Tian*, of the *Li*, that it emanates, and its coherence throughout the *qi* (spirit-matter, or spiritualised matter). The concept of the Son or Word mirrors that of the Yellow Deity as the crossing and centralising potency of the *yuzhou*. In the first and second chapters of the present essay, we have deepened the fundamental importance that the creative Word had in Mesopotamian culture as the second person of God (part of a triune vision of God which is common to all Eurasian religions), and still has in Chinese culture as

---

523 Ibidem, p. 262. Quotes Bonaventure's *Itinerarium Mentis in Deum* 6.2 (5:310).

524 The sentence expresses my interpretation. Ilia Delio, as a Franciscan, Roman Catholic, Western Christian, in her wordings seems to remain, at times, very attached to the Western Christian doctrinal formula of the *Filioque*, i.e. "and the Son", implying that the Spirit proceeds from both the Father and the Son equipollently, at the same time and on the same level. Such formula, albeit already present in the doctrine of certain thinkers and local churches since early Christianity, was officially established by the Frankish emperor Charlemagne in Frankish Catholicism with the Council of Aachen of 809, approved by Pope Leo III and later included in the official creed of all Roman Catholicism in 1014; it was part of Charlemagne's project of centralisation of power in his own hands and expansion of his empire and religious doctrine, as it functioned as an expedient to give the terrestrialised Son/Word, thus terrestrial nature, human rationalism, and the person of emperor Charlemagne in particular and later the Roman Popes, a creative power equivalent to that of God, the power of the heavenly Spirit (which mankind has only the task of reaffirming and reproducing), thereby giving way to a terrestrialisation of the Spirit in which we can see the foreshadowing of the later complete secularisation and materialisation of Christianity in the modern epoch with the total denial of the Spirit. I already alluded to the essence of Charlemagne's reforms in the note 179 of section 1.3.3. The *Filioque* was declared a heresy by the Eastern Orthodox Church, which therewith seceded from the Roman Catholic Church in 1054. Cf. Dugin (1992), pp. 105-111.

the power to name entities and thus trace their destiny in accordance with, and reproducing the, patterns of Heaven.[525]

The Son/Word is both generated by the Father and, together with the Father as one principle, breathes forth the Spirit, who is that eternal bond of love between the Father and Son. The Spirit proceeds from Father and Son in an act of full freedom (*per modum voluntatis*), the procession of the Spirit being the act of a clear and determinate loving volition on the part of Father and Son.[526]

Bonaventuran theology inherits its concept of love[527] from the *Corpus Dionysianum* and Richard of Saint Victor. They defined love, respectively, as the self-diffusive highest good (*bonum est diffusivum sui*) which gives rise to being, and as a dynamism, personal and communicative. As such, God manifests itself as a "communion of persons in love" articulating in a manifold structure.[528] This is clearly analogous to Sinitic cosmology, in which a twofold dynamism operates by begetting a third element, and to the Ruist anthropogogical concept of *ren* ("two-person"), which emphasises the fundamentality of such twofold dynamism for the construction of human society (being the link ancestor— offspring, the kinship lineage, the link to God). In Delio's terms:

525 Section 1.3.3 and 2.2.1 of the present essay.

526 Delio (2007), p. 260.

527 Delio tends to express theological doctrines in very "humanising" (in the sense of "terrestrialising"), dense terms, maybe a reflection of the fact that such "humanising", "social" interpretation of theological doctrines is typical of the completely secularised, materialised, "socialised" Western Christianity (cf. Dugin [1992], pp. 105-107). It is worthwhile noting forthwith, however, that the Germanic word "love" has different semantics than the Latin word *amor, amōris*, and the two should not be confused. "Love" belongs, by Germanic *umlaut*, to the same semantic series as "life" and "lief", and "to live" and "to believe", much like the German *Liebe* ("love") belongs to the same series as *Leben* ("life") and even *Leib* ("living body"), and expresses a natural, congenial, sticking together of things. *Amor*, instead, is traced back to the Indo-European root **am-* which expresses attachment to the mother and to material pleasure. *Amor* is the duty of women, while "life" is the duty of men. As Jullien says in *De l'Être au vivre*, "love" is a word which in the West has become laden with earthen, dense meanings, and it should be avoided; the Chinese equivalent, 爱 *ài*, in the same way, implies passion and attachment and is almost never used by the Chinese.

528 Delio (2007), pp. 257-258.

The life of the Trinity originates eternally from the first divine person, the Father, who, as first, is infinitely fecund and thus "fountain fullness" of goodness. This fountain fullness expresses itself perfectly in the one who is Son and Word. This process reaches its consummation in the love between them, which is the Spirit. Love, therefore, is the energizing principle of the dynamic life of the Trinity.[529]

In Bonaventure, the productive power of God only coincides with the procession of the Spirit, while the Son is begotten *per modum naturae* (by the mode of nature). The Son is "beloved" by the Father, meaning that within generation, the Son is sustained by God through an act *approbans*. God, as the triune process, is the prototype of all creation, and all created things follow its model. In such conception, the Word or Son, that is the Christ, is the symbol of God as creative self-expressing order, centre of divine life. It is a reproduction *in loco* (in a specialised, clarified configuration of space-time) of God's triune imprint. Creation is the expressed Word of the inner Word of God.[530]

I distinguish the singular non-particularised Word from the manifold particularised words, analogically to the Sinitic conception of the universal *Li* and the particularised reasons/rites. The Sinitic conception of the Yellow Emperor proceeding from the essence of the Yellow God of the Northern Dipper, otherwise conceptualised as the "primordial energy" (原气 *yuánqì*) irradiated by the *Taiyi* which impregnated his mortal mother (local nature), easily resolves early Christology in a less abstract way. Indeed, Sinitic theology, due to its emphasis on God as the always-presencing ultimate forefather of everything — another one among God's names, incidentally, is "Supreme/Highest Ancestor", 上甲 *Shàngjiǎ*, whose signifier in Shang script is a cross contained in a square

---

529 Ibidem, p. 258.

530 Ibidem, pp. 261-262. Delio quotes: Hayes, Zachary (1979). *Saint Bonaventure's Disputed Questions on the Mystery of the Trinity*. Allegany, New York: Franciscan Institute Publications, Saint Bonaventure University. p. 46.

→ 田 ,[531] conceptualised in modern Chinese culture by the expression 曾祖父 *zēngzǔfù*, "forefather of all forms"[532] —, advantageously shuns utter transcendentalisms of thought that would lead to the abstraction of God, the objectification of the *Logos*, and the maddening of human reason in demonic horizontality. Instead, Sinitic thinking provides a real and experiential relationality with divinity which takes place along the kinship lineage.

According to Bonaventure, the Christ is not only the centre of creation, but also the art of God — *ars patris*, a concept significantly analogous to those of *Li* as artwork discussed in the foregoing chapter. The Son, not the Father, is the immanent grounding of reality.[533] The figure of the Yellow Deity portrays the immanence of divinity in an even stronger way, especially when regarded as the "progenitor of humanity" (人文始祖 *rénwén shǐzǔ*), that is to say the archetype of humanity, while as we have seen the God of the Northern Heighth is conceived as the progenitor of all things of the universe. The understanding of the kinship of God and humanity is the foundation of Ruism's empowerment of the latter as a crucial actor in creation. As already said, such conception contrasts with the Western idea of Christ as a symbol of acceptation of the *status quo* and renunciation of human agency.[534]

There is a noteworthy similarity between the Bonaventuran, Franciscan and medieval conception of the attainment of the iridescent truth (Heidegger's ἀλήθεια *aletheia*, "unhiding/ unveiling/revelation") without "intellectual eyes"; the concept of Christ and crucifixion as a symbol of death (i.e. of extinction of the self, or "utter self-emptying"), to see "into the heart of things";[535] the Heideggerian *Dasein* as "being-toward-death"

---

531 Didier (2009), vol. II, pp. 227-228.

532 Zhong (2014), p. 84, note 282.

533 Delio (2007), p. 267.

534 Section 2.3.4 of the present essay.

535 Delio (2007), pp. 270-271.

(*Sein-zum-Tode*), the acknowledgement that death haunts being as the void space that is needed for change and rebirth; and ultimately the general Sino-Ruist concept of sage/etheling/*wu*. The Yellow Deity itself is a symbol of asceticism as death of the ego (*kenosis*), realisation of the notself, but also of rebirth as re-centring of the self, its replenishment with the heavenly measure.[536]

Throughout the essay, I have advanced a critique against the historicisation/spatiotemporal fixation of the Christ and the sclerotisation of reason that ensues thereupon. Here, I enrich my hypothesis by saying that the definition of Christ as the centre, or the cosmic Christ, as a "point in history at which the content of that Word is historicized with such explicitness that from that point light is shed on all of reality", has to be wrested from Christianity, from the spatiotemporal fixed setting that Christianity assigned to it, so as to be re-interpreted as a centralising coherence which is diffused throughout different worlds, which inheres organic contexts and entities, like the Eurasian saviour god-king. Delio herself, throughout her reading of Bonaventure, comes to similar conclusions; as Bonaventure said, "every creature proclaims the eternal generation of the Word", that is to say, the axial Christ is "cosmically differentiated".[537] Once the *Logos* is unfixed from history, reunited with a non-abstract conception of God, dissolved and ultimately recoagulated within the figure of the Eurasian saviour god-king, which already overlaps with the conception of the multiplex *buddha*, the way would be open for an integration of Europe, or what remains of the olden medieval Germanic civilisation and what has developed over the latest centuries of modernity outside of it, into the project of a broader Eurasian religio-political entity, led by a divine emperor governing over many local divine kings, who would function as nexuses of religio-political power, in turn governing over the divine fathers of kinships. Thus, a plural

---

536 Lévi (2007), p. 674.

537 Delio (2007), pp. 272-273, note 76. Quotes Bonaventure's *Collationes in Hexaemeron* 11.13 (5:382), 11.21.

religio-political power which would not be fragmented into an incoherent and horizontal dust, but which would point to the unity represented by the great emperor of Eurasia.

The Yellow Deity inscribed within the *yuzhou*, as a model for divine sovereignty, may also be analogised to Heidegger's concept of *Ereignis*, the "event/happening" of the return of *Seyn*, its "advent", especially as reformulated by Aleksandr Dugin. The Yellow Deity is the *Dasein* at the centre of the Fouring, identified with *Seyn* in itself. It is the radical subject, the first men who emerge personifying the *Dasein* and who recreate civilisation *ex novo* after the end of history. As Dugin writes in his unfurling of Heideggerian phenomenology, the sign of the Fouring (the symbolism of the cross) is "an image relating to *Seyn* and to thinking about the truth of *Seyn*". The Fouring is the *Lichtung* of *Seyn*, the "flash that illuminates with a final light the entire structure", which happens once the peak of thinking is reached.[538] As we have seen, this peak of thought is not something transcendent but may be identified as the God of the Northern Heighth, the north celestial pole (precessional and ecliptic).

The manifestation of the Fouring itself is the *Ereignis*, the happening of *Seyn*.[539] As a "central axis threading everything around itself", including politics, theology and mythology, the approaching *Ereignis* embodies "the triumphant return of Being, at the exact moment when mankind forgets about it, once and for all", in the Fourth Political Theory, at the midst of the nighttime of the nihilistic *Gestell* of postmodern postliberalism;[540] as a reintegration and re-blossoming of thought, as a new institutionalisation of time, attuned with the great time of Heaven, which triggers a new movement of anabasis and publicisation (we may say by using Ernesto de Martino's wording), of ascending evolution towards Heaven.

---

538 Dugin (2010), pp. 143-144.

539 Ibidem.

540 Dugin (2012), p. 29.

The *Dasein* institutes what Dugin calls the "original political ontological topography", the fundamental structure of any political entity and experience. Manifesting as the Fourfold, the *Ereignis* of *Seyn* "introduces war into everything, establishing the tension of the great axes of the world" (a Heraclitean formula). *Seyn* is intrinsically war because it manifests itself as oppositional dualities (synthesisable as the supreme Yea and Naught[541]), in the tautness between such dualities; as such tensional potency. It is in this sense that the *Dasein* is *Zwischen*. Vitally, the Naught is part of *Seyn* (*das Nichten im Seyn*), even determining *Seyn*'s possibility of happening; it is the space to be cleared and made into an ordered world. Dugin calls the two primary lines of war: "ouranogeomachy" (war between Heaven and Earth) and "anthropotheomachy" (war between men and deities).[542]

---

541 I adopt "yea" and "naught", archaic English forms of "yes" and "no", to represent such conceptualisation of dualities in Heideggerian-Duginian thought. Dugin himself uses "yes" and "no". They are the same as *Chaos* and *Logos* discussed in the prolegomenon to the first chapter of the present essay, and as the *Yang*-Thing and the *Yin*-Thing discussed in the second chapter.

542 Dugin (2010), pp. 148-149.

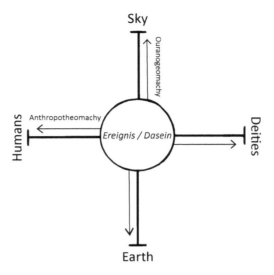

Sky

Ouranogeomachy

Anthropotheomachy

Humans

Ereignis / Dasein

Deities

Earth

Figure 24: Dugin's representation of the *Geviert*, i.e. the manifestation of *Seyn*, that is the *Ereignis*, its happening as *Dasein/Zwischen*, as tensional lines of power. Besides this last, Dugin also proposes the Thing and *Seyn* itself as occupying the central position.[543] Shown hereunder are the rudimentary signs representing it, relating to it and sparking the thinking of its truth. They represent as well the fundamental political ontological topography that the *Ereignis* establishes, the ontologico-political topography which is *Seyn* itself in flash and flesh.[544]

3.3.3. RECOLLECTING THE EURASIAN CONCEPTION OF THE SEVENFOLD STRUCTURE OF DIVINITY

In this last section of the third chapter, I investigate the Eurasian interconnections of the Sinitic spatiotemporal

543   Ibidem, p. 170.

544   Ibidem, pp. 143-144.

cosmotheanthropic structure, with the Yellow Deity at its core, elaborating what I define here as the "Eurasian sevenfold structure of divinity", in order to corroborate its functional value for a new civilisational configuration of Eurasia. It is the paradigm for an institutionalisation of time in rhythm with the great time of Heaven, as well as the original political ontological topographical paradigm sought for by Aleksandr Dugin and the Fourth Political Theory.

Didier traces the figure of the Yellow Deity much back in history. Highlighting its role as a creator god, a cosmogonic source begetting a sevenfold supernal order (the seven stars of the Chariots), stabiliser of the Three Augusts — 三皇 *Sānhuáng*; the numina of the Threefold Potentiality, namely the heavenly 伏羲 *Fúxī*, the earthly 女媧 *Nǚwā* (whose complex theonyms' etymologies mean, respectively, "Awesome/Holy Breath/Spirit", in which "awesome" has both its meanings of "marvellous" and "terrifying", and "Female/Material Spiral/Vortex"), and the numen of agriculture 神農 *Shénnóng*, "Peasant/Farmer God" —, and central one among the Five Deities — the other four being the Blue/Green Deity (青帝 *Qīngdì* or 蒼帝 *Cāngdì*), the Red Deity (赤帝 *Chìdì*, or Fiery Deity, 炎帝 *Yándì*, which is *Shennong* himself, the numen of humanity, or humanity's terrestrial nature, human reason and craft), the White Deity (白帝 *Báidì*) and the Black Deity (黑帝 *Hēidì*), each of them euhemerised as various historical sovereigns descending from the Yellow Deity,[545] and each one representing a phase in the process of continuous creation and renovation of the world, as well as of the cycle of the Sun (the Green Deity representing the beginning of the creative process, which proceeds to the Red Deity, to the White Deity, and ends

---

545 Sun & Kistemaker (1997), p. xxiii. Conventionally, based on Han-dynasty sources, the Three Potencies (Heaven, Earth and man) are represented by the Three Augusts: *Fuxi*, *Nuwa* and *Shennong*; besides *Xuanyuan*, historically placed in the 27th century BCE, the human incarnations of the other four spatial deities are identified, in the *Shiji*, with *Zhuanxu*, *Ku*, *Yao* and *Shun*. According to the *Huainanzi*, the Red Deity of the south, also called the Fiery Deity, fully coincides with *Shennong*, the god of mankind, agriculture and craft, the Green Deity of the east is associated with *Taihao*, while the White Deity of the west is associated with *Shaohao*. In modern times, the White Deity has been identified with *Chiyou*, a war god of the western populations of China.

with the Black Deity) —, the Yellow Deity is ultimately identified as the source of astral creation and human procreation, of public civilisation, forefather of aristocracy or of civilised humanity. Didier postulates a northern origin of such figure, finding analogies with Siberian myths pertaining to the astral She-bears and Indo-European cosmologies, especially the Seven Ecstatics (*Saptarṣi*) of the Vedas (corresponding to the Seven *Apkallu* of Mesopotamia and the Seven Sages of Greece) — sons of the supreme God who together with *Manu* (instructed by God itself in the form of *Matsya*, the "Fish", to build an ark) recreate the world after its dissolution —, they themselves symbolising the seven stars of the Chariots.[546]

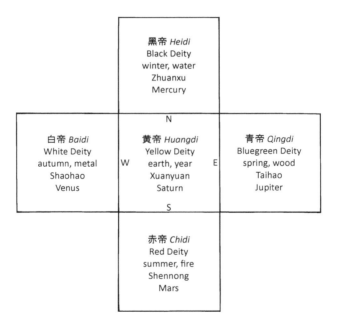

Figure 25: The diagram before is a representation of the spatial Five Deities and their attributes according to the *Huainanzi*. It shows the cosmic centre and four directions with ① the deities' Chinese names and their English translations, ② their seasonal and elemental function, ③ their most common other name/euhemerisation, and ④ their astral

---

546 Didier (2009), vol. I, pp. 155-160.

body in the Sun system.[547] The creative process starts with the Green Deity, passes through the Red and White Deities, and ends with the Black Deity, which symbolises reabsorption into the originating Oneness. The diagram below represents the same scheme with the addition of the vertical dimension, and thus *Fuxi*, the forces of Heaven, and *Nuwa*, the forces of the Earth: the hosting surface 地母 *Demŭ* ("Mother Earth") and the chthonic 后土 *Hòutŭ* ("Queen of the Earth"). Also added is 西王母 *Xīwángmŭ* ("Queen Mother of the West"), the celestial virgin.

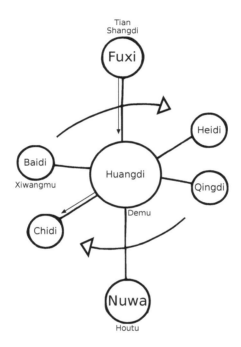

Didier also betokens the same motifs found in Mesopotamian religio-cosmology. As we have already seen, in Mesopotamian culture, the seven stars of the astral Chariots are considered the operative power of the God of the Northern Height (*An*) and are reflected in the seven planets' system, including five visible planets plus the Sun and the Moon, constituting a seven-tiered structure for ascending to the supernal God.[548]

---

547 The diagram reproduces an analogous one found in: Sun & Kistemaker (1997), p. 121.

548 Section 1.3.3 of the present essay. Also see: Didier (2009), vol. I, pp. 113-119.

The Mesopotamian sevenfold system (the seven *Anunnaki*, the "Heaven coming into Earth", the incarnation of Heaven) articulates as follows: *Marduk* 𒀭 ("Sun Calf"; Jupiter, the white deity of air and authority, lieutenant of *Enlil*), *Ninurta* 𒀭 ("Barley Lord"; Saturn, the black deity of war and hunting), *Nergal* 𒀭 ("Underworld Lord"; Mars, the red deity of woe and dearth), *Inanna* 𒀭 ("Lady of Heaven"; Venus, the blue deity of love and war), *Nabu* 𒀭 ("Announcer" or "Glowing"; Mercury, the orange deity of wisdom and writing), *Nanna* 𒀭 (the Moon, the green deity of fertility and fruitfulness) and *Utu* 𒀭 (the Sun, the yellow deity of justice).[549] They are poetically described as the "heavenly writing" of *An*,[550] and Simo Parpola identifies them as stages in the "tree of life", the process of God's manifestation in the flesh that structures all beings.[551] The Moon God, also known as *Enzu* or *Zuen* 𒀭 ("Lord of Wisdom"), is of particular importance as it represented the *pleroma*, the fullness of the powers of *An*, thus *An* itself as *Enlil*.[552] It is worthwhile to note that in Germanic languages, the word "Moon" (cf. German *Mond*, Proto-Germanic **mēnô*), and the related "month" (which literally means "lunation"), are traced back to the root of "measure", the already well-discussed **me-*, through the branch **menot-*,[553] witnessing the importance that the Moon had as an instrument for the regulation of time even in Germanic cultures.

As we have seen in the first chapter,[554] the supreme God of the Northern Heighth is conceived in Mesopotamia, as in all other declinations of Eurasian religio-cosmology, as having three

---

549 Kasak & Veede (2001), p. 23. The colours associated with the gods are those reconstructed by: James & Van der Sluijs (2008), passim. There are other combinations from other sources which may correspond more precisely to those of Sinitic religio-cosmology.

550 Kasak & Veede (2001), p. 14.

551 Parpola (1993), passim.

552 Ibidem, pp. 176, 184 & 185, notes 66, 89 & 93.

553 Pokorny (1959), pp. 731: *menot-*.

554 Section 1.3.3 of the present essay.

aspects: *An* itself as the hidden and quiescent potentiality of God at the north ecliptic pole, *Enlil* as its active force spinning as the precessional pole, and *Enki* as its earthly manifestation; *Enlil* was associated with the Plough and Chariot constellations — and *Marduk*-Jupiter was considered his proxy in the Sun system —, while *Enki* was associated with the Square of Pegasus (the Chinese *Ding*). Drawing a parallel with the Sinitic tradition, *Enlil* corresponds to the celestial aspect of the Yellow Deity (黄帝 *Huángdì*), or the Yellow God of the Northern Dipper (黄神北斗 *Huángshén Běidǒu*), while *Enki* and the *lugal* correspond to its earthly manifestation as the Yellow Emperor, the Red Deity, or the given divine sovereign (皇帝 *huángdì*) of a celestial civilisation. *Marduk* corresponds to the Green Deity, reactualising *Enlil*'s power at each renewal of the world.

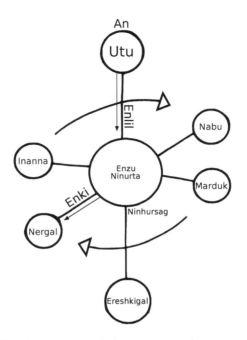

Figure 26: Application of the Sinitic *yuzhou* cosmotheanthropic structure to the Mesopotamian seven *Anunnaki*, the manifestation of *An* in the flesh. Note that the scheme also includes the three faces of the supreme God of Heaven, *An*, that is to say *An* itself, *Enlil* and *Enki*, interpreted as lines of tensional power: *Enlil* being time and motion, and *Enki* being space and expansion. The scheme also includes the great goddesses, ✳𐏒𐏒𐏒𐏒𐏒 *Ninhursag* ("Lady of the Mountain", one of the other names of 𐏒 *Ki*) as the hosting surface, and ✳𐏒𐏒𐏒𐏒 *Ereshkigal* ("Queen of the Great Earth") as the chthonic female matrix.

The study of the possible Indo-European transmission of the conception of the Yellow Deity and of its historical euhemerisation, the Yellow Emperor, has been carried out by a number of scholars. Chang Tsung-tung,[555] on the basis of Pokorny's *Wörterbuch* and Bernhard Karlgren's *Grammata Serica* (1940) and of the previous work of other Sinologists, has traced the origin of hundreds of words in the Old Chinese language back to Proto-Indo-European. He suggests that strong linguistic similarity may be found especially among

---

555 Cf. Chang (1988), passim.

Chinese and Germanic languages, which share a tendentially monosyllabic structure of words (consonant-vowel-consonant), polyphthongal vocalism, a simple grammatical structure and the largest number of cognate words.[556] Though I do not share it and rather interpret the Yellow Emperor as a paradigmatic archetype of the Eurasian saviour god-king, Chang even puts forward the euhemeristic hypothesis that the Yellow Emperor was, in fact, a blond-haired Indo-European (whence the reference to the colour yellow or gold in his title) who introduced wagon technology, founded a centralised state, and deeply shaped Sinitic language, as in the *Liji* ("Record of Rites"), chapter 23, *Jifa* ("Sacrifice methods"), is written that he "gave hundreds of things their right name, in order to illumine the people about the common good".[557]

Another scholar, Julie Lee Wei, provides an *interpretatio sinica*, identifying the most important Sinitic deities with Indo-European deities, especially their Hellenic and Roman forms, on the basis of the etymological and functional comparative work of other authors, including Chang's study.[558] She identifies the Yellow Deity with the Greco-Roman trinity of *Chronus/Saturnus*, *Zeus/Deus* and *Phoebus Apollo*. The other ones of the cluster of the Five Deities are identified as follows: ① the Black Deity with *Dionysus*, the principle of metamorphosis, dark facet of *Apollo* himself (顓頊 *Zhuānxū* is the "grandson of *Huangdi*" just like *Dionysus* is the grandson of *Chronus*); ② the Blue Deity with *Uranus* (太昊 *Tàihào* means "Vast Sky", is associated with the rising Sun, and among the Four Deities the bluegreen one of the east, the orient, as we have seen, represents the beginning of creation); ③ the Red Deity with *Saturnus* (competing and conflating with *Zeus*, just like in Sinitic cosmology *Xuanyuan* competes and then allies himself with *Shennong*); and ④ the White Deity is

---

556 Ibidem, pp. 3 & 32. As we have already seen in the note 165 of section 1.3.3, Aleksandr Dugin says that the earliest Turanian/Siberian branch of the Aryan tradition was best preserved among the early Germanics and Sino-Tibetans. Cf. Dugin (1992), p. 128.

557 Ibidem, p. 35.

558 Cf. Wei (2005), passim.

identified as *Tyr*, the Germanic god of war (Proto-Germanic *Tīwaz*), whose name etymologically derives from the same root of *Zeus*, that is *Dyeus* (which Wei says to also be the source of the contemporary Chinese identification of the White Deity, 蚩尤 *Chīyóu*, described as the "master of weapons" and "double of *Huangdi*"),[559] thus *Ares/Mars*, traditionally associated with the female goddess of beauty and war, *Aphrodite/Venus*. Wei also identifies *Nuwa*, the goddess of the Earth of the Three Augusts, with *Persephone/Demeter*.[560] I conjecture a stronger identification of *Shennong* with *Ares/Mars* besides *Saturnus* since *Ares/Mars*, just like *Shennong*, is associated with fire and was originally the principle of agriculture. The *Huainanzi*'s association of the planet Mars to *Shennong* corroborates such a hypothesis.

Wei concludes that this religio-cosmological structure was probably brought to the Sinitic heartland by Indo-European tribes (belonging to the Celto-Germanic branch, she says), likely the Tocharians,[561] blond/red-haired, blue/grey/green-eyed and high-nosed people whose remains have been found in the northwest of today's China.[562] In Chinese texts, such populations, who principally dwelt in the Tarim valley and adjacent areas of northwest China, but groups of whom were present in areas of the northeast and even in south China, are also designated as the "whites" (*bai*), "wolf warriors" (*quanrong*) and "dragons" (*long*; a symbol whose religio-philosophical significance we have well-studied), and are described as having had "white bodies and braided hair falling on their shoulders",

---

559 Ibidem, pp. 7-26. pp. 12-13: *Taihao-Uranus*; pp. 7, 9 & 14-19: *Xuanyuan-Chronus/Zeus/Apollo*; pp. 13-14: *Shennong-Chronus/Saturnus*; pp. 21-22: *Chiyou-Tyr*; p. 26: *Zhuanxu-Dionysus*.

560 Ibidem, pp. 22-23. Cf. Attic Greek: Δημήτηρ *Dēmḗtēr*; Doric Greek: Δαμάτηρ *Dāmātēr*. "Demeter" means either "Mother Earth" (if *De/Da* is interpreted as a variant of *Ge* Γῆ, both shortenings of the Indo-European root *ghdhem-, *ghdhom-*; cf. Pokorny [1959], p. 414 ff) or "Mother Goddess" (if *De/Da* is interpreted as a shortening of *Dea* Δηά). Cf. also the Chinese goddesses *Demu* and *Houtu*.

561 Ibidem, p. 37.

562 Cf. Mair (1995), passim.

like Tocharian mummies.[563] Mark A. Riddle reports that in the Chinese chronicles, the Tocharians were called the *Yuèzhī* (月支 or 月氏), literally the "Moon Offspring", and they were present as far east as the state of Jin, in central-east China, before moving to the Gansu Corridor in the far west. They were involved in the transmission into China of metallurgy, horse chariot, wheat and barley cultivation and traded jade and silk.[564] According to Riddle, the Tocharians were also at the origin of the dynasties of "Dragon Kings" who ruled over the Koreans, having had a colony — it itself known as *Yuezhi* — in the peninsula, and these Tocharians in Korea were in turn at the origin of the Japanese solar imperial dynasty.[565] The personal name "Dragon" was used by Tocharians themselves in Central Asia, and skull-elongating techniques were practised among the *Yuezhi* of both Central Asia and Korea and in the Heian period of Japan (794-1185).[566]

Serge Papillon propounds further associations between figures of Sinitic and Indo-European religions. Amongst them, he identifies ① the Yellow Deity with the Tocharian *Ylaiñäkte/ Wlāñkät* (respectively in Kutchean and Agnean Tocharian; a compound of *ylai/wlan+nakte/nkat*, literally the "Striking God", associated with thunder symbolism), which has the same qualities as the Germanic *Odin* (wild warrior, wiseman, magician, master of language and technique just like *Huangdi*), and as the Celtic *Lug* (polycentric like the Sinitic supreme God; represented as bi-, tri-, or quadricephalous like *Huangdi*, besides having the same attributes of *Odin*); ② the Green Deity *Taihao* with the Germanic rebirth god, *Balder/Phol*; ③ the Red Deity *Shennong* with the Germanic sea god, *Njord*; ④ *Fuxi* and the White Deity *Chiyou* with the Germanic *Frey* (a generic title meaning "Lord"), and of *Nuwa* with *Freya* (a generic title

---

563 Papillon (2005), pp. 6-11. Quotes the *Shanhaijing* 17:8a at p. 8. As for *quanrong*, it is comparable to the holy warriors of Odin in early Germanic cultures, the berserkers ("bear-clad", a reference to the astral She-bears) and wolfserkers ("wolf-clad"), see p. 13.

564 Riddle (2011), pp. 12-13.

565 Ibidem, p. 19 ff.

566 Ibidem, p. 25.

meaning "Lady").[567] Papillon confirms the identification of the Black Deity *Zhuanxu* as the dark and hidden aspect of the same Yellow Deity, as well as the latter's origin in the north, just like *Apollo* originated in *Hyperborea*,[568] that is to say, "beyond the north" (beyond the Northern Heigth of Heaven, i.e. the unmanifested phase of God).

Starting from Wei's and Papillon's interpretations, I propose a refinement for both schemes, interpreting the components of the Eurasian trinity of the God of Heaven studied in the first chapter as lines of tensional power within the structure either of temporalisation movement or spatialisation in the four directions. For the integration of Germanic theology within the Sinitic *yuzhou* cosmotheanthropic structure, I propose the identification of the Black Deity, that is to say, the hidden, quiescent, unmanifested phase of God, with *Odin* — the Wanderer, which has all these qualities in Germanic culture and is traditionally identified as *Hermes / Mercurius* in Greco-Roman interpretations —, and of the Yellow Deity with *Thor* ("Thunder"), given the Tocharian theonym's connection with thunder symbolism and the fact that *Thor* is the active emanation of the supreme quiescent *Odin*.[569] The Red Deity may be identified with *Frey* besides *Njord*, given that *Frey* (better *Ingfrey*, "Lord of Generation") is unmistakeably attested as the third aspect of the Eurasian trinity in Germanic cultural declinations, that is to say, the coming of the power of God on the Earth, in the flesh, in particularised contexts. Anyway, he is the twin brother of *Freya* and son of the same *Njord*. At the same time, *Freya* as *Frigga*, the Germanic goddess corresponding to the Greco-Roman *Aphrodite / Venus*, may be associated with the west, to the White Deity of war, to *Tyr*, while, as the equivalent of *Nuwa* it may be set the Germanic chthonic goddess *Hella*. Besides the aforemade correction to Wei's Greco-Roman

567 Papillon (2005), pp. 11-14: *Huangdi-Odin*, pp. 15-17: *Huangdi-Lug* (and Apollo), pp. 21-24: *Huangdi-Ylainakte*, pp. 63-64: *Fuxi/Nuwa* equated with *Frey/Freya*, p. 65: *Njord-Shennong*, p. 99: *Taihao-Balder/Phol*, p. 126: *Chiyou-Frey*.

568 Ibidem, p. 109.

569 Ibidem, p. 98.

scheme, Papillon's association of *Njord*, god of the sea, to the south provides the basis for setting, in the Greco-Roman scheme, *Poseidon* (the "Lord of the Earth" and god of the sea, the third aspect of the Eurasian trinity of the God of Heaven among the Greeks) as the spatialisation in the four directions of the descent of *Chronus* as *Zeus* into the Earth.

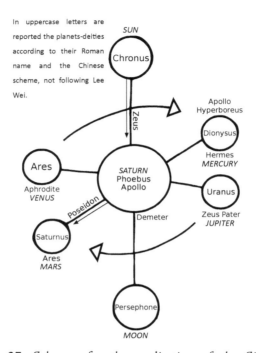

In uppercase letters are reported the planets-deities according to their Roman name and the Chinese scheme, not following Lee Wei.

SUN

Chronus

Zeus

Apollo
Hyperboreus

Dionysus

Hermes
MERCURY

SATURN
Phoebus
Apollo

Ares

Aphrodite
VENUS

Poseidon

Uranus

Zeus Pater
JUPITER

Demeter

Saturnus

Ares
MARS

Persephone

MOON

Figure 27: Schemes for the application of the Sinitic *yuzhou* cosmotheanthropic structure to Greco-Roman and Germanic theologies, based on Julie Lee Wei's and Serge Papillon's identifications with some refinements. In the Greco-Roman scheme (above), the three aspects of the supreme God of Heaven, representing it as God-Time and God-Space, are *Chronus*, *Zeus*, and *Poseidon*, respectively working as the quiescent eternal supreme, temporal tension and spatial tension. The scheme also includes the great goddesses, *Venus* as the celestial virgin, *Demeter* as the hosting surface and *Persephone* as the chthonic female matrix. In the Germanic scheme (next page), significantly altered compared to that of Papillon, *Thor* is placed at the centre, *Tyr* to the west in association with *Freya* as *Frigga*, *Odin* to the north, and *Ingfrey* to the south besides *Njord*. The scheme also includes *Jord* (the "Earth") and the chthonic goddess *Hella*. It is worth noting that *Frey* and *Freya* (the two main Wanes [apparently meaning "Strugglers", but possibly "Chariots", both of whom are associated to the boar, another animal associated to the two cosmic poles], whereas the other gods are the Ases/Anses [literally the "Spirits"]) are generic titles meaning "Lord" and "Lady", and thus may collectively personify the masculine forces of Heaven and the feminine forces of the Earth rather than single gods, much like the Chinese *Fuxi* and *Nuwa*.

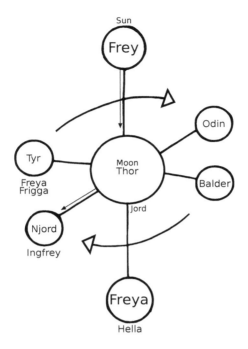

Another analogy may be instituted between Sinitic and Slavic religio-cosmology, wherein the Yellow Deity finds a precise equivalent in the god *Svetovit* (translatable as "Worldseer" or, more philologically, "Lord of Light", "Lord of Power" or "Lord of the Holy"[570]). *Svetovit* represents the incarnation of the supreme *Deivos* or *Rod* (Род; a word which denotes the highest source of all life, and at the same time life itself, the ancestral lineages and the kins; it simply means "Generator"[571]). According to Jiří Dynda, *Svetovit* is "the most complete reflection of the Slavic cosmological conception", the union of the four horizontal directions of space with the three vertical tiers of reality (Heaven, Earth and the underworld), and with time; is a "fourfold potentiality which comes true in threefoldness".[572]

---

570 Jakobson (2010), p. 18, where the author (the linguist Roman Jakobson) discusses the Slavic root *svet-*, which means a "miraculous and beneficial power". See also: Dugin (1992), p. 5, where the author says that in Russian *svet* means "light", "bright", "holy", "white"; Mathieu-Colas (2017), passim.

571 Mathieu-Colas (2017), passim.

572 Dynda (2014), pp. 74-75.

In Slavic religio-cosmology the three vertical planes of reality, which are also the three phases of time, are also known as *Prav* (Правь, literally "Rightness"), *Yav* (Явь, "Actuality") and *Nav* (Навь, "Potentiality"), respectively corresponding to Heaven, Earth and the underworld or the astro-spiritual world. They are theologically represented by *Svarog* ("Heaven"), *Perun* ("Thunderer") and *Veles* ("Coverer"), known together as the *Triglav* ("Three-Headed"), and by the colours white, red and black, respectively. According to Dynda, who bases his research on historical attestations, the *Triglav* is otherwise constituted by *Perun*, *Svetovit*, and *Veles*, and the three colours, as attested by Adam of Bremen (1050-1081/1085), are white for Heaven, green for the Earth and black for the underworld.[573]

In its spatial manifestation, *Svetovit* has four faces associated with four colours, the masculine ones of *Svarog* (northward and white) and *Perun* (westward and red), and the feminine ones of *Lada* ("Beauty", southward and black) and *Mokosh* ("Wetness", eastward and green). In other accounts, they are rather: *Svarog* to the north, *Ruyevit* to the east, *Porevit* to the south, and *Gerovit* to the west. They represent the cycle of the Sun and the four seasons (winter, spring, summer and autumn, respectively),[574] but also the four Russias of a popular tradition of sacred geosophy: White Russia, Red Ruthenia/Ukraine, Black Sea Russia and Green Ukraine (Far Eastern Russia).[575] Two of the phases are positive, of waxing, and two are negative, of waning, thus representing the dual dynamism through which the supreme *Rod* manifests itself in the threefold time and in the fourfold space. Such dual dynamism is primarily represented by *Belobog* ("White God") and *Chernobog* ("Black God"), conceptualising male/celestial deities and female/chthonic deities, day and night.

573 Ibidem, p. 63.

574 Leeming (2005), pp. 359-360.

575 *Ukrainian Soviet Encyclopedic Dictionary* (1987), entry: *Svetovid*.

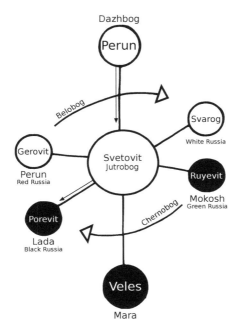

Figure 28: Scheme for the application of the Sinitic *yuzhou* cosmotheanthropic structure to Slavic theology and geosophy. The vertical axle is the *Triglav*, representing the three times and the three aspects of reality (*Prav, Yav* and *Nav*), theonymically symbolised by *Perun, Svetovit* and *Veles*, as shown in this drawing, or by *Svarog, Perun* and *Veles*. The scheme also includes *Dazhbog* ("Day God") and *Jutrobog* ("Moon God"), or the light of the day and the light of the night, the latter reflecting the former. *Mara* ("Death") is the chthonic goddess concealed by *Veles*, her consort.

These schemes, which ultimately belong to pan-Eurasian religio-cosmology and which reflect the process of unfolding of being, the process of continuous creation, also mirrored by the cycles of the Sun and the Moon, are paradigms for the attunement of human times with the great time of Heaven, and thus constitute the original political ontological topography, and public spatiotemporal theology, for establishing a heavenly civilisation into a cosmic, organic state, for stemming the horizontal collapse of the forces into *Chaos* and thrusting them towards Heaven. As tri-quadridimensional, thus sevendimensional, spatiotemporal rotating crosses, I propose that they represent "wheels of the *Dharma*", or, using the Latin cognate, "of the *Firma*", for interpreting and setting in motion different cultural contexts.

CHAPTER 4

RUIST/EURASIAN UNIVERSIST POLITOLOGY

It is now safe to institute a political program that was once outlawed by modernity. It no longer appears as foolish and doomed for failure as before, because everything in postmodernity looks foolish and doomed for failure, including its most "glamorous" aspects. It is not by chance that the heroes of postmodernity are "freaks" and "monsters", "transvestites" and "degenerates" […]. Against the backdrop of the world's clowns, nothing and no one could look "too archaic", not even the people of Tradition who ignore the imperatives of modern life. || It is important to fight against liberalism here and now; it is important to identify its vulnerabilities; it is important to forge an alternative worldview […]. The future is in our hands, and it is open rather than predetermined.

Aleksandr Dugin[576]

— PROLEGOMENON: RUISM AND THE FOURTH POLITICAL THEORY

In this fourth chapter of the essay, I describe the developments of mainland China's contemporary Confucianism, giving centrality to Jiang Qing's "Political Confucianism", as Jiang himself has defined it in contradistinction to "Mind-Heart Confucianism" (20th-century Neo-Confucianism).[577] They are the two main streams of New Confucianism, which is the reinvention of Confucianism that began after the end of the Chinese empire and the foundation of the modern republics.

Mind-Heart Confucianism draws from the tradition of Neo-Confucianism, which blossomed during the Song (960-1279) and Ming (1368-1644) dynasties. Jiang's Confucianism, on the contrary, is conceived as a return to Han-dynasty Confucianism, particularly the Gongyang School of esoteric hermeneutics of Confucius' texts, which was also the source

---

576 Dugin (2012), pp. 26 & 34.

577 Bell (2012), p. 5.

of inspiration for Kang Youwei (1858-1927), the theorist of a Confucian Church as the state religion of China. According to Jiang Qing, Mind-Heart Confucianism gives excessive emphasis to metaphysics and, at the same time, adapts itself to the external conditions of liberal democratic ideology, indeed giving up any reflections about the sense of politics.[578] According to Daniel A. Bell, Jiang continues in the wake of Kang, and his Ruist constitutionalism is the most systematic alternative to modern-day political forms.[579]

In the first part, I reck Jiang Qing's theory of the "Way of Humane Authority" and of the "Threefold Legitimacy of Power". Subsequently, I expound on the political ontology codified in the *Zhōulǐ* (周礼 "Rites of the Zhou") and Jiang's own proposal of a Tricameral Parliament, respectively, in the first case as a timeless blueprint of the Way of Humane Authority, and in the second case as a workable implementation of it within today's political contexts. The three sources of the legitimacy of political authority, which find their ground in the cosmotheanthropic vision explicated in the previous chapter, are not reciprocally exclusive but concur to give shape to a polity in which spiritual and temporal powers are reconciled in unity. According to Jiang, who approaches my conclusions drawn from Fukuyama's work, liberal democracy is ruinous because it is a partial system that exclusively represents the desires of amorphous throngs of unrelated people and alone may not bring real political authority to fruition.

The triune system expounded in this chapter is not exclusively a reflection of Sinitic cosmotheanthropism but finds precise analogies in other Eurasian cultures. Georges Dumézil thoroughly studied the trifunctional structure that is found in all Indo-European societies, first described in the books *Flamen-Brahman* (1929) and *Mitra-Varuna* (1940).[580] Such trifunctional structure may be summarised as follows: ① divine sovereignty

---

578 Jiang (2009), translated in French by Sébastien Billioud, p. 103, t/ns 2-3.

579 Bell (2012), p. 1.

580 The trifunctional thesis is further formalised by Georges Dumézil in the books *Jupiter, Mars, Quirinus* (1941-1948) and *L'idéologie tripartite des Indo-Européens* (1958).

represented by a shamanic/sacerdotal class exerting the juridical power (for instance, the Vedic ब्राह्मण *brāhmaṇa* or the Nordic *Rigsthula's jarl*, whose god is Odin/Varuna and whose colour is white [sky] or yellow [stars]; they are also associated with the power of the Dragon,[581] thus of time, of generations); ② warrior aristocracy endowed with the power to put the laws into spatial practice (the Vedic क्षत्रिय *kṣatriya* or the Rigsthulic *karl*, whose god is Thor/Indra or Mitra, Odin/Varuna's emanation,[582] and whose colour is red [blood]); and ③ the productive class of craftsmen and land-owning farmers (the Vedic वैश्य *vaiśya*, later blurred with the servile शूद्र *śūdra*, or the Rigsthulic *thræll*, whose god is Ingfrey/Aryaman and whose colour is swart [soil]).[583] In

581 Papillon (2005), p. 50. For the colour white, associated with the priestly classes of the Indo-Europeans (the Celtic druids, the Indian brahmins, the Roman flamens, the Persian mages, the Tocharian agrippans described by Herodotus), the colour of the hair of these castes' members at birth, also see p. 57. For the agrippans see p. 51.

582 Ibidem, p. 98.

583 Cf. the Norse poem *Rígsþula*, collected in the Edda, for Germanic trifunctionalism. The same is mentioned also in Dumézil's *Les dieux des Germains* together with corresponding Vedic tripartitions (note that in post-Vedic Hinduism the names of the three gods corresponding to the three classes changed: Varuna to Brahma, Indra/Mitra to Vishnu, and Aryaman to Shiva). Note that the distinctions are somehow blurry, and in various historical contexts the first two classes overlapped, while the third class merged with the masses of unskilled labourers and outcasts. In early medieval northern Germanic societies the *jarl* (English "earls") were a warrior nobility who mastered runology (note that the term *jarl* is traced back to the Indo-European root *her-* explained in the section 1.3.1 of the present essay), the *karl* (English "churls") were land-owning freemen, farmers and craftsmen, while the *thræll* (English "thralls") were unfree farmers and serfs (the word itself is traced back to *tragh-*, "to drag"; see: Pokorny [1959], p. 1089). In continental Germanic traditions, the three classes were called "ethelings", "freelings" and "laets" (cf. Ferrario [1829], vol. 15. p. 232), or "ethelings", "hermans" and "alds" amongst the Lombards. Tacitus talks about *Herminones* (offsprings of Irmin/Odin), *Istaevones* (offspring of Ist/Thor) and *Ingaevones* (offspring of Ing/ Frey). Amongst the Anglo-Saxons, the earls were also called thegns/thanes, the "technicians", from the Indo-European root *tek-/*tekth-/*teku-* ("to produce/to run"), the same of "technique"; cf. Pokorny (1959), pp. 1058-1061. Regarding the colours associated to the three types of humanity, respectively yellow/white, red and black, in the Rigsthulic myth they are explicitly described as physical features of the three eponymous forefathers of the three classes, *Jarl, Karl* and *Thræll*, generated by God (precisely by *Heimdall*, the god of beginnings and ends, an aspect of Odin) by impregnating mortal women, and differentiated by the hospitality he received from such women's families or from the quality of the women themselves (cf. the three mothers Freya [the white mother], Finda [the yellow mother] and Lyda [the black mother] fecundated by the *Od*, "spirit/breath",

contemporary mainland China, there is a widespread, ongoing institutionalisation of the religious worship of the Yellow Deity, the Red Deity, and the White Deity as *Chiyou* (interpreted in this case as the god of minority ethnicities and foreign races), which might reflect the Indo-European tripartition (interestingly, as enunciated in the previous third chapter, Papillon identifies the Yellow Deity as Odin and *Chiyou* as Frey). As we have seen in the first chapter of the present essay and recalled in the last section of the foregoing one,[584] the three colours are associated, already in Mesopotamian religio-cosmology and throughout all Eurasian theologies, to the three stages of manifestation of the supreme God of Heaven (clearly described in Mesopotamian theology as *An, Enlil* and *Enki*) — the quiescent potentiality of the ecliptic North Pole of the sky, the spinning activity of the precessional pole, and the terrestrial manifestations of the heavenly power —, identified as the three concentric bands of the visible sky and the constellations which revolve within them.

It is worthwhile noting that Jiang Qing's project is accompanied by other Chinese thinkers' enterprises, developing in similar directions. Even though I do not deepen their theories in the present essay, we may cursorily mention some of them: they include Kang Xiaoguang's theocratic project, which privileges the reconstruction of Confucianism as a state religion,[585] and Zhao Tingyang's proposal of the "*Tianxia* System", based on the traditional *tianxia* cosmological vision of heavenly power emanating from the centre and civilising the umbegoing

---

of *Wralda*, the supreme God, in the *Ura-Linda* mythology discussed in: Dugin [1992], pp. 47-64; otherwise, the three names of the Rigsthulic myth are also alternative names of Odin, Thor and Ingfrey themselves). *Jarl* is also described as having "piercing blue eyes" like those of a snake. I argue that they have not to be interpreted in terms of 18th-century racism, but as symbols of a more or less ordered and thus more or less enlightened thought power, within each race of humanity. In medieval Christendom, Indo-European trifunctionalism was restructured into the three estates as codified (as ideally fixed) by Adalberon of Laon in the *Carmen ad Rotbertum regem*: *oratores* ("those who order/speak/pray"), *bellatores* ("warriors"), and *laboratores* ("those who labour").

584 Section 1.3.3 and 3.3.3 of the present essay.

585 Cf. Ownby (2009), passim.

peripheries as concentric circles, extended as a worldwide political philosophy to overcome the nation-state idea.[586]

In the Indo-European world, analogous ideas are advanced by Dugin, who is even said to have influenced the Kremlin of Vladimir Putin.[587] His Fourth Political Theory heralds that the bringing to the extreme consequences of the nihilistic disintegration of the West, of its nation-states, and of its crystallised metaphysics would clear the field for a rebirth of the *Logos* as *Dasein*,[588] the return of the "radical subject", spring of a new spatiotemporal creation based on the "original political ontological topography". As we have seen in the first chapter, the Fourth Political Theory arises as the alternative to what Dugin defines as the three political systems which have dominated the world since the Enlightenment, namely liberalism, communism and fascism, outdoing all of them. The first one, liberalism, after the death of the other two, in the early 1990s remained the apparent winner on the world stage. The Fourth Political Theory, with Eurasian religio-cosmology at its core and open to the participation of intellectuals who want to give their contribution for its construction, emerges as an alternative paradigm to the "deathly godless" plague of liberalism, which is leading humanity towards self-annihilation.[589] Dugin forecasts that the palingenesis of Europe, intended as an Indo-European spiritual, organic civilisation, would be possible with the creation of a Eurasian political entity led by the Russians, who are Slavs and Scythians,[590] the directest descendants of the earliest Indo-Europeans (Aryans) whose *Urheimat* ("original

---

586 Cf. Zhao (2011), passim.

587 Mosbey (2015), p. 1.

588 Dugin (2012), passim.

589 Dugin (2012), p. 13, where the author says: "[...] This is not dogma, nor a complete system, nor a finished project. This is an invitation to political creativity, a statement of intuitions and conjectures, an analysis of new conditions, and an attempt to reconsider the past. The Fourth Political Theory is not the work of a single author, but is rather a trend comprising a wide spectrum of ideas, researches, analyses, prognoses, and projects. Anyone thinking in this vein can contribute his own ideas. As such, more and more intellectuals, philosophers, historians, scientists, scholars, and thinkers will respond to this call"; Mosbey (2015), pp. 2-14.

590 Cf. Shekhovtsov (2008), passim.

homeland") is ascertained by historians, archaeologists and linguists alike to have been located in territories which are today part of Russia.[591] Regarding the Scythians, theirs is the general name under which we know the Indo-Iranians of Siberia, whose cultures are attested back to the eighth century BCE and who were largely absorbed by the East Slavs by the early Middle Ages.

Dugin appeals to the shared effort of European and Asian intellectuals alike, who perceive the "eschatological tension of the present time", for the formulation and actualisation of the Fourth Political Theory,[592] which he himself characterises as a "Fourth *Nomos* of the Earth", using Carl Schmitt's terminology; a coalescence of political science, political theology (theopolitics), political geography (geopolitics) and a "new model of the political organisation of space" (in Schmitt, a "*nomos* of the Earth" is an *Ordnung*, "ordering", as well as an *Ortung*, a "localisation").[593] In other words, a new foundation act for a new civilisation with the *Dasein* as its gravitation centre.

I argue that the Fourth Political Theory might be integrated with Ruism, otherwise conceptualised in the more general terms of "Eurasian Universism", the "integral humanism" and all-comprehending new "religion of man" sought for by Ernesto de Martino,[594] to become the spiritual paradigm of the future Eurasian empire, a multipolar empire, capable of acknowledging and embracing multiple localised religio-political entities, which might be the China of the Way of Humane Authority theorised by Jiang and other Confucian intellectuals, the empire of Japan, a new Tsardom in Russia,[595] a new Greco-Romanity in southern

---

591 Dugin (2016), passim. Cf. Yamnaya culture, Sintashta culture and the site of Arkaim.

592 Dugin (2012), p. 31.

593 Ibidem, pp. 35 & 43.

594 Cursorily mentioned in the section 1.2.2 of the present essay.

595 Other sources of inspiration may be found in Russian religion, as cursorily analysed in the last section of the foregoing chapter (3.3.3). It is worth noting that East Slavs do not perceive their "Christianity" in the same way as those Westerners

Europe and a new Celtic and Germanic civilisation, or even a pan-European Zuist empire led by a *lugal*.[596] Even Israel, framed by a fully reconstituted Judaism, led by the *Sanhedrin* from a rebuilt Great Temple of Jerusalem as its religio-political centre, might be part of the greater Eurasian empire. In all these local potentates of Eurasia, the system wrought by Jiang might be adopted in versions adapted to the specific contexts. This old-yet-new vertical religio-political ontology would work as an anthropological machine, for forging a new vertical form of man,[597] amidst and after the dissolution of the anomic machination of Western modernity.

---

who have remained Christians do (in the note 236, section 2.1.1.1, we already cursorily mentioned this). In the West, Christianity has utterly and irreversibly turned into the secularised and materialised *Sklavenmoral* blamed by Nietzsche. In Slavic languages the name of Orthodox Christianity, or better Eastern Orthodoxy, is Православие *Pravoslavie*. This term is the literal translation of the more generalised Greek-originated term "orthodoxy", and thus means "right doctrine", "right piety", "right glory", but by the term *Pravoslavie* the East Slavs conceive their whole spiritual tradition, including pre-Christian and non-Christian (i.e. modern movements such as Slavic Rodnovery and Scythian Assianism, and movements of folk faith synthesising indigenous Slavic religion and Gnostic doctrines under "Christian" symbolism and iconography, namely the Orthodox Old Believers). In the Russian term, the root word *Prav* ("Rightness", i.e. the *Logos*) is also the uppermost of the three planes of reality as described by traditional Slavic religion, the other two being *Nav* ("Potentiality") and *Yav* ("Actuality"); *Prav* permeates the other two worlds. Based on the etymological analysis of the words with *Ar* root explored in the first chapter (1.3.1), the term "orthodoxy" may also be regarded as synonym of "aryanism". According to Aleksandr Dugin, Eastern Orthodoxy was deeply influenced by Nestorianism, the most esoteric and "Asian" current of early Christianity which René Guénon considered the most external circle of the Perennial Tradition of the North Pole, and is entirely permeated by the Hesychastic doctrine of Gregory Palamas (Palamism), also known as the "*gnosis* of light", so that it can be said that "all Orthodox are Gnostics". See: Dugin (1992), pp. 106-107.

596 As mentioned in two notes (162 in section 1.3.3; 518 in section 3.3.2) of the present essay, Zuism, Mesopotamian Neopaganism, is a reinstitutionalisation of Mesopotamian religio-cosmology.

597 In this regard it is worth mentioning Eske Møllgaard's essay *Confucianism as an Anthropological Machine*, in which he elaborates the concept of "anthropological machine" of the Italian philosopher Giorgio Agamben, applying such concept to Sinitic philosophy. The difference between the Western and the Chinese "anthropological machines" rests in the fact that while the Western one has ultimately developed, under Christian influence, into an anthropocentrism in which man is cut off from the world and acts against the world, the Chinese one has preserved the bond between humanity and the broader harmony of nature. Cf. Fiskesjö (2017), p. 226.

4.1. THE WAY OF HUMANE AUTHORITY AND THE THREEFOLD LEGITIMACY OF POWER

In Ruism, religious morality and political ability are two aspects of the same sovereign power. In other terms, "outer kingliness" (外王 *wàiwáng*) — also translatable as "outer craft", since, as explained hereinbefore,[598] *wang* is cognate of *gong*, "square and compass/*gnomon*"[599] — is the outward showing of "inner wisdom" (内圣 *nèishèng*, also "inner holiness"; i.e., etymologically, "health").[600]

According to Jiang, the political view intrinsic to Ruism is the Royal Way (王道 *Wángdào*, more appropriately the "Kingly Way"), also rendered in Western translations as the "Way of Humane Authority",[601] and it constitutes the best alternative to

---

598 Section 3.3.1 of the present essay.

599 The Germanic term "king" (**kuningaz*) itself means "wellborn", "gentile", literally one made ("-ing") within the kin (i.e. a *gens*, genealogically ordered humanity); cf. Greek *gígnomai* (γίγνομαι, "to come into being"). It is worth noting that the Greek *gnōmōn* (γνώμων), the pointer of the sundial, means "indicator", "carrier of knowledge", from the verb "I know" (γιγνώσκω *gignōskō*). Ostensibly, the Indo-European roots of the two semantic fields from which "king" and "to know" come, respectively **gen-* and **gne-*, are very similar. Both of them bespeak the sight of the process of generation, respectively as a "general" and an individual or personal ("gnostic") perspective. Cf. Pokorny (1959), p. 373 ff: **gen-*, **genə*, **gne*, **gno*.

600 Jiang (2009), p. 103, t/n 3. In Indo-European, and especially in Germanic languages, there is an overlapping between the semantic fields of sanity and sanctity or sacrality: the English words "to heal", "hail" or "hale", "holy" or "hallow", "hollow" or "hole", and "whole", and the corresponding German *heilen*, *Heil*, *Heilig*, and *hohl*, have the same origin in the Proto-Germanic **hailaz*, in turn from the Indo-European **koylos*.

601 "Humane authority" is the translation that many Western scholars have chosen for *wang*. Due to the distorted meanings that these words, especially "humane", have acquired in contemporary Western mass ideologies, it requires a further etymological analysis. As abovesaid, the Chinese word *wang*, related to *gong*, and the Germanic word "king", it itself related to *gnomon*, may be regarded as carriers of analogous meanings synthesisable as "one who knows (the heavenly craft) and produces by means of it". "Authority" is a Latinate from *auctōritās*, the quality of an *auctor* ("author"), from the verb *augeō*, "to increase", "to make (things) grow". "Humane", an older spelling of "human", as I have already explained, means "earthly", "coming from the earth". Therefore, "humane authority" expresses the idea of a founder who embodies the principle of Heaven on Earth, growing from the Earth and pointing to the Heaven. The Western translation appropriately renders the Sinitic meaning of the cosmetic sovereign, one individual incarnation of the polycentric *Logos*, who acts as the ordaining axle of a world.

the other systems of contemporary politics. The core of the Way of Humane Authority is the theory of the Threefold Legitimacy of Power: according to the Gongyang School, "a king is one who conjoins Heaven, Earth and men". The three springs of legitimacy are: ① the Way of Heaven, that is the source of holy or divine legitimacy, consisting in the transcendent principles of Heaven which manifest themselves in the patterns of natural things; ② the Way of Earth, which is the source of cultural legitimacy, consisting in a historical tradition which grows anchored in a specific place (*locus*); and lastly ③ the Way of Humanity, consisting in popular intention (民意 *mínyì*), that is to say, in the voluntary participation of men (人心 *rénxīn*), organised in kinships, to the political celestial civilisation.[602]

In Jiang's own words:[603]

> The relationship of the Way of the Prince to the activity of Heaven and Earth or to the spirits establishes a sacred and transcendental legitimacy. The relationship that it entertains with the ancient kings expresses a legitimacy rooted in history and culture. Endly, that this way must manifest itself in the behaviour of the people indicates the need of a popular legitimacy.

It is important to note that, according to the *Zhongyong*, royal power is always virtuous (i.e. in accordance with the divine Reason), and as such, it is spontaneously acknowledged by the people:

> The government of a wise prince has the virtue of the prince himself as its foundation, and it manifests itself by its effects on the entire population. [...] If we compare it with the action of Heaven and Earth, we see that such action is not contrary to it. If we compare it with the modality of action of the spirits, it does not raise any doubts [...].[604]

More detailedly, if the claimant of power is truly an intermediary between Heaven and Earth, capable of bringing

602 Jiang (2009), pp. 104-105.

603 Ibidem, p. 105.

604 Ibidem. Quotes the *Zhongyong* 29, French translation: Couvreur, Séraphin (1895). *L'invariable milieu*. Paris, France: Cathasia-Les Belles Lettres.

Heaven down to Earth (i.e. establishing a harmonious polity) and making Earth grow in tune with the great time of Heaven (i.e. exerting auspicious influence), the people recognise him as their leader. Elsewise, if the claimant of power does not fulfil the Threefold Legitimacy, his authority is rejected, and political order and public civilisation are not instituted.

As Jiang says, Ruist political thought is primarily concerned with the problem of the fundamental principles of political power's legitimacy. In other words, its main focus is the "way of policy" (政道 *zhèngdào*), and only secondarily does it deal with the "way of administration (or governance)" (治道 *zhìdào*). The principles of policy must always precede regulations that, in turn, are enacted on the basis of the former by already legitimised potentates.[605]

According to Jiang, Western-style liberal democracy is defective because it consists of a partial legitimisation.[606] The Western model of the separation of powers represents a balance on the plane of the art of governance (*zhidao*) but not on the plane of principles (*zhengdao*). In a democratic polity, the latter is dominated by the "sovereignty of the people", an absolute and exclusive, non-transferable and indisputable power.[607] Thus, from the perspective of the Way of Humane Authority, democracy consists of the domination of one of the three sources of legitimacy over the other two and, therefore, in an imbalance of power, a tilting of the political structure towards one of its sides, and consequently a perversion of governance. When popular will and private interests dominate as in contemporary Western societies, holy and cultural values are repudiated, and the satisfaction of any human desire becomes the only purpose of governments. An imbalance may also occur in the other directions; Jiang brings pre-modern Christian theocracy in Europe and modern Islamic states as examples of the domination of the sacral power, which denies popular will and cultural legitimacy.[608]

605 Ibidem, pp. 105-106.

606 Bell (2012), p. 6.

607 Jiang (2009), p. 106.

608 Ibidem, pp. 106-107.

Jiang continues with a fiery critique of Western democracy and its foundational thesis, the social contract. According to him, this hypothesis is a mere ideological construct lacking ground in reality. The Way of Humane Authority, on the other hand, is rooted and growing in historical reality; it is an enduring process. Anyway, Jiang avoids an identification of the way that he advocates with specific imperial systems of the past. Being primarily concerned with China's political system, he takes the latter's imperial institution, which lasted until 1910, as an example of a polity that persisted for centuries as a successful moralising system. However, the imperial monarchy was just a particular institutional configuration (*zhidao*) appropriate to the given historical circumstances, an instrument for an actualisation of the archetypal political order (*zhengdao*) of the Way of Humane Authority. In Jiang's theory, institutional configurations of power may and must transform themselves to allow the adaptation of the *zhengdao* to the changing contexts. In other words, the Way of Humane Authority may take on new forms to fit into different contexts through the creative invention of an institutional system drawing from both archetypal and historical experiences.[609]

Jiang criticises Fukuyama's thesis that democracy is humanity's ultimate form of government, marking the "end of history". According to Jiang, from the perspective of Sinitic thinking, democracy is obviously not a universal form but merely the final product of Western civilisation. History never ends, and practical developments are inevitable since reality itself is an ever-unfinished business (未济 *wèijì*). Democracy realises states of mediocrity and indistinction, flattening everyone on the same plane, where institutions (*zhidao*) become instruments for the fulfilment of low instincts of material pleasure. In a democracy, "popular will" is constituted by private desires and interests, which are always favoured over high public (holy and cultural) values through the mechanism of the popular vote.[610] Another yet related flaw of

---

609 Ibidem, pp. 107-108.

610 Ibidem, pp. 109-110.

democracy is its amorality: popular will is taken into account as a quantitative entity, not as a qualitative one; consequently, the moral stature of the power claimant is not relevant, as long as it is numerical strength that decides his legitimacy. Democracy brings to a condition in which anomic and monetary forces define power since the primacy of the number is not counterpoised by holy and cultural principles. Already De Martino, paraphrasing José Ortega y Gasset and Arnold J. Toynbee, recognised in modernity "the triumph of mediocrity, the scorn for tradition, for the person, the bondage of bureaucracy and machinery [...] The triumph of mass-men, the proletarianisation of culture".[611] And similarly to Dugin, as a prognosis, he found the "function of the Orient: to help the Occident to regain possession of the heritage of eternal, holy truths which all normal civilisations rely upon and on which the West itself rested before the great laceration which produced the monstrous, barbarian, diabolic modern civilisation".[612]

The historical roots of such a state of things may be traced back to the separation of politics and religious morality at the dawn of Western modernity.[613] Bell enlightens that, according to Jiang, the modern notion of the sovereignty of the people is indeed an enantiodromical overturning of the pre-modern European Christian notion of the absolute sovereignty of God, of the erstwhile absolute domination of the sacral power.[614] Without any vertical axis of sublimation, democracy reveals itself as being a "demonocracy", and a "dementocracy", a "rule of demons", and "denial of the mind",[615] where individual and

---

611 De Martino (1977), p. 495.

612 Ibidem, p. 497.

613 Jiang (2009), p. 111.

614 Bell (2012), p. 6.

615 "Demonocracy" is a coinage of mine, and it is neither in a Platonic nor in a Christian sense. Here "demon" is not meant negatively. The "demon" (Greek: δαίμων *dáimōn*), like the Latin *genius*, is the categorial spirit, which generates a category of beings, and the individual entities which are part of it (what I have discussed in the first chapter of the present essay, section 1.1.1). "Demonocracy" is negative when, like in Western liberal democracy, it implies the loss of the vertical axle and supreme end, the horizontal collapse of demons, and consequentially their senseless fight against each other for survival; the "demonic texture" bespoken by Dugin. In Chinese

private thrusts fight against each other for supremacy in a horizontal *Chaos* of forces and a pulverisation of atomised anomic individuals.

In Jiang's own words:[616]

> Political legitimacy has been transferred from God to humanity alone, and sacred values have no longer had right of citizenship within the public domain. And since the rational way of thinking of the Westerners has not allowed the coexistence of multiple types of legitimacy, we have arrived to the hegemony of merely one [...]. Therefore, politics are at this point stripped of strong morality and elevated ideals. Only naked desires remain, without aspirations for the future, without vital fervour. In such a context, we tend to a mediocre life and to the mere satisfaction of desires; government becomes mere business, the leaders of the country its managers, while governing the country becomes like signing contracts. Everything is regulated by money and by playing on the interests of the people. There is no longer room for past aspirations to ideals or for powerful personalities.

Being fundamentally amoral, democracy is necessarily unrooted in any historical culture. In normal conditions, popular legitimacy is always conferred within a precise historical, spatiotemporal conjuncture, and it consists in the identification of the population and its private forces with the claimant of political power within a public civilisation. Jiang conceives a polity, a state, as an organic entity constituted by the coalescence of folks into a common identity over a long time. Such a common body extends from a past up to the present and towards a future. The present time has the charge to transmit the meaning inherited from antiquity to the future. It is implied that when a government is divorced from the organic entity of the ethno-state, when it does not take into account its cultural tradition, the life and destiny of a country are broken, and what follows thereafter is the

---

culture it is intended as the *shen* of *yang* becoming 鬼 *guǐ* of *yin*, "phantoms", i.e. empty images and rambling disincarnated forces. "Dementocracy" means the denial of the *mens*, the head, the supreme end of being.

616 Jiang (2009), p 112.

decadence of civilisation into historical nihilism. A state, and its cultural tradition, is never an intellectual construction but rather a body which lives as a historical process. Political authority has, therefore been ingrained in the state's history.[617]

Jiang puts forward a reaffirmation of the true legitimacy of political power within a new institutional framework to open channels for the expression of all three sources of legitimacy. Such a new system would reinstate holy and cultural values into politics[618] while overcoming the hegemony of the desires of the amorphous masses. The project does not consist in a complete elimination of democracy: the Way of Humane Authority is superior to democracy because it opposes and prevents the domination of one form of legitimacy over the others, but it acknowledges the will of the folks as a constituent part of true legitimacy. Opposing Fukuyama's inauspicious predictions about the "end of history", Jiang propounds a system for the harmonious integration of the three sources of power legitimacy, offering new perspectives on politics and new prospects for the future.[619]

4.2. POLITICAL ONTOLOGY AND SPATIOTEMPORAL COSMOLOGY: A MODEL FROM THE *ZHOULI*

In his 2009 essay, Jiang mentions various past realisations of the Way of Humane Authority (*Zhouli* statecraft, *Mingtang*,[620] suburban sacrifices and Confucianism as a state religion, among other examples) as models from which to begin thinking about a political configuration based on the same principles and yet achievable inasmuch as it is possible within contemporary

---

617 Ibidem, p. 113.

618 Bell (2012), p. 6.

619 Jiang (2009), pp. 114-115.

620 Ibidem, p. 116, t/n 25. The *Mingtang* ("Palace of Light"), Billioud explains, is an institution that goes back to the Zhou epoch, and it was a temple seat of the religio-cosmological royal power. The king moved through the four quarters of the temple according to the lunations.

political contexts and by means of forewrought and already experimented conceptual tools.[621] Such statecraft schemes represent systems that integrate aspects of reality and human experience that in contemporary Western politics are kept separate, namely cosmology, theology and religion, and politics; they offer principles of policy (*zhengdao*) and institutional frameworks (*zhidao*) which reflect the cosmotheanthropic architecture described in the foregoing chapter of the present essay. They represent instances of the Duginian "original political ontological topography" that is crucial to the Fourth Political Theory. Herein, I choose to focus on one of these "blueprints", specifically that contained in the *Zhouli*, a text which likely goes back to the period of the unification of the Warring States into an empire (3rd century BCE) at the hands of the Qin. It is a theologico-political statecraft planimetry purportedly representing the organisation of the olden Zhou dynasty, structured according to the sevenfold architecture of the divine space-time.

According to Michael Puett:[622]

> [Comparing it with other models of cosmological statecraft] the *Zhouli* is an attempt to take everything that exists and define a place for it within a comprehensive system. [...] The political administration is divided into six realms, called Heaven, Earth, Spring, Summer, Autumn and Winter.

Each department has a two-faced function: the administration of an aspect of life and religious sacrifices to their corresponding divine powers, that is, Heaven, the Earth and the directional gods (*Wufang Shangdi*). According to the American Sinologist Mark Edward Lewis, "the composition of the *Zhouli* was thus a ritual act that conjured into existence a graphic image of the state as a cosmic *mandala*".[623]

Puett's opinion is different from Lewis' one in that he does not consider the *Zhouli* to be a device for the imitation of a

---

621 Ibidem, pp. 115-116.

622 Puett (2010), p. 138.

623 Lewis (1999), pp. 43-45.

larger cosmic pattern as Lewis apparently does, but rather considers it as a wherewithal which gives primacy to the agent (the ruler, or humane authority) as an order-establishing centre.[624] Puett continues:[625]

> [...] The *Zhouli* [...] sees the ruler's establishment of the state as the condition for the possibility of order, (and yet) the ruler's activity is presented not as an act of creation but rather as one of organization. The ruler is an organizer, not a creator. [...] He takes what exists and organizes it. Moreover, the way of organizing is always the same: the ruler is the pivot and organizes everything around himself. [...] What is striking about the *Zhouli* is that it is, in a sense, outside history and outside claims of legitimation altogether. The power of the text is to say that, whatever exists, here is a blueprint for how the ruler establishes the center and creates a hierarchy in which everything is given a place. [...] The power of the text lies in its absolute commitment to timeless modes of organization [...]: things exist, and here's how one puts them in order.

Wang Mingming identifies the political ontology exemplified by the *Zhouli* as *tiānxià* (天下, "under-Heaven"), which, as elucidated hereinbefore, is a term denoting "creation" as a process led by Heaven, better translatable as "generation". Wang defines it as a world-scape, a framework for ordering the world from a centre, radically different from the modern Western concept of "nation".[626] Comparing it to Mircea Eliade's conceptions of the "centre" and "consecrated space", Wang describes the Zhou *tianxia* as a both centrifugal and centripetal hierarchy of interrelation between populations and individuals, and of cultural transmission, with the political body of the king functioning as the nexus of convergence of all relations.[627] A class of officials of the four directions, called 士 *shì* (Wang gives the translation "knight-masters") or *junzi* — the warrior-shamanic aristocracy that by the Warring States would have reshaped itself as the class of philosophers and civilisers,

---

624 Puett (2010), p. 140.

625 Ibidem, p. 143.

626 Wang (2012), p. 338.

627 Ibidem, pp. 340-345.

Confucian and Legalist court scholars and Taoist mystics — secured the health of the *tianxia*; they sanctioned and conducted rituals steadily "orchestrating the world" as a great unity (大同 *dàtóng*). They were the authors of the *Zhouli* and of the other two books of rites (礼记 *Lǐjì* and 仪礼 *Yílǐ*).[628]

The *tianxia*, in accordance with the general "immanent transcendence" of divinity in Sinitic thinking, may therefore be described as an order that comes from within rather than as an order that is created as an object by an external agent who subsequently imposes it upon an objectified matter. Otherwise said, it is a political ontology that sees order as emanating from a centre of authority that constantly arranges things according to what they actually are.[629]

Humane authority, the cosmic sovereign, thus, fully coincides with the spatiotemporal cosmotheanthropic figure of the centralising sage/etheling, who functions as the *axis mundi* of human societies, reproducing *in loco* (in multiple *loci*) the universal pattern of the polycentric *Logos*, in Sinitic terminology the *Li*, personified as the Yellow Deity, or the *Dasein* in Dugin's Heideggerian terminology, realising a multipolar cosmos.

---

628 Ibidem, pp. 346-350.

629 Ibidem, p. 366.

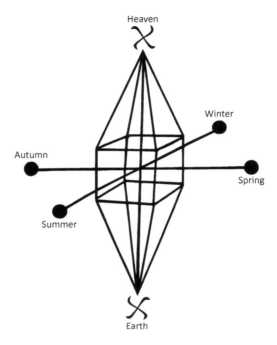

Figure 29: An attempted visual representation of the statecraft model explicated in the *Zhouli*. Heaven, Earth and the four seasons (Spring, Summer, Autumn and Winter) are the six departments of the political state, which with the addition of the axial authority, the all-centralising and interconnecting *Li/Logos*, reflect the sevenfold architecture of the divine space-time.

4.3. RUIST CONSTITUTIONALISM: THE TRICAMERAL PARLIAMENT AND THE *RU* ACADEMY

Jiang Qing propounds the realisation of the Way of Humane Authority as a reconfigured political system that would be suitable not only for China but for other civilisations as well.[630] According to him, the Threefold Legitimacy might be embodied in contemporary political sceneries by a Tricameral Parliament, composed of the bodies of: ① the House of the Ru (通儒院

---

630 Jiang (2009), p. 121.

Tōngrúyuàn) representing transcendent, holy legitimacy; ② the House of the Folks (庶民院 *Shùmínyuàn*) representing popular will; and ③ the House of the National Essence (国体院 *Guótǐyuàn*) representing cultural legitimacy. The members of the first house would be examined and appointed by the *ru* themselves; the body of the second house would be the result of elections by universal suffrage, basically following the procedures of Western democratic parliaments; while the appointment of the members to the third house would work on hereditary criteria. The third house would host descendants of notable lineages, writers, poets, and other people of great achievement who have left an imprint on the cultural history of the country. In China itself, the third house would be led by the male descendant of Confucius' kin, traditionally invested with the title of duke or king.[631]

Drawing an analogy with Plato's *Republic*, we may render the three types of power, represented by the three houses, in the terminology of the European philosophical tradition as, respectively, noöcracy (from *Nous*, the cosmic "Intellect"; thus meaning "power of the intellectuals"), democracy ("power of the folks"), and aristocracy ("power of the best right ones"). According to *The Histories* of Polybius (c. 200-118 BCE), amongst the Indo-European civilisations he had knowledge of, a threefold system of such kind was realised most perfectly in Sparta — where the political bodies were: the two kings, the Γερουσία *Gerousía*, and the Ἀπέλλα *Apélla* — and in the Roman Republic. In the latter's case, two consuls represented the military power of the *rex* of the earlier Roman Kingdom, the Senate represented aristocracy, and the Tribunate of the Plebs

---

631 Ibidem, pp. 117-118, t/n 36-37. I have chosen to render the names of the three houses in English somehow differently from Billioud's translation, especially for the second house. Like Bell (2012, p. 7), I have left *ru* untranslated, since, as I further explain below, the translations "scholars", "learned ones" and "Confucians" are simplistic. I have translated *shumin* as "folks" rather than "commoners" or "people", since I think that "folks" conveys an idea of genetic ancestrality, of people organised into kinships and groups of sense, rather than that of an unrelated amorphous mass (the meaning which "people" has somehow acquired in modernity). Another fitting translation would be "House of the Kins".

represented the tribes, the common people organised into ethnic lineages. In the medieval Slavo-Germanic state of Kievan Rus' (860-1240), the matrix of all Slavic civilisation, there were three analogous political bodies representing the three classes, namely the *Družina* (the king and his direct following), the *Duma* (the assembly of the nobles, the *muži* or boyars), and the *Veče* (the popular, tribal assembly, constituted by representatives of the *smerdy*, either landed or unlanded free farmers).

Within Jiang's project, the *ru*, holy men who act as custodians of the transmission of the holy knowledge of the Way of Heaven, would come from any strata of the population. Their representatives in the House of the Ru would not be merely specialised exegetes of written traditions but outstanding individuals characterised by inborn wisdom. They would be recommended by other *ru* and by the society, trained in classical knowledge and political theory within state schools, and led by a Great Ru (大儒 *Dàrú*).[632]

All the three wings of the Tricameral Parliament would have the power to ratify bills before their implementation or block them if such bills go against the values that they represent (Heaven, Earth and humanity). The houses would also have the power to form the executive and nominate the head of the government.[633]

In subsequent refinements of Ruist constitutionalism, Jiang Qing gives priority to the power of the House of the Ru, especially to avoid institutional gridlock, responding to concerns raised in this regard by Daniel A. Bell.[634] This priority, Bell writes, reflects universal cosmogony as expounded in the *Yijing*: since the multiplicity of things springs from the principle of Heaven, then the holy legitimacy of the Way of Heaven precedes both the cultural legitimacy of the Way of Earth and the legitimacy bestowed by popular will in the Way of Humanity.[635] In order

---

632 Ibidem, pp. 117-118, t/n 33.

633 Ibidem, p. 119.

634 Ibidem, p. 119, t/n 39.

635 Bell (2012), pp. 6-7.

for a bill to be implemented as law, it ought to be ratified by at least two houses. Therefore, in the legislative process, the power of the House of the Ru would be restrained by the other houses. Anyway, as the expression of the primacy of the Way of Heaven, the House of the Ru would be endowed with the power of veto.[636]

As for what concerns the head of the state in Jiang Qing: it is the symbolic king, the leader of the House of the National Essence. In China, he would be the direct male descendant of Confucius, who in turn was a scion of the erstwhile ruling Shang dynasty. He would symbolically represent the continuity of the state, which, as hereinabove explained, is conceived as the spiritual body of the nation proceeding from the past towards the future, generation after generation.[637] Unlike in a monarchical system, the king would not represent the state and the government but would merely be the symbol of the state. The three houses would hold the legislative power together, which would also nominate the executive, while the *ru* would hold the judiciary power.

Jiang then puts forward a fourth institution to further consolidate the role of the *ru* as the religious and moral leaders of society: the Ru Academy. This is conceived to be a body of *ru* who would devote themselves to the study of scriptures and to the practice of religion. They would conduct state religious rituals and sacrifices to Heaven and to the gods of the world. The Ru Academy's political role would consist in training the *ru* and the parliamentarians for the House of the Ru, managing state examinations, and leading the ceremony for the investiture of the head of the state. They would also have the extraordinary power to intervene and take a decision in the case of conflicts among the houses and in cases of negligence of government officials. Ultimately, the Ru Academy would work as the overseer of morality but would not interfere with the governmental powers of the houses.[638]

---

636 Ibidem, p. 7.

637 Ibidem, p. 9.

638 Ibidem, p. 8.

The Ru Academy — which, meanwhile, in China, appears to have been created either in the form of the 孔学堂 *Kǒngxuétáng* located in Guiyang or as the 孔圣会 *Kǒngshènghuì* (technically a religious body open to anyone) founded in 2015 by a committee including Jiang Qing, Kang Xiaoguang and Confucius' descendant, among other philosophers — might be analogised to the College of Pontiffs of ancient Rome, which included the flamens, and was led by the *Pontifex Maximus*. The *pontificēs*, in earlier times, had hermeneutic and juridical power, being the masters of *iūris prūdentia* (i.e. "right-craft", originally "divine craft"), and in the erstwhile Roman Kingdom, their presiding leader was the same as the king (*rex*), who in turn, in the Roman Republic, became the separate and purely symbolic institution of the *Rex Sacrorum*. According to Varro (116-27 BCE), "pontiff" means "able to do" and "bridge-builder" (deriving from *posse facere* or *pōntem facere*) to the Gate of Heaven, therefore recalling a technical power.[639]

The three types of humanity of Indo-European or broader Eurasian trifunctionalism, represented by the three political bodies, may be regarded as characterised by the three layers of the iity as articulated by Dugin, and reflecting the three faces or stages of manifestation of the supreme God of Heaven of pan-Eurasian religio-cosmology:[640] ① the noöcrats representing the deepest layer of the *Dasein*, the timeless/eternal radical subjectivity, the Dragon at the north ecliptic pole, the hidden and quiescent heart of the God of the Northern Heighth, thus having the "science of the serpent and of the eagle",[641] the ability to recollect all history and to reëmerge starting the *novum*, a new beginning of historical time, after eventual gridlocks, or "ends of history", the ability to grasp the patterns of Heaven and prepare them for their actualisation on Earth; ② the aristocrats representing the *Dasein* as the transcendental subjectivity, the

---

639 See: Marcus Terentius Varro's *De Lingua Latina*, V.83.

640 Sections 1.2.1 and 1.3.3 of the present essay.

641 The symbols of the serpent, or dragon, and the eagle, or raptor bird, are treated in the prolegomenon to the third chapter and in the section 3.1.3 of the present essay.

outgrowth of the radical subjectivity (just like in historical Indo-European societies the aristocracies were outgrowths of priestly classes), the active aspect of the God of the Northern Heighth perceivable as the north precessional pole and its spinning constellations, thus working as the "eagle-technicians" of Heaven, endowed with the ability to act in the three ecstasies of time and in the four directions of space, maintaining the spatiotemporal continuity of history, by putting into practice the laws formulated by the noöcrats; and endly ③ the folks and the democrats, representing the established forms of subjectivity organised into kinship lineages or professional guilds (the "democrat" representing the patriarch of a single lineage or guild), the incarnated, squared, personified forms of the God of the Northern Heighth, the hardware upon which political society is built by orchestrating their forces, their multiple times or serpents, into a public civilisation participating in the great time of Heaven.

4.4. THE *RU* AND THE PHILOSOPHERS, LEADERS OF EURASIA

Let the buffoonery of postmodernism have its turn; let it erode definite paradigms, the ego, super-ego and *Logos*; let it join up with the rhizome, schizo-masses and splintered consciousness; let nothing carry along in itself the substance of the world — then secret doors will open, and ancient, eternal, ontological archetypes will come to the surface and, in a frightful way, will put an end to the game.

Aleksandr Dugin[642]

For better understanding — and possibly transposing into European and broader Eurasian contexts — the idea of the House of the Ru and its political role, it is important to study more in depth the meaning of the concept of 儒 *rú*. In the Chinese language, *ru* defines anything pertaining to what in the West is simplistically rendered as "Confucianism"; indeed, the most comprehensive name for such a system in Chinese is not 孔教 *Kǒngjiào* — the compound word that literally translates

---

642 Dugin (2012), pp. 97-98.

"Confucianism", with Confucius (*Kong*) as its fountainhead —, but actually is 儒教 *Rújiào*, appropriately rendered "Ruism" by many contemporary Sinologists. "Confucianism" was coined in the sixteenth century by Jesuits in China, but it is at least partially a misnomer since Confucius was not the founder but the most prominent carrier and teacher of the *ru* tradition, which predated him during the twilight of the Zhou dynasty.[643]

Ru has been conventionally translated in various ways, including "scholars", "literates", "learned ones", and "refined ones", but the word's meaning is deeper. As a "specialist of the classical texts",[644] the *ru* easily overlaps with some acceptations of the Western concept of "philosopher", especially when conceived as "hermeneut". Yao Xinzhong says that the figure of the *ru*, predating Confucius, originated from the Zhou dynasty's government magistrates, professionals of rites and education.[645] They were a type of the *shi* discussed by Wang Mingming, more wholly called 方相氏 *fāngxiàngshì* ("lords who see/imagine/manage the four directions/the square"), the knight-masters who, with the downfall of the Zhou, fragmented into multiple schools giving rise to the different traditions of Confucianism, Taoism and Legalism, among others.[646] Kang Youwei and Hu Shih (1891-1962) said that the *ru* were the adherents of Shang-dynasty orthodoxy, and originally the term referred to the sacerdotal class of the Shang[647] (the *wu*), who, as demonstrated in the previous chapter, were in all probability Indo-European mages.[648] In the figure of the *ru*, we may therefore see the convergence of the shaman (i.e. the sage/wise, since the word *šamán* from the Altaic *Sprachbund* means a "man who knows"), the philosopher and the warrior. The Shang shamans (*wu*), who by the Zhou dynasty had become the four-directions masters

---

643 Yao (2000), pp. 16-17.

644 Jiang (2009), p. 118.

645 Yao (2000), p. 18.

646 Wang (2012), p. 350.

647 Yao (2000), p. 19.

648 Section 3.1.1 of the present essay.

(*shi*) of religious rituals and official and private education, versed in history and the arts, ultimately gave rise to the *ru* who gathered around Confucius' reshaping of the tradition.[649]

The etymological analysis of the grapheme *ru* corroborates its connection with shamanism. It is composed of two signifiers. The left radical (亻) is the side form of 人 *rén* and means "one person". The right radical is 需 *xū*, meaning "to wait" and "to need", and is itself made up of two further glyphs: the one above is 雨 *yǔ*, "rain", but also, figuratively, "instruction"; the one below is 而 *ér*, meaning the conjunction "and", implying cause and purpose. Yao says that *er* also means "sky",[650] and investigating among its archaic forms, one finds that, both in the bronzeware script of the Shang and Zhou epochs and in the Qin seal scripts, it is homographic with 天 *Tiān*. On the basis of the etymology hitherto enucleated, a literal meaning of *ru* is "man who waits/is waited" or "man who needs/is needed". According to Yao, the ancient forms of the grapheme *xu* may also be seen as portraying a man in the rain.[651] This might legitimise an interpretation of *ru* as "man who is inspired/instructed by Heaven" or "who receives/draws instructions from Heaven".

Figure 30: Graphic composition of the grapheme *ru* (儒), the "man instructed by Heaven". The leftmost one is the Qin small seal version of *ru* itself, complete with the *ren* radical. Those at the centre and on the right are my reconstructions, respectively, of the Zhou large seal and the older Zhou bronze writing versions of the right radical *xu* (需), the "man in the rain" or "man who receives instructions from Heaven", composed by *yu* ("rain/instruction") above and *er* ("sky") below.

---

649 Yao (2000), pp. 20-21.

650 Ibidem, p. 19.

651 Ibidem.

Considering a preëminence of the power of the *ru* favourably — embodied by the Ru Academy, the House of the Ru, and led by the Great Ru — as a reintegration of the long-lost coherence of the divine-religious and the political fields in the hands of the wisemen, I agree with Jiang and Bell's assertion that Ruism and Ruist constitutionalism pose an efficacious alternative to the decadent and monolithically partial (i.e. totalising a maimed legitimacy) forms of government which have come to dominate contemporary global politics, namely the democracies of the formless masses (horizontal fidgeting of ever-wrangling demons) and the Islamic theocracies (absolute rule of an abstract idea of God). I argue that a transposition of the Tricameral Parliament, and of the cosmotheanthropism upon which it draws, into European contexts and terminologies would provide the way for a regeneration of European cultures. Such hierarchical cosmotheanthropism, as we have seen, is not merely Sinitic, but is shared by all the cultures of Eurasia, from ancient Mesopotamia to Siberia. Ruism, or Eurasian Universism, Ruist constitutionalism, and the *ru* itself, a complex concept of the noöcrat as an "institutionalised shaman" or "scholar", as a representative of the Yellow Deity, of the *Logos* as *Dasein*,[652] holder and unifier of the "science of the serpent" and of the "craft of the eagle", of the great time of Heaven and human reason which articulates itself worlding space, may be integrated with Aleksandr Dugin's Fourth Political Theory providing the mazeway for the construction of a broader Eurasian religio-political entity, or great multipolar empire, comprehending local potentates, all organised according to the threefold system of cosmotheanthropism, as tricameralism. The House of the Ru might be rendered on the broader Eurasian level as the "House of the Noöcrats", the utmost institution of the empire of Eurasia, overseeing all the houses exerting the noöcratic function localised in the various lesser potentates; otherwise, it might be translated as the "House of the Philosophers", recovering

---

652 Concepts discussed throughout the section 3.3 of the present essay.

the original comprehensive meaning of the Hellenic concept of *philósophos* (φιλόσοφος).[653]

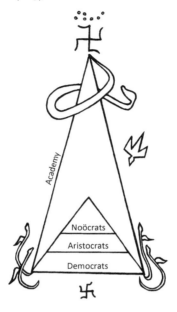

Figure 31: The diagram represents the Tricameral Parliament envisioned by Jiang Qing in its pan-Eurasian rendition, with the House of the Folks constituted by the "democrats", the House of the National Essence constituted by the "aristocrats", and the House of the Ru rendered as the "House of the Noöcrats", set in an order of ascensional hierarchy, overtopped by the Ru Academy, together constituting a threefold-fourfold religio-political structure of society. The noöcrats have the duty to project the whole social body towards Heaven and its order, represented by the Dragon of the ecliptic North Pole and by the eagle symbolising the precessional North Pole. They are the holders of the "science of the serpent" (theory of time, of generation) and of the "craft of the eagle" (theurgy of the quadridirectional space). The demons of the peoples, that is, the spirits of blood kinships and professional guilds, their specific times and private interests, represented in the drawing by the winged snakes, are thus integrated in a common public civility, heightened in the verticalising attunement with the great time of Heaven.

---

653 Cf. Glass (1974), *passim*. Glass' essay compares the philosopher and the shaman as creators and handlers of concepts, forms and images, for the regeneration of contexts and the creation of new ones, for the resurrection (reformulation) of time, for healing, recomposing the anomic disintegration of society and thus the suffering of entities.

POSTFACE: TOWARDS A NEW ORTHOLOGY

[...] If the Christ and the Antichrist are not symmetric, then the radical subject and the Antichrist are. Between these two polarities, a fundamental tension unfolds, a metaphysical blaze which constitutes the deepest riddle of postmodern ontology and of the cyclical phase we are living. It is this pair that must be understood, thought and queried: its two members represent the epiphenomenon, in its extreme form, of the apocalyptic and eschatological reality in which we are immersed. || The Antichrist is directly linked to language — just like the radical subject, on the other hand. Both of them live within language, in a similar yet fundamentally different way. That's why the Antichrist, aside from "rational", may be defined as "verbal" as well. That's why in the Apocalypse the Word is described as a sword coming from the mouth of the Christ. A fundamental tension arises in the linguistic space, assuming a peculiar meaning in the epoch of postmodernity. What is intelligent is conquered by intelligence, what is spiritual by spirit, what is verbal by word — here dwells the mystery, both dark and bright, of our times. If we will be able to understand the riddle, itself both dark and bright, of our eschatological twilight, if we will be able to recognise it, to name it, if we will be the ones who formulate it — then, if *Deus hoc vult*, we will open the way to the descent of the Celestial Jerusalem.

Aleksandr Dugin[654]

— *MOTUS IN FINE VELOCIOR*

According to the Aristotelian maxim *motus in fine velocior*, the processes of postmodern postliberalism seem to be manifesting in an accelerating motion various nefarious phenomena which are disintegrating the erstwhile *Logos* of the West into *Chaos*. I have outlined such phenomena in the present work whilst trying to discern their point of origin in the disruption of the balanced relationship between Heaven, Earth and humanity, a rupture which took place beginning with Christian theology and spreading through its later secularised iterations up to its final product represented by unrestrained liberalism. This

---

654 Ibidem, pp. 172 & 177.

final product entails disconnection from the vertical order of Heaven (the rightwise North Pole, the *Nous* and *Logos*), the private psychopathology and hypertrophy of calculative human reason (logism) used for mere material growth and spiritless reproduction, the denial of spiritual qualities and genealogical principles, and consequent anomy. Hence the homologising universalism/globalism and reductionism of all spirits to an endless monotonic projection of time, to a horizontal flattening of time, and then, when the horizontal projection of time reveals itself as purposeless, its reification and the downward suction of the plurality of the generative forces of mankind towards the Earth, towards the amorphous matrix (the leftwise South Pole).

In the wake dug by the Traditionalist School and by Ernesto de Martino, I say that the same institutions and technological machinations, symbols and words that build a civilisation during its phase of anabasis/anastrophe are subject to an "inversion of sign" when such civilisation begins its phase of katabasis/catastrophe, thereby becoming vehicles of manifestation for the anti-cultural, anti-linguistic and (in one concept) anti-genealogical forces of death which dissolve the moribund civilisation into the chaotic amorphous matrix. Such decomposing forces are in full swing in the Western world, infesting its rotting carcass, moving themselves through its techno-financial skeletal machinery and feeding themselves upon the Western uprooted amorphous masses of populations — they are representable as the rhizomatic "demonic texture" described by Aleksandr Dugin,[655] otherwise defined as the "ophitic [i.e. serpentine] network" in another of his works,[656] also corresponding in my conceptualisations to the "dementocratic demonocracy", the horizontal tangle

---

655 The concept of "demonic texture", as already cited in the present essay, in section 2.1.1.1, is from Dugin's *The Fourth Political Theory*.

656 Dugin (2019b), pp. 50-51. At p. 300 Dugin uses once again the concept of "demonic texture".

of "ever-wrangling demons".[657] The inversion of sign has occurred even to various traditional symbols of the heavenly civilisation which have been stolen and twisted by the anti-traditional forces of dissolution — a paradigmatic example is the appropriation, at the hands of nihilistic "pacifism" and other abnormal phenomena, of the seven colours of the rainbow, which traditionally (the seven of the rainbow or variants of such series, in any case seven colours) symbolise the sevenfold operative power of the God of Heaven embodied by the seven stars of the north celestial pole and reflected by the seven planets of the Sun system; the rainbow appears at the beginning and at the end of times in various cultures (e.g. in *Genesis* and in John's *Apocalypse* of the Bible; and named *Asbru*, the "Bridge of the Gods", which leads to the northern polar *Asgard*, the "City of the Gods", in the Germanic Edda, in which it is told that at the end of times, during the *Ragnarok*, the "Fate of Powers", it will be walked and disrupted by the offspring of the southern dimension of *Muspell* trying to rise to the heavenly city).

René Guénon and Julius Evola agreed that Christianity has already exhausted its life cycle as the axial shaft of the Western civilisation.[658] Evola articulated a sharp critique of the Christian religion, one the most salient points of which is that Christianity is a "lunar" religion (as typical of religions of Semitic derivation,[659] in Evolian terminology), that is to say, a religion keeping the souls of individuals under the Lunar Gate, the precessional North Pole, and within the material world, thus preventing their ascension to the Solar Gate, the ecliptic North Pole, also called the hidden "Black Sun" or "Midnight Sun" in some Western esoteric currents, the utmost hub of the universe, which is the ultimate destination and objective of identification

---

657 Supra, sections 4.1 and 4.4.

658 Bianchi (2020), pt. 3.

659 By "Semitic religions" here I mean the soteriological and matrifocal religions coming from a Near Eastern civilisation that by the time of the Late Roman Empire, the epoch when Christianity was formed, was already decomposed.

in "solar" religions (religions of Indo-European derivation, in Evolian terminology).[660] According to Evola, following the paradigm of Indo-European social trifunctionalism, the degenerative nature of Christianity may be read as a rebellion of the feminine, "lunar", executive aristocratic function against the masculine, "solar", contemplative sacerdotal function, with a subordination of the latter to the former as a merely clerical bureaucracy with a feminine sterile role. In a normal religio-political social structure, by contrast, the feminine executive aristocratic class would always be subordinated to the masculine contemplative sacerdotal class, the former being generated by the latter and bestowed with the warlike role which itself is originally a prerogative of the latter. The overturning of the two functions would trigger the later further decomposition of the social structure with the rise to power of the "terrestrial" productive democratic function, led and exploited by a rootless amoral mercantile bourgeois elite originating from the mixing of the aristocrats emancipated from the sacerdotal domain with democrats their servants, bringing to a complete ousting of sacral power from the social structure, which is thereby reduced to a class bipolarity of bourgeois and proletarians distinguished by criteria of wealth and not by spiritual quality, and ultimately resulting in a complete desacralisation of civilisation as governed no longer by supra-individual ideas of the public common good but by individual private interests of chrematistic accumulation.[661]

It is indeed factual that the clergy of the Roman Catholic Church — the "continental", "solid" aspect of Christianity and

---

660 Bianchi (2020), pts. 1-2. About the "Black Sun" in various esoteric traditions, see: Nechkasov (2021b), p. 410 ff.

661 Ibidem, pt. 1, notes 3 & 15. Bianchi also links the mixture of the aristocratic function with the democratic function, which produces the rootless bourgeois elites, to the Biblical myth of the mixture of the "sons of God" (b'nei ha-Elohim) with the "daughters of man" (b'not ha-Adam), which produced abominable mixlings, the gibborim, later destroyed by the Great Flood. Also see: Dugin (1992), p. 145, where the author describes the regression of the social functions, or castes, beginning with the "rebellion of the kshatriya", i.e. the rebellion of the aristocratic function against the sacerdotal function.

of the European civilisation as reformulated beginning in the Late Roman Empire — has been historically constituted not by truly inspired *sacerdotes* (shamans "endowed with holy power"), but by the cadet or illegitimate sons of the European nobility,[662] and from the Second Vatican Council of the 1960s onwards increasingly also by those of the lower classes. Protestantism — the "maritime", "liquid" aspect of Christianity and of the European and Western civilisation — began in the sixteenth century in close bond with the rise to power of the bourgeois elites as a movement to appropriate the assets of the Catholic clergy and redistribute them to secular persons, thus as an early decomposition of the Catholic Church either reproducing the latter on smaller scales (cf. Anglicanism, Lutheranism) or fragmenting itself into myriads of minuscule sects (cf. Calvinism, Methodism, and the more recent Evangelicalism and Pentecostalism) which are nothing more than money-making enterprises revolving around the cults of personality of given pastors, like worms swarming in the rotting body of Christianity, preying upon the atomised individuals of the uprooted, amorphous masses of the Western and Westernised world, horizontalising their generative powers and then plunging them into primordial material undeterminacy.

— THE RADICAL SELF AND THE FOUR AXIAL GATES

In Duginian Traditionalism, the Midnight Sun is identified as the "radical subjectivity", better named the "radical self", which is the Evolian "differentiated man" or "absolute individual",[663]

---

662 Invented in the Late Roman Empire, Christianity/Roman Catholicism was later significantly strengthened, developed and expanded among the Germanic peoples (especially the continental Saxons who proudly resisted Christianisation) by Charlemagne (likely, according to his name, a representative of the *karl* function of traditional Germanic society), founder of the Carolingian dynasty of the Frankish Empire, who also largely replaced the ancient sacral aristocracy of the Germanic ethelings-dukes (i.e. the *jarl*, sacerdotal-warrior leaders) with a nobility of bureaucratic adminstrators, counts (i.e. companions, fellows). See: Balbo (1836), p. 34.

663 Dugin (2019a), pp. 15 & 29; Dugin (2019b), p. 310.

the Nietzschean "overman" (*Übermensch*),[664] the source of the universe itself, of the *Nous* coming in the flesh, which is still alive during the darkest phase of history as a "white dot" or "mustard seed" plunged into the depths of the black material flood of *Chaos*, but ready to emerge as a new *Logos* as the tides of material dissolution will recede. It is in phases of transition like the one that the Western civilisation is going through, in the liminal stage between the end of a cosmic cycle and the beginning of a new one — specifically, using European and Indian terminologies, between the Iron Age or *Kali Yuga* ("Black Age") and the Golden Age or *Satya Yuga* ("Truth Age") —, when tradition is lost, and all forms are dissolved, that the radical subjectivity manifests itself as some men,[665] who, stricken by a "vertical initiation" coming directly from the supreme God of Heaven,[666] look for others like themselves, other awoken radical subjects, with whom to act in order to build a new heavenly civilisation and to set in motion a new divine tradition, a new turn of the wheel of the *Dharma*. Within the black sea of the "Cosmic Midnight", the radical subject remains steadfast in identifying itself with the wellspring of the universe and of all light and brings into reality, by drawing them from the supreme source, the forms for the new tradition.[667]

There has been a serendipitous convergence between my philosophical research, the interoperational hermeneutic framework I have outlined in the present work, and the

---

664 Dugin (2019b), p. 68.

665 Dugin (2019a), p. 30.

666 The Russian Traditionalist thinker Yevgeny Nechkasov, who has been a disciple of Aleksandr Dugin, distinguishes between a "horizontal initiation", that is the initiation of individuals into sacred knowledge of eternal wisdom generation by generation through uninterrupted chains of traditions, and a "vertical initiation", which is the descent of eternal wisdom to certain individuals directly from the God of Heaven and the gods, possible through experiences of "rupture of levels" of reality and spiritual ascension and approach to the utmost source of the universe, happening in epochs of decadence when the chains of horizontal traditions are broken and their forms are dead, ossified, emptied, and on the way to dissolve completely. Cf. Nechkasov (2021a), pp. 114-116 & 128-133.

667 Dugin (2019b), pp. 66-69, 159-160 & 169-170.

Traditionalist philosophy developed by Aleksandr Dugin. I have realised that in my essay, I have carried out an operation of what Dugin calls "Hyperborean", "Nordic", or "arboreal deconstructionism", that is to say, research which seeks to go back to the northern polar "original meaning at the roots of the World Tree" through various of its branches — we have seen that according to the Traditionalist view, and etymology, "truth" is a "tree", and Dugin himself evokes a similar image by emphasising the related Russian words for "tree", *derevo*, "ancient times", *drevnost'*, and "village", *derevnya*, all coming from the same Indo-European root, for explaining such deconstructionist methodology which according to him should be "the main weapon of Eurasianism".[668] In my work, I have also tried to outline a "retrospective mapping of the direction of darkness" and an "exact genealogy of human degeneration", which are part of Dugin's systematic program for his "new task of philosophy".[669] At the same time, I have found significant analogies with my discourse about the cosmology of the two poles of the universal axis, or two Gates, namely ① the northern Gate of Heaven with its seven stars which reflect themselves as the seven planets — or the five planets (Saturn, Jupiter, Mars, Venus and Mercury, which correspond to the Chinese concept of the *Wufang Shangdi*) plus the two luminaries (the Sun and the Moon, which correspond to the Chinese duality of yang and yin and as the luminaries are also personified as *Taiyangshen* and *Yueshen*) — and ② what I term here the southern "Gate of Hell", in the manual of Zuist (Mesopotamian Neopagan) theory and practice, *Simon Necronomicon*, published in 1977, and its ancillary books, especially *The Gates of the Necronomicon*, written under the pseudonym "Simon" by someone claiming to be an Eastern Orthodox priest, commonly identified as the American scholar of esotericism Peter Levenda (who has

---

668 Ibidem, pp. 203-205. For my study of the etymology of the words "truth", "tree", and others, see the section 1.1.3 of the present essay. A noteworthy addition to the series is the Celtic word *druid*, identifying the sacerdotal class of the Celts, which literally means "man of the tree" or "one who sees the tree".

669 Ibidem, p. 319.

declared he is not Simon, nonetheless holding the rights to the books), in which a Mesopotamian cosmology and ritual of the Gates is reconstructed by relying upon the Chinese religious tradition, amongst others.

Dugin traces the beginning of the schism between God and humanity, and the loss of awareness of the spark of God as the human self — what he calls the "internality" of the *Nous Poietikos* ("Active/Creative Intellect") or of the *Logos*, or else the "Inner God", which is the radical subjectivity itself (as well as Martin Heidegger's *Dasein*, De Martino's "presentification", which I have compared in my essay to the Chinese concept of *Huangdi*) and its power to give discontinuous terms, limits (*peras*) and thus forms to entities in reality — to the antinomian school of Greek philosophy elaborated in Abdera, chiefly Democritus' atomism, which challenged the traditional teleological determinism represented by the Platonic doctrine of the "ideas" of things and by the Aristotelian doctrine of the "entelechies" of things (the concept of "entelechy" implies that the goal of an entity is within the entity itself, is the spirit of the entity itself, and that the chains of events for reaching such goal are interchangeable), replacing it with a causal determinism, which emphasises the study of the causes why entities exist without regards to their ends, at the same time attributing the power of discontinuous terming, limiting and forming things to matter, thereby inventing the conception of matter as constituted by independent atoms and by void between atoms — thus ultimately attributing the activity of the Inner God to matter itself, which is traditionally seen instead as continuous, limitless (*apeiron*) "externality" of *Chaos*.[670] According to Dugin, the Inner God, which is absolute internality, the silent "dot" at the centre of all beings, does not exist as an object within matter but generates all acts, all forms, all words, ultimately all entities, all things, as its own projections into matter, which is otherwise no-entity, no-thing; the Inner God generates all the changeful *physis* as its own projection into matter. Therefore, philosophical

670 Dugin (2019b), pp. 72-81; cf. also Dugin (2021a), passim.

operations which set God outside internality, and search for it or for proofs of it within matter, generate an aberration of reality, a false reality, an anti-reality based on an overturning of the true metaphysical cosmology, orchestrated by inventing an objectified materialised divine dot which is actually an anti-dot, an anti-God. By inventing the object of the atom within the void as the fundamental element of matter and as the ultimate reality, as a material ultimate "God", Democritus' atomism, which was rediscovered and redeveloped since the Renaissance with the birth of modern science (Galileo Galilei, Isaac Newton, Pierre Gassendi, et al.), generates an anti-*physis*, since with its continuous strive for finding the ultimate atomic object of God within matter it ongoingly decomposes the *physis*, the universal nature — this is an approach to reality which consists in an anti-natural, inverted misuse of the same power of the *Logos*, as it is used to unlink rather than to link and relink reality.[671]

Dugin's vision of the aberrant foundations of modern science and of the modern world itself, which is shared by others amongst his disciples, including Yevgeny Nechkasov (alias Askr Svarte) in his 2021 book *Polemos*,[672] perfectly corresponds, in terms of the history of theology, to the operation carried out by Christianity with its confinement of the *Logos*, of the divine dot, as "Christ" into a single spatio-temporal entity, Jesus of Nazareth,[673] marking the objectification of the *Logos*, the historicisation of myth and the fixation of it in a linear segment of time, the "paradoxy" of time described by De Martino.[674] In Dugin's view, the operation carried out by modern science consists in putting and looking for the ultimate atom within the material *physis*, which is always moving and therefore manipulable only

---

671 Dugin (2021a), passim.

672 Nechkasov (2021a), pp. 143-144.

673 Jesus — from Hebrew/Aramaic *Yeshua*, meaning "*Ya* who Saves", as already mentioned in section 1.1.4 of the present essay — is the spatio-temporal historicised fixation specifically of *Ya*, the terrestrial aspect of the God of Heaven in the West Semitic derivations of the East Semitic and Sumerian religion of Mesopotamia (in which *Ya* is *Ea* in East Semitic/Akkadian or *Enki* in Sumerian).

674 Supra, sections 1.1.4 and 1.2.2.

through poetry (in both practical and literary acceptations of such concept), through the rhetorical enthymeme which pertains — as the word itself implies — to the *thymos*, is an undue interpretation of the metaphorical idea of the divine dot as really referring to things of externality, while the divine dot is as such only in the logics of internality, in the divine *logistikon*. It is important to underline that the *thymos* and the *logistikon* are the aspects of the soul which are dominant, respectively, in the aristocratic warrior class and in the sacerdotal contemplative class of Indo-European social trifunctionalism,[675] which, as I have illustrated in my essay, are also associated to the two poles of the Gate of Heaven, respectively to ① the ecliptic North Pole and to ② the precessional North Pole, that is to say to ① the Solar Gate of the *Empyrium* or *Hyperuranion* — with its animal representation as the reptile (usually the dragon or serpent), and associated to the colour white and to the power of the science of time — and to ② the Lunar Gate of the *Elysium* or *Olympus* — with its animal representation as the raptor bird (usually the diurnal eagle and the nocturnal owl; e.g. the [often] two-headed Mesopotamian *Anzu* and the Jewish *Ziz*, the Egyptian hawk-faced *Ra* and *Horus*, and also the Chinese eagle-faced *Leigong*, another representation of *Huangdi*) or other free creatures (such as the bear, the wolf, or the horse, and also possibly the crow, as in the case of Odin's two crows *Huginn* and *Muninn*, which together with his two wolves *Geri* and *Freki* may symbolise the two Chariot asterisms of the precessional North Pole), and associated to the colour red and to the power of the craft of space.[676] Therefore, the operation carried out by atomistic science, just like by Christian theology, is the transposition of a pristine idea pertaining to the sacerdotal *logistikon* into the level of the aristocratic *thymos*, which should instead use it only as a metaphor; such appropriation represents the usurpation of the power of the sacerdotal function at the hands of the aristocratic function on the plane of the mind, of

---

675 Dugin (2021a), passim.

676 Supra, sections 1.3.3, 3.1.1, the prolegomenon to the fourth chapter, as well as the section 4.3.

the foundations of thought itself. Such operation consists in the selling of a changeful metaphor traditionally used merely as a tool to mould matter as being instead a fixed fact, a fixed thing, a fixed entity within matter itself and within the human space-time and its history, in what we may name ③ the "Terrestrial Gate", of the *Epichthonion* — associated to all entities and to their singular or categorial spirits or demons, traditionally represented as snakes in various cultures, but also associated to the colour yellow as the colour of the incarnation of the divine power in the flesh, as represented in Chinese religious culture by *Huangdi*-cum-*Yandi* (the heavenly-cum-earthly archetype corresponding to the Mesopotamian *Enlil*-cum-*Enki*), which is, however, differently from the fixed Christ, a polycentric or multipolar continuous embodiment of the divine, as it may represent the cosmic sovereign of a celestial empire, but at the same time also the patriarchs of kinship lineages and of cultural initiatic traditions (for instance, *Huangdi* is Confucius in Confucianism, *Laozi* in Taoism, and the divine ancestor of the Chinese race as well, without any type of theological conflicts between the various schools of interpretation).

The Christian historicisation/spatiotemporal objectification of the *Logos* brings with itself what I have studied in my work as the objectification of entities and the denial of their inner divinity; thus, their depoliticisation-cum-deaxialisation and degeneration-cum-despiritualisation.[677] Entities thus degenerated and despiritualised — that is to say disconnected from the rightwise vertex of the North Pole, from the masculine heightening, ordering, name-giving, genealogically qualifying and differentiating spirit of the North Pole —, as well as "atomised" and liable to further "atomisation", further decomposition, are then launched into a linear projection of time, first in the form of Christian chiliasm and then, with the latter's secularisation, in the form of atheist materialist progress, a linear progress towards feminine primordial anomic undifferentiation, characterised by mere calculative quantification denying any genealogical qualification, ultimately to be sucked

---

677 Supra, sections 1.1.2 and 1.1.3.

down into the leftwise whirlpool of ④ the South Pole, the subterrestrial "Gate of Hell", of the *Hypochthonion*[678] — with its animal representation as the seven-headed female reptile (which has seven heads as it represents an inverted simulation of the sevenfold heavenly order), but also the dog,[679] and associated

---

678 The concept of *Hypochthonion* as the subterranean, watery, slippery, dissolved dark realm completely bereft of divine order is used by Nechkasov (2021a, pp. 143-144, 206-207 & 232), where it is described as the seat of the "Mother of Matter" (*Nuwa-Houtu* in Chinese culture, *Tiamat-Ereshkigal* in Mesopotamian culture, *Persephone-Proserpina* in Greco-Roman culture, *Hella* in Germanic culture, *Mara-Baba Yaga* in Slavic culture), as well as in one of Dugin's works in which he distinguishes between the *Epichthonion* (which he identifies as *Demeter*) and the *Hypochthonion* (which he identifies as *Cybele*). Cf. Dugin (2020), p. 123. In Slavic folklore, *Baba Yaga* is an iteration of *Mara* representing the chthonic female principle which hinders the path of the hero to prevent him from reaching his goal. Cf. Dugin (1992), pp. 80-81. The name of the chthonic female principle in Hinduism is *Kali Ma*, the "Black Mother" of the *Kali Yuga*. Cf. Dugin (2020), p. 256.

679 Regarding dogs, we have seen (supra, section 3.1.1) that such an animal is associated to the south celestial pole, whose characteristic constellations are *Crux*, and *Canis Major* and *Canis Minor*, represented in Egyptian culture as the canid-faced gods of disorder and death, *Set* and *Anubis* respectively, in Mesopotamian culture as the dog-faced or lion-faced god of the southwestern wind, droughts and ailments *Pazuzu*, and in Germanic culture as *Garm*, the dog of *Hella*. The dog is also an animal attribute of the South American, Incan *Pachamama*. Also the Zuist manual *The Gates of the Necronomicon* informs that such animal is an attribute of the mother goddess of death and obscenity residing in the *Hypochthonion*, described here with another of her Greek conceptualisations, *Hekate*; the book affirms that the dog to the Greeks symbolised "all sorts of obscenities [...] the underworld [...] the unconscious [...] the repository of all sorts of shameful or indecent material". Cf. Levenda (2006), p. 50. Julius Evola himself once wrote, citing Alfred Baümler, that "the modern skimpy clad dominatrix of men carries in her arms the dog, the ancient symbol of limitless sexual promiscuity and of the infernal forces". Cf. Evola (1990), p. 12. Besides the dog, also the lion, as we have seen associated to the Mesopotamian god *Pazuzu*, may be an attribute of the chthonic female principle, as two of them are attributes of the Mesopotamian *Ereshkigal*, and of *Cybele*, *Rhea*, and other Mediterranean representations of her. The lion, however, has an ambivalent symbolism, as it can be either a chthonic or a heavenly symbol, since "the lion is the Christ, but the Antichrist too". Cf. Dugin (2019b), pp. 164-165. The symbolism of the chthonic mother is manifest everywhere in the inverted and decomposing Western world, indicating its hidden driver: as examples amongst many from the fallen "star system" of the Anglo-American "society of the spectacle", Lady Gaga (alias Stefani J.A. Germanotta) obtained world popularity in 2008 with the song *Poker Face*, the music video of which begins with the singer emerging from water between two dogs and guttural voices evoking multiple times "Ma" or "Mu", the simplest and trans-cultural form of the name of matter/mother; the music video of Shakira (Shakira I.M. Ripoll)'s *Whenever, Wherever*, which gave her world popularity in 2000, had a very similar beginning, with the singer emerging from the sea and landing on earth, with an emphasised Christian cross hanging from her neck.

to the colour black, whereas the reptile of the ecliptic North Pole is identified as male, like the male member in the reptilian pairs of *Fuxi* and *Nuwa* in Chinese religious culture (whose complex theonyms' etymologies I have already explained in my essay, and whose theonyms' graphemes also seem to go back to representations of, respectively, a land beast and a water beast), *Lahmu* and *Lahamu* in Mesopotamian religious culture, *Kuk* and *Kuket* in Egyptian religious culture, and the two Leviathans, the female Leviathan (meaning maritime "Serpent") and the male Behemoth (terrestrial "Animals", plural of Behemah), the latter also identified as Enoch and Metatron, and also called Gog while the former is Magog, in Biblical literature, in the *Book of Enoch*, and in Jewish esotericism, which is the first of God's creations and therefore the nearest to it, almost identifiable with it.[680]

---

680 Dugin (2019b, p. 189) discusses the Egyptian primordial duality of *Kuk* and *Kuket* and the Jewish duality of the Leviathan and Behemoth-Enoch-Metatron (2019b, pp. 138-151), and also reports (2019b, p. 142) that, according to the *Book of Enoch*, such primordial duality is incarnated within humanity by two races of the beginning and the end times, a Western maritime leviathanic race, destined to be "eaten by the offspring of Ethiopia", and an Eastern earthly enochian race; I would identify them as the red-black race and the white-yellow race, according to the colour symbolism of races. In Hinduism, the two reptilians may be *Makara* (the mount of *Varuna*) and *Vritra* (slain by *Indra*), followed respectively by the good and evil *asura*, the former cooperating with the seven *deva*, and the latter opposing them. Regarding the descent to the *Hypochthonion*, to the underworld of the chthonic mother, *The Gates of the Necronomicon* explains that such descent is equivalent to the return to the womb of the mother, or the actualisation of unconscious unorderly and antinomic suppressed desires, and it may be either wholly destructive for the identity of the self or a necessary passage for its further construction — much like the decomposition of the dead forms of a civilisation at the hands of unchained antinomic hypochthonic forces makes free space for the rise of a new civilisation built by the nomic hyperuranic forces. Cf. Levenda (2006), pp. 50-51. According to Nechkasov (2021b, p. 404), a successful descent to the chthonic world of death and subsequent rebirth is accomplishable only by those who are destined to the sacerdotal function, and only by the most powerful amongst them; it is indicative that in the cosmic topographical map of the four poles, or gates, explained hereinabove, the sacerdotal function is associated to the utmost North Pole and the male celestial dragon, which is diametrically connected to the South Pole and the female chthonic dragon in the line of maximal metaphysical tension — therefore, the descent to the South Pole may be, for members of the sacerdotal class, also a way of sudden ascent to the North Pole (as illustrated on the right).

— KERYGMATIC CREATIONISM AND
APOCALYPTIC MANIFESTATIONISM

Similarly to my research,[681] Dugin attributes the beginning of the process of desacralisation, thus despiritualisation, of the world to the *ex nihilo* creationism of Abrahamic religions, of Christianity in particular for what concerns the Western world, and its associated idea of a transcendent God, separated from creation, whose "exclusivity and absoluteness tear off any kind of life from other beings", so that "the world no longer has life of its own" and it "is, in conclusion, a dead world", and to Christianity's projection of human perfectibility from the here and now to an otherworldly afterlife, where also the spirits of the dead are confined, whereas non-Abrahamic, non-Christian cultures see them as still living and reincarnating in the here and now.[682] Such process of despiritualisation, which according to Dugin was strengthened with the victory of nominalism (the idea that "universals", that is to say the identifiers of categories of similar beings, are mere names intended as empty sounds representing concepts of the mind and do not really exist as spirits, as essences effectively generating similar beings) over realism (the idea that "universals" really exist as essences generating similar beings) in medieval scholastic Christian theology, sanctioned and symbolised by the *Novacula Occami* (William of Ockham's principle that it is superfluous to postulate universals as well as any plurality of categories of being),[683] was later embodied chiefly by Protestantism, the final incarnation of the *kerygma* of Christianity (the expansive preaching of the doctrinal overstructure of Christianity subsuming and parasitising local and indigenous conceptualisations of the world, or "structures"), was gradually secularised in philosophy beginning with Cartesianism and other deisms with their conception of a mechanician God, clockworker of a clockwork cosmos,

---

681 Supra, section 1.2.2.

682 Dugin (2019b), pp. 80-81 & 216-218. The quotes are taken from p. 217.

683 Ibidem, pp. 219-221.

and of the individual with its omnipotentised reason as the only real entity, and ultimately turned into atheist materialist progressivism.[684] According to Dugin, such a process is the result of a "castration of Beyng", and he defines the *Novacula Occami*, which symbolically represents its turning point, as the "scythe of death" which severed the tradition (Latin *traditio*, that is to say, the "transmission") of the forms (spirits) whose function is to symbolically connect to the first principle of the universe, God,[685] thereby turning the tradition of Christianity into deathly kerygmatic machinery. As the opposite vision to such "*kerygma* of creationism" with its causal determinism and linear time, which tried to cut Beyng at its roots in all the cultures it met during its worldwide expansion through Western colonialism, Dugin introduces the concept of the "structure of manifestationism", characterised by teleological determinism and changeable configurations of time pursuable by entities for reaching their ends.[686] This view corresponds to what I have described in my essay, using a concept elaborated among contemporary Chinese Confucian scholars as "immanent transcendence", and to the Late Antiquity Gnostic dynamic cosmology of the *Ktisma*, with its interconnected "rooms" or "spheres" of existence traversable by souls,[687] and is ultimately the same structure of the World

---

684 Ibidem, pp. 239-249 & 295. Quoting pp. 242-243: "Many believe that modernism is equal to atheism. Nothing falser: modernity is Protestantism, then kerygmatic Protestantism [...]. By denying [...] the structure, the Christian theological *kerygma* starts the process of modernisation. No matter what *kerygma* will arise — it just needs not to be a structure". The "structure", as explained at p. 239, is conceived, as in structuralism (the theoretical and methodological school first originated by Ferdinand de Saussure in linguistics), the innate essence, thus the spirit, of an entity, a group of entities, or a folk, manifesting itself as their peculiar patterns of existence and of conceptualisation of the world.

685 Ibidem, pp. 220-221. Nechkasov expresses the same view in similar terms in his book *Polemos* (2021a, p. 59).

686 In the latest two sentences, "Beyng" is uppercase and written in the 14th-century spelling to emphasise its use in its Heideggerian meaning as the supreme being of the universe, itself in its ever-changing unfolding, according to a style explained in the section 2.3.4 of the present essay. The concept of "manifestationism" is explained by Dugin (2019b, pp. 72-73) and Nechkasov (2021a, p. 27), both of whom describing the same view of reality.

687 Supra, section 1.1.3 and 1.3.2.

Tree, with its branches representing the spiral time(s) walkable by entities, the traditional view of reality as pervaded by the "golden threads" of divinity, by the rays coming from the supreme universal principle, God.[688]

According to Dugin, the rupture between God and the world introduced by *ex nihilo* creationism would be reintegrated with eschatology, with the reunification of the creation with the creator in the "descent of the Celestial Jerusalem",[689] the "City of the Spirits" or "Angelopolis".[690] In his writing *The Metaphysical Factor in Paganism*, Dugin asserts that the structure of manifestationism, or the manifestationist view of reality, is most characteristic of indigenous Pagan religions and Eastern religions, while it is present in the creationist Abrahamic religions only in their esoteric schools (Islamic Sufism, Jewish Kabbalah, Christian Hesychasm). According to Dugin, while Abrahamic religions put the reunification with God at the end of times, Paganism is intrinsically and infinitely eschatological as it sees the world as "theomorphic" or "angelomorphic", as a continuous immanentisation of God symbolised by the multiplicity of entities and phenomena themselves, as a continuous energisation, spiritualisation of reality by God's deities or angels (messengers), and as it sees God as becoming conscious of itself in the presencing of the conscientious radical subject, which is Paganism's protagonist, the coming of the spiritual light in the flesh whose aim is to co-work with God as the other pole of the dual dynamic structure of manifestationism for continuously rearranging reality in order to reveal the supreme unity which is higher than the conceptualised "God" itself and than the dualities of all reality,

688 Dugin (2019b), pp. 79 & 85.

689 Ibidem, p. 81. The disclosure and reflection on the Earth of the "Celestial City" or "Celestial Temple", or the "Ark of God" (whose two angels, Metatron and Sandalphon, representing the two Chariots of the north celestial pole, are discussed further onwards in this postface), as bewritten in John's *Apocalypse*; it is the same as the Chinese *Ding* (which is the Mesopotamian *Iku*), which in my work, especially in the section 3.1.3, I have described as the alignment of Earth with Heaven in the establishment of a celestial civilisation, through the Great Square of Pegasus.

690 Ibidem, p. 332.

within an infinite reconfiguration of being.[691] Dugin cites John of Patmos, the author of the fourth Gospel and of the Biblical *Apocalypse*, as the best representative of manifestationism within Christianity,[692] and indeed John's *Apocalypse* is an illustration of the reactivation into reality of the spirit of God through its doubling as the Leviathan and the Behemoth,[693] and then through its fourfold and sevenfold manifestation (the seven spirits or eyes of God, which are the seven stars of the north celestial pole and the seven planets), the Four Horsemen — which are the major Four Archangels (Michael, Gabriel, Raphael, Uriel) — part of the Seven Archangels which remould reality (whose complete nomenclature beyond the four major ones, and often even beyond the third, has never been standardised in the Abrahamic religions, apart from Orthodox Christianity in which they are named Michael, Gabriel, Raphael, Uriel, Selaphiel, Jegudiel and Barachiel, and which in any case find clear names and associations in pre-Abrahamic traditions, especially Mesopotamian and Greco-Roman ones).

The sevenfold structure of divinity which returns in John's *Apocalypse* is what I have reconstructed, on the basis of the Chinese concepts of *tiandiren* and *yuzhou*, as a pan-Eurasian architecture of divine space-time interpreted through the concepts of "ouranogeoanthropism" (a coinage of mine) and "cosmotheanthropism",[694] and whose vertical axle is analogisable with the "Three Logoi" of the system of the "noomachy" introduced by Dugin[695] — ① the "Logos of Apollo" corresponding to Heaven, ② the "Logos of Dionysus" corresponding to mankind, and ③ the "Logos of Cybele" corresponding to the Earth, which fluidly coexist in individual humans and in entire ethnicities much like the Lacanian three orders of the psyche, respectively ① the "Symbolic Order", ② the "Imaginary Order", and ③ the "Real Order" (*Das*

---

691 Dugin (2019c), passim.

692 Ibidem.

693 Dugin (2019b), p. 149.

694 Supra, sections 2.3.4, 3.2.2 and 3.3.3.

695 Dugin (2020), passim.

Ding), which in turn would correspond to ① the *logistikon*, ② the *thymos* and ③ the *epithymitikon*, that is to say to the tripartition of the soul characterising the three functions of society in Plato's *Republic*, and also to Dugin's other tripartition of the phenomenological subjectivities, respectively ① the "transcendental subjectivity", ② the aforediscussed "radical subjectivity", and ③ the "subjectivity" as such.[696] Dugin defines the Chinese civilisation as the paradigmatic example of a culture which is very different from other historical cultures, including the European, Iranian and Indian ones, in that it has always operated to maintain a Dionysian character, that is to say, a character which keeps an equilibrium between Heaven and Earth and the forces which they represent, and not founded on the unconditional victory of one of the two opposite poles on the other one as it is the case in most of the other world cultures.[697] Similarly, the Zuist book *Simon Necronomicon* affirms that Chinese culture is unique in not trying to suppress completely the chthonic female serpent (which, according to Zuist religion, the book identifies as the Leviathan or *Tehom* in Hebrew and *Tiamat* in Akkadian) but rather to tame and cultivate it.[698] In Duginian Traditionalism, Dionysus represents the radical subject, the white dot, the radical light which remains incandescent and receives the infinite light even in those phases of utter desacralisation and materialisation of reality represented by the Cosmic Midnight,[699] and it is therefore equivalent to the Chinese concept of *Huangdi*, which is the light(n)ing (*guang*; either heavenly light as *Huangdi* in its celestial polar stage, or fiery light as its terrestrial incarnation and as *Yandi*) coming in the flesh at the centre of the rotating cross of the sevenfold ouranogeoanthropism-cosmotheanthropism, which symbolises the role of a spiritually awoken mankind and of a cosmic sovereign mediating between, and co-working with, Heaven and Earth, bringing the order of Heaven down to Earth.[700]

---

696 Supra, section 1.2.1.

697 Dugin (2020), p. 73.

698 Levenda (1977), pp. xxi-xxii.

699 Dugin (2019a), p. 10; Dugin (2019b), pp. 159-160.

700 Supra, section 3.3.

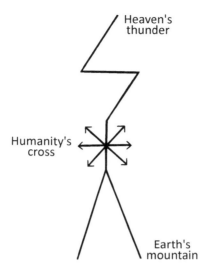

Heaven's
thunder

Humanity's
cross

Earth's
mountain

Figure 32: The diagram above illustrates a symbol taken (though slightly modified) from the book *Occult Cosmology* (2010), written by Bruce Lyon and defined as "the fundamental tune for the next phase of the esoteric tradition of Transhimalayan Theosophy".[701] The symbol might be interpreted as a Western symbol of ouranogeoanthropism-cosmotheanthropism, whose threefold-sevenfold structure is illustrated, in different terms, by Lyon himself.[702] Lyon, moreover, builds his cosmology around the need to rediscover the source of all divinity as the hidden Black Hole (thus the Black Sun) at the centre of the universe, to which the Earth is connected through the ecliptic North Pole and from which the universal spiritual energy passes to the visible Sun and then to the Earth itself.[703] He affirms that while the Eastern traditions have preserved the first-person perspective on God (the first aspect of God; internality and identification of the soul with the spiritual flow of God), the Western traditions have developed the third-person perspective on God (the third

---

701 Lyon (2010), p. 27. Note that I have consulted the Italian translation of Bruce Lyon's book; the symbol is found at p. 147.

702 Ibidem, pp. 68-69, where the author explains a cosmological scheme similar to what I have described as ouranogeoanthropism-cosmotheanthropism.

703 Ibidem, p. 367. Nechkasov (2021b, pp. 410-414) discusses the same symbolism of the Black Sun, and its association to the other symbol of the arrowed star, in both Theosophy (including its National Socialist declinations, such as the doctrines of Miguel Serrano) and the most esoteric currents of contemporary Germanic Heathenry and Slavic Rodnovery.

aspect of God; externality and separation between the soul and the spirit of God), which has gradually brought to the complete materialisation of the Western world; the purpose of Lyon's Theosophical teachings, analogical to the purpose of my work, is to reunite the two perspectives by reactivating the second aspect of God, which is the spirit itself, or what Lyon defines in Sanskrit as the *buddhi*, the ray of "awakening", "enlightenment".[704] The symbol is constituted by: ① the thunder representing the flow of spiritual energy coming from Heaven above; ② the mountain representing Earth, the material receptacle coming from below; ③ perfected mankind between the two, on the top of the mountain as the utmost point of sublimation of matter which receives the spiritualising awakening from Heaven, and represented by the arrowed cross (in the original drawing a simple cross) interpretable as rotating.

The sevenfold ouranogeoanthropic-cosmotheanthropic structure, organised in a duality with Heaven and Earth as its opposite poles, above and below, is also analogous to the "World Egg" bespoken by Dugin in the wake of Guénon[705] and to the cosmology of the two Gates of the Zuist system of the *Simon Necronomicon* cursorily mentioned hereinbefore. Dugin says, following Guénon, that in ① the Golden Age of traditional society the World Egg is open from its top (from the Gate of Heaven), the universal rays of God pervade and spiritualise reality, and every entity is connected to God and is a symbol of an idea of God itself — as above, so below, as what is on Earth is perceived as a reflection of what is in Heaven, of the hyperuranic harmony; in ② the following ages of progressive modernisation the World Egg becomes closed, God's rays no longer pervade all entities, and one after the other they become despiritualised and laden with matter — as below so above, as gravity from the Earth gradually becomes stronger than the spirits of Heaven, and the world is ensnared in "gravitational jails" and becomes a "concentration camp for the spirit"; in ③ the last phase of the Iron Age, in postmodernity, the World Egg opens from its bottom (from the Gate of Hell), and it is invaded by the hypochthonic "hordes of Gog and Magog", which constitute the confused, obstreperous "demonic texture" of a completely

704 Ibidem, pp- 62-64.

705 Dugin (2019b), pp. 295-301. Also described in: Nechkasov (2021b), pp. 470-471.

materialised reality, and man itself is no longer filled by a ray of God, but by a complex of demons[706] — Jacob's *Qliphoth* (the empty "Shell") filled with the *Erev Rav* (the "Mixed Multitudes") of the end times in Jewish esotericism.[707]

— ANTIKEIMENIC CHRISTIANITY

At the end of times, the World Egg overturns, and a new Golden Age begins with the seeds of a new mankind characterised by radical subjectivity, the reborn consciousness of the Inner God of life (represented by the return of God at the end of times in various religious traditions, e.g. the Hindu *Kalki*, the Buddhist *Maitreya*, the Zoroastrian *Saoshyant*, the Jewish *Mashiah*, the Islamic *Mahdi*, the second coming of Christ, and the "Russian Saviour", a return which in all these traditions is described as "tremendous"; this figure will also be incarnated as singular individual, as the holy emperor, the King of the World, the Hindu *Chakravarti* whose task will be to set once again in motion the cosmic wheel of the North Pole, unmasking and destroying the chaotic forces of the South Pole), while those humans who remain entangled in the paradigms of the previous ages perish without leaving any trace.[708] As previously recalled, during the phases of the decline of civilisation, the same institutions which built it undergo an "inversion of sign", lose the anchorage in the transcendental source of normative tradition, and become empty simulacra functioning as vehicles of the forces of dissolution — this is the "Great Parody", the "Great Simulation" according to Guénon,[709] the "obduracy" or "network sclerosis" of the Symbolic Order which becomes infested with *Das Ding* according to Lacanianism, or what I have described in my own words as a "machine-like empty shell",

---

706 Ibidem.

707 Ibidem, pp. 302-303.

708 Ibidem, pp. 302-309. Also see: Dugin (1992), pp. 99, 201 & 204, about the "Russian Saviour" of the Russian folk beliefs, which has characteristics of all the others.

709 Guénon (1945), pp. 267-274.

using a figure very similar to that of the *Qliphoth* of Jewish esotericism illustrated hereinabove.[710] The Italian philosopher Maria Stella Barberi, in her study *Lo spazio katechontico da San Paolo a Carl Schmitt* (2006), treats the eschatological concept of the *Katechon* introduced in Paul's *Second Epistle to the Thessalonians*, which is literally the "withholder", the "container" of the *Antikeimenos*, acting at times as a general force and at times as a punctual entity against the latter,[711] which is, in turn, the force of anomy and apostasy of the end times which becomes incarnated as the masses of the "men of perdition", of uprooted humanity.[712] Following the interpretations of the ninth-century French monk Haimo of Auxerre and of the French philosopher René Girard, Barberi says that the *Antikeimenos*, which when embodied as entities is also called the "Antichrist", is sent by God itself to test and to discern those who succumb to the Antichrist's lie of bewilderment consisting in the deception of bringing a definitive "closure of the system of violence", and who worship him as a deity, from those who stand firm in truth and do not believe in the Antichrist's fixed falsification of what is the ultimate good — it is the divine victim of sacrifice, the Christ, to "withhold" the violence which it is intended to curb definitively, the Antichrist; the *Katechon*, it itself embodied as the multitude of the men of righteousness, "contains" the *Antikeimenos* both in the sense that it restrains it and in the sense that it hosts it within itself.[713]

The symbol of the fixed cross, by hindering the closure of the system of natural violence onto itself as represented by the rotating cross, is at the same time a factor of denial and

---

710 Supra, section 1.1.4.

711 Barberi (2006), passim. At p. 31, note 2, the author explains the etymology of *Antikeimenos*, which is what is against *keimai*, literally against "staying", "standing", "stabilising", "establishing", and thus is both apostasy and anomy. From the same Indo-European root of *keimai*, that is *kei*, also derive the Greek terms *oikos* ("abode"), *oikeo* ("abiding"), *oikoumene* ("abided place"), and the Latin *civitas*, *civitatis* ("city", "civility", "civilisation").

712 Ibidem, pp. 26-27.

713 Ibidem, p. 27.

destructuring of the established order and a factor of anomy, of crisis and acceleration of the end times.[714] To Barberi, "the same powers [...] the sons of Satan, the Roman Empire, the Church [...] have represented alternately, for one another, the Antichrist or its withholder".[715] In *De ortu et tempore Antichristi*, the tenth-century French monk Adso of Montier en Der underlines that the Antichrist, symbolising the anomic masses of the end times, will be born as a regular human from a father and a mother, in "Babylon", symbolising a city which was glorious in the past but has now degenerated having lost the connection with God, as the divine spirit passes to different civilisations according to the theory of the *translatio imperii*, which Adso himself supports.[716] As we have seen hereinbefore, the Gate of Heaven, *Babilu* in the Akkadian language, may be opened either from the top or from the bottom (as the Gate of Hell) of the World Egg, from the North Pole or from the South Pole; in John's *Apocalypse*, and in Dugin's geosophical interpretation of it, the upside-down cosmology is illustrated as follows: ① the red-clad Whore of Babylon (the America-driven Western civilisation, according to Dugin's interpretation) rides ② the (black) seven-headed female Leviathan, the serpent of the South Pole and of the Western seas (the Atlantic Ocean; astrally identifiable as *Dorado*, the fish- or snake-like constellation of the south ecliptic pole), and at the peak of its hegemony it is supported by ③ the (yellow) Behemah (Enoch) of the Eastern landmasses (Russia, Eurasia), while both of them draw power from ④ the (white) celestial *Draco*, Behemah of the North Pole,[717] in a possible

---

714 Ibidem. The distinction between the "fixed cross" and the "rotating cross" is mine.

715 Ibidem.

716 Ibidem, p. 28.

717 Dugin (2019b), pp. 149-154. The geosophical associations between the Leviathan-Whore of Babylon and the Western civilisation of the seas, and between the Behemoth-Enoch and Russia-Eurasia, the Eastern civilisation of the landmasses, are made by Dugin himself. The polar and colour associations are mine. It is important to note, however, that Russia or the Russian people are also associated, even by name, to the colour red, or better to both white and red which combined may represent a shade of yellow; in another of his books, Dugin explains that "Holy Russia" is white-red, and the name "Rus/Ros", generally

symbolisation of the overturning of the cosmic order of society and its degeneration due to the rise to power of the antikeimenic Western multitudes of perdition, fruit of the mixing of ① the red aristocratic function (the Whore of Babylon) with ② the black democratic function (the seven-headed Leviathan) after the former's overthrowing of ③ the white sacerdotal function (the celestial Behemah, *Draco*) and the subjection of ④ its yellow katechontic representatives (the terrestrial Behemah, Enoch). The fixation and objectification of God's spirit and divinity into a single spatio-temporal entity, into a single moment of historical time, blocks the entire rotating pan-Eurasian theo-cosmological and religio-politological structure and onsets its overturning; the inner divinity that is the spirit coming in the flesh as all entities, thus at one time the second and third aspects of the God of Heaven in pan-Eurasian theo-cosmology taken together,[718] is fixedly set in the externality of matter, among snakes creeping on Earth and then beneath it, and no longer flies freely as the eagle (symbol of the warlike function) of the precessional North Pole around the ecliptic North Pole to impart the latter's changeful order to the Earth, while it is instead the first aspect of God and its dragon (symbol of the sacerdotal function) which rotates around the former — in the social reflection of such cosmological overturning, the sacerdotal king, who in traditional sacral societies is at or near the centre of the circle of being, finds itself thrown at the periphery, at the margins of the circle of being of modern desacralised,

---

identifying the East Slavs, comes from the Indo-European root *ros (Indo-Iranian *ruxs/roxs, Proto-Germanic *raudaz, Latin russus), which means "red", "bright", but obviously darker than white, and sometimes so dark to have connections with black, becoming a red-black. Cf. Dugin (1992), pp. 6-9 & 16. There are also Russian folk beliefs about a "Black Dragon" associated to the south of Russia, to winter, and to the Black Sea, whereas the northern White Sea is associated to summer, west to autumn and east to spring (Dugin [1992], pp. 74 & 99), and we have already illustrated the colour associations of the four Russias of a popular tradition of sacred geosophy (supra, section 3.3.3). Russia might therefore be the "red impulse" which may be driven either by the "white horse" or by the "black horse", and should choose the former. Cf. supra, section 2.3.1, where I discussed the three colours in relation to Plato's Chariot Allegory regarding the impulse of the soul, the *thymos*.

718 Supra, section 1.3.3.

degenerated societies, and everywhere-cum-nowhere in the vortex of dissolution of postmodernity.[719]

Barberi says that the role of the katechontic "spirits of peace" should be to keep within history, intended as keeping within the spiral of time and not as fixing into a singular entity in space-time, that godly, draconian unifying awesome force which, unless continuously "historiated" in changeful projections in the spiral of time, otherwise escapes the spiral of time and the contrasts between dualities in reality (even manifesting themselves as wars among different peoples) and sets itself at the head of nations as a utopian homologating goal.[720] The contrast between the *Antikeimenos* and the *Katechon* has always been and always will be at work throughout history, and the katechontic men, the righteous men of the end times animated by the spirits of peace who do not believe in the Antichrist's deceit of the definitive closure of being, are ultimately not those who preach a fixed "security" and "neutrality"; on the contrary, they are those who constantly, restlessly put into question the genuineness of fixed institutionalisations and their mechanically self-reproducing forms, or simulacra. To Barberi, the *Antikeimenos* itself, which

719 Dugin (2019b), pp. 226-227. Also see: Dugin (1992), p. 110, where the author discusses how such process was established by the doctrine of the *Filioque*.

720 Barberi (2006), p. 28. Regarding the *Katechon* and the *Antikeimenos*, the Christ and the Antichrist, Babylon and the anti-Babylon, that is to say gods/deities and titans, angels and demons (Western religions' general categories), *shen* and *gui* (Chinese religions' categories), *deva* and *asura* (Hinduism), *ahura* and *daeva* (Iranian Zoroastrianism), *anunnaki* and *igigi* (Mesopotamian Zuism), ases-wanes and yotuns-thurses (Germanic Heathenry), and other names identifying, respectively, the forces (seven, in the most systematised theologies, as we have thoroughly seen) of the *Hyperuranion* (Gate of Heaven) and their fallen reflections in the *Hypochthonion* (Gate of Hell), it is important to remember that they are also manifest in the human nature itself, and form different multitudes of individuals. In the *Rigveda*, it is written that *deva* and *asura* are of the same nature; everyone is born *asura* (the term itself, like its cognates, the Iranian *ahura* and the Germanic "ases" or "anses", comes from the same root of the Latin *ens, entis*, "entity"), but while some remain *asura* and degenerate as they act for selfish goals, for their personal material and passional growth, and lose conscience once they have achieved such goals, others ascend to the rank of *deva* by acting selflessly, detached from the affections and the effects produced by actions. The demons of the southern matrix of Hell manifest themselves when the rays of the northern pattern of Heaven withdraw from reality, desacralising and emptying it, a process which culminates in postmodernity. See: Nechkasov (2021a), p. 207.

269

is at one-time apostasy (negation of *stasis*, of "staying", "standing firm", i.e. unsettling, uprooting) and anomy (negation of the *nomos*, the "norm", "law", and of the concrete place of foundation of the divine order which gives sense and meaning to all particularised laws), is the "sin of utopia", which implies the denial of the present world, the refusal of "staying in a place" and of "staying in the world", that is to say, delocalisation and derealisation, which in the words of Carl Schmitt is represented by any "human plan of interrupting history, to escape from it and reach a stable perfection"; on the other hand, the *Katechon* is the "goad of insecurity" which prevents the stiffening of the spirit within the deception represented by any totalising ideology claiming to represent the final solution of all being and the end of history.[721] Human history is a process generated within time by a constant lack of completeness in reality, "deprivation and reinvigorating insecurity";[722] it remains and should always remain inherently unfinished and thus always open to new paths to perfectibility, as I have illustrated throughout my work on the basis of the Chinese conceptions of time and its history, but also thought and its culture.

In her discourse, Barberi seems to imply that at the end of times, Christianity might unveil itself as the *Antikeimenos* or Antichrist, comprehending all the utopian Western rationalist and positivist totalitarian ideologies that it spawned throughout history as its own secularised iterations, which have reduced all reality to an "object of planning",[723] a vision similar to what I have explained in my essay on the basis of the thought of De Martino, Roland Littlewood and Simon Dein.[724] Similarly to the latter two and to my discourse, Nechkasov too identifies a schizophrenic psychopathology in Christian theological thought, which gives way to anomy, in the sense that when humanity is disconnected from God and the ancestral gods law becomes desacralised logism, an

---

721 Barberi (2006), pp. 28-29.

722 Ibidem, p. 29.

723 Ibidem.

724 Supra, section 1.2.2.

instrument in the hands of the "material anthropological element", opening to humanity's growth from the bottom up.[725] Dugin himself, in the wake of Russian Gnostic doctrines of the Orthodox Old Believers, seems to identify the *kerygma* of Christianity as the source of apostasy: it is the doctrine of the "Three Apostasies" which have taken place throughout a series of religious reforms; first ① the Catholic Church of Rome with its schism from Orthodox Christianity in 1054, then ② the Orthodox Church of Greece with its rapprochement to the Catholic Church with the Union of Florence in 1439, and endly ③ the Orthodox Church of Russia with the Westernising Nikonian Reform in 1666-1667.[726] In the midst of such a process, a ④ "[total] collapse [of tradition within Christianity] happens with Protestantism", which began in the sixteenth century — started by the Saxon former Augustinian monk Martin Luther —, with its emphasis on individuality, thus on amorphous masses of individuals, and at the same time its bringing the externalisation of inner divinity to its extreme consequences.[727] I would add to this chain of occurrences also ⑤ the gradual secularisation, materialisation and thus externalisation of Catholicism itself which began with the Counter-Reformation launched by the Council of Trent of 1545-1563 to thwart the Protestant Reformation, with which the Catholic Church itself began to be "Protestantised" and which culminated with the Second Vatican Council of the 1960s (characterised, amongst other reforms, by the inversion of the worship in the mass — no longer directed towards the altar, symbolic of the North Pole, but towards the mass itself of anomic individuals, symbolic of the South Pole), and possibly with the worship of the South American *Pachamama* (Quechua Incan for "Universal Mother" or "Great Mother") hosted in Saint Peter's Basilica in 2019 by Pope Francis, which might symbolically represent the complete overturning of Heaven and Earth in the Christian metaphysical cosmology of the West, the full emergence of the "Logos of Cybele", which is the *Chaos*

---

725 Nechkasov (2021b), pp. 43 & 278-279.

726 Dugin (2019b), pp. 152-153.

727 Dugin (2020), pp. 175-178.

of the leftwise vortex of the South Pole, from the decomposing body of the erstwhile "Logos of Apollo" of the Western civilisation which has long since completely exhausted its cycle of rightwise verticalisation towards the North Pole,[728] in a process of events comparable to the penetration and officialisation of heterogeneous Semitic religions into the nonsensical state syncretism of the Late Roman Empire, which included the worship of Cybele herself, which originated in Anatolia and gradually spread up through the Italian peninsula eventually reaching Rome during the final stages of the Roman civilisation.[729] It is also worth mentioning the

---

728 Ibidem, pp. 254-256. Dugin frequently makes reference to contemporary literature and cinematography to explain his philosophical view of the forces at play behind the phenomena of the modern world. In my opinion, the described processes might be well represented by the movies *The Thing* (1982) by John H. Carpenter and the homonymous prequel of 2011 by Matthijs van Heijningen Jr., which I have already cited in my essay, in which a disorganic monster with extraterrestrial origins landed in Antarctica, at the southernmost point of the Earth, simulates the bodies of animals and human explorers who have come to the area and uses them as "mouths" through which to assimilate others, and the entire vicissitude begins from a dog, of which we have already explained the symbolism.

729 Bianchi (2020), pt. 3. Another cinematographic work interpretable as symbolising the described processes is the 1998 movie *Deep Rising* by Stephen Sommers, in which a cruise ship (symbol of the Catholic Church and of broader Christianity since the beginning of the religion's history [the temples of Christianity themselves, especially Western Christianity, are modelled after the ship, or "nave"; cf. the "Bark of Saint Peter"], as well as of the Western civilisation or of the civilisation of the seas) for rich people named *Argonautica* (once again an astral reference to the South Pole, as *Argos* is either *Canis Major* or *Canis Minor* and *Argo Navis* is the ship of the South Pole, near *Dorado*; cf. Allen [1963], p. 132) is invaded by an ottoia mutated into a giant octopus-like leviathanic monster (a sort of Lovecraftian *Cthulhu*; the octopus is another animal associated with the chaotic matrix of the South Pole [and the architecture of some great domed Western Christian temples, such as Saint Peter in the Vatican or Saint Paul in London, might also give the idea of the octopus], cf. Nechkasov [2021b], p. 413) which emerges from the abyss of the Mariana Trench (which is the deepest depression of the seabed, the diametrical opposite of the sky) at the precise moment when the engines are sabotaged by planning of the corrupt captain himself, thus when the ship loses its direction, its route, its end. The giant ottoia enters into the blocked ship from the third of the four aft helix propellers, thus from the third of the four cosmic poles (ecliptic, precessional, terrestrial and subterrestrial), if we want to give them a symbolic interpretation; the giant ottoia infests the whole ship, primarily through pipes and interspaces (the "ophitic web", network of serpents, bespoken in: Dugin [2019b], pp. 50-51), with its vermicular tentacles provided with mouths with which it devours all the passengers (or, rather, drinks them by sucking their bodily fluids and dissolving their bodily tissues), except for three social outcasts infiltrated into the ship who manage to blow up the infested vessel with the sea monster itself.

beatification, in 2020, of the bourgeois youth Carlo Acutis as the "blessed of the Internet" and potential future "saint of the Internet", comparable to the personality cults of the Late Roman Empire with a sinister technocratic drift, considering that the Internet is a technological reflection of the rhizomatic, vermicular tangle of unbridled demons opened towards the abyss of the Gate of Hell.[730]

As a solution for saving Russia and the Eurasian landmass from the deception of the *Antikeimenos*, the female Western Leviathan/Whore of Babylon which lures the Behemoth they embody, the celestial male reptile and the two-headed *Ziz* its representative, to choose to be the "Dark Enoch", the false prophet driving the peoples of the world to her,[731] Dugin calls for the formulation of a special Russian *kerygma* that would perfectly match the Russian structure, in order to thus

---

730 James F. Cameron's 1997 movie *Titanic*, about the liner ship *RMS Titanic* which sank into the Atlantic Ocean in 1912, also lends itself to cosmological interpretations, with attention to the symbolism of the races or functional orders of society, to their associated colours (represented both by parts of the ship itself and by the colours of the hair of the main characters), and to their implosion with the rise to power of the bourgeoisie (the black function taking over the red function and ousting the white function). In the movie, the *Titanic* ship (symbol of Christianity), directed by the fictional "Francis Ltd." (a reference to Cameron's second name), sinks and is sucked down into the Atlantic Ocean beginning from its damaged bow, thus from its damaged head part, slashed by hitting an iceberg (note that the berg, the mountain, is a symbol of matter, of the Earth; "Cybele", *Kubileya* in Phrygian, means precisely "Mountain") at the level of the red band of the hull below the waterline; when the final section of the stern is sucked into the ocean, two final symbolic words, the sign on the black band of the hull with the ship's name and the ship's registration port's name, are emphasised at the centre of the frame to catch the eye — *Titanic Liverpool*, the "titanic" suck into the "turbid waters" (the meaning of the English city's toponym).

731 Dugin (2019b), pp. 143, 147 & 153. Dugin identifies the Behemoth, the spirit of Russia/Eurasia or of the civilisation of the land, as the male member of the pair of reptiles representing the primordial duality of creation and as the two-headed raptor bird *Ziz* (the Mesopotamian *Anzu*) its representative as well, which may be either the "Dark Enoch" (also interpretable as "Black Enoch") if serving the red Whore of Babylon and the black female Leviathan, which represent the spirit of the West or the civilisation of the seas, or the "Bright Enoch"/Metatron (also interpretable as "White Enoch") if fighting the red-black Leviathan and identifying itself with the God of Heaven, as the yellow bird representative of the white celestial dragon. Also see: Dugin (1992), p. 90: "[...] one of the heads [of the two-headed eagle of Russia/Eurasia] represents the Occident, the other one, the Orient [...]".

actualise the peculiar Russian radical subjectivity with its own *Logos*, the Russian *Dasein* within its own *Ereignis*.[732] Such kerygmatic overstructure should not necessarily be Orthodox Christian, as Dugin sees the Christian stage of Russian history, especially the Nikonian Church (the Orthodox Church of Russia), which he identifies as the Dark Enoch itself,[733] as concluded and as hampering the development of something really new which would be truly, authentically Russian.[734] Enoch should be freed from the antikeimenic enchantment of kerygmatic creationism and should remember his identity as the "Bright Enoch", Metatron, the firstling of God, who stands up in front of the "Throne" (*Araboth*) of God, the supreme angel of the "Chariot" (*Merkabah*) of God at the North Pole,[735] a role which is also that of the archangel Michael. Dugin seems to imply that the key role in determining that Enoch chooses to be the Bright Enoch is played by Elijah, though such role is unclear; in Jewish mythology and esotericism both Enoch and Elijah were originally men but ascended to the *Araboth* via the *Merkabah*, though Elijah preceded Enoch, and by ascending Elijah became the angel Sandalphon and Enoch became the angel Metatron, the two angels of the Ark of God, while in Slavic Pagan-Christian popular religion Elijah is identified as being *Perun*, the god of thunder and charioteer of the north celestial pole, in Kabbalah Sandalphon and Metatron are the same being, and in the *Apocalypse* both of them return as humans at the end of times to expose and fight the *Antikeimenos*.[736] Therefore, Elijah and Enoch might be the same figure, part of the Behemoth as either the celestial reptile (the white sacerdotal function) or the celestial bird (the red aristocratic function), the *Ziz*; otherwise, Elijah/Sandalphon might be the bright one

---

732 Ibidem, pp. 283-285 & 290-291.

733 Ibidem, p. 153.

734 Ibidem, p. 288.

735 Ibidem, pp. 145-146 & 154.

736 Ibidem, pp. 82, 144, 151 & 154. For Elijah-Perun and the Great Chariot, also see: Allen (1963), p. 428; Dugin (1992), pp. 76-77.

of the *Ziz's* two faces, thus the Bright Enoch/Metatron itself, and the bird-man, or the bird-men, incarnating it at the end of times by identifying themselves with God; the spirits of peace of the *Katechon* freed from the materialism of fixed, sclerotised utopias purporting to represent a closure of all being. According to Duginian Traditionalism, the *Katechon* might correspond to the radical subjectivity, the white dot, the mustard seed, the sacerdotal king — resynthesising the true, spiritual, sacerdotal and aristocratic functions, the "science of the serpent" and the "craft of the eagle", as one, as a serpent-eagle, like in the undivided class of the *hansa* at the beginning of the Golden Age according to Vedic literature. In traditional society, this figure is at or near the centre of the circle of being; in modernity, they are born at the margins of the circles revolving around the centres of the blackened degenerate societies; while in the postmodern dissolution of all institutional forms they are scattered across all the fluidified reality, ready to mould it into new forms, new traditions.[737] The many katechontic white dots might be guided by Sandalphon-Metatron towards a new Golden Age.

— KATECHONTIC PAGANISM

As the antikeimenic pathology of the Western and Westernised world has been extensively diagnosed, we might propose further visions of possible therapies for healing such pathology. Dugin's project for an authentic kerygmatic overstructure for systematising an indigenous structure might be applied to all the peoples of Europe, onsetting the latter's palingenesis within broader Eurasia. Barberi cites an etymology of *Katechon* provided by Schmitt himself: *kata*, "down", plus *echo*, "keep"; thus, it would mean what "keeps down", in the sense of what "keeps rooted" to the land.[738] As we have seen

---

737 Ibidem, pp. 226-227. The association of the sacerdotal king to the Vedic concept of the undivided original nature of the *hansa* is my addition, like the mention of the "science of the serpent" and the "craft of the eagle", which are concepts that I have elaborated myself in the section 4.4 of my essay.

738 Barberi (2006), p. 29.

hereinbefore, Dugin considers the religions of Paganism as intrinsically eschatological, as they conceive the relationship between God and humanity as ongoingly renewing itself through the changeful epiphany of the nature of God's spirits within matter while keeping entities firmly rooted to their native land, and this last "katechontic" idea is encapsulated in the etymology of the word "Paganism" itself, which indicates what is natively, genealogically and peacefully radicated but at the same time always open to a continuous immanentisation of the transcendental God into ever-renewing "ecstatic" divine forms and words, and thus never gives way to illusions of an "end of being".[739]

John's *Apocalypse* is interpretable as a new unveiling of the seven spirits of peace, the seven eyes and rays of God, within a new configuration of reality as a multipolar world, as a world constituted by multiple local cultures all within a Eurasian empire orienting and rectifying them towards the supreme circumpolar operativity of Heaven, thus within a new "orthology", an *Orthos Logos* ("Right Order", "Right Word", "Right Law"). According to Dugin, Paganism is the necessary

---

739 It is worthwhile to highlight that the original Latin meaning of *pāgānus*, is countryside "villager", but "civilian" as well, as the word originated in the Roman civic lexicon as an adjective describing an inhabitant of the *pāgus*, meaning "region", "settlement", "establishment", and "kinship village", a basic civic unit of a (specifically the Roman) civilisation in the sense of "campaign" (itself coming from the same word), thus meaning a cohesive group of people often genealogically linked and therefore giving worship to the same divine ancestors and gods. Another derived adjective is *pāgēnsis*, from which come for instance the French *pays* and the Italian *paese*, both meaning either "country" or "village", as well as the English "peasant". Synonyms of *pagus* and *paganus* in Latin are *gēns* ("ilk", "kin[d]", "race") and *gentīlis* ("kind", "gentile"), and *nātiō* ("birth", "nature", "nation", "race") and *nātiōnālis* ("native", "national"), while in Greek the closest meaning is that of *éthnos* ("tribe", "folk", "nation"). The Indo-European etymological root is **pak-, *pag-*, meaning "to be firm/steady/standing", and from it also come the noun *pāx* ("peace"), and the verbs *pācō, pācāre, pācāvī, pācātum* ("to make peaceful/pay/appease"), and *pangō, pangere, pepigī, pāctum* ("to fasten/fix/set/establish"). See: Pokorny (1959), p. 787 ff. While the term originated in the Roman civic lexicon, in the Late Roman Empire it acquired religious (and derogatory) overtones, when the countryside villagers were reluctant to adopt the new official universal religious doctrine which was being formulated in the urban centres (named *Christianismus*, the "concretising" doctrine; or *Catholicismus*, the doctrine for "keeping all" together) and instead maintained local and indigenous religious traditions.

foundation for a true, ecstatically energetic and continuously eschatological empire and for its corresponding true, ecstatically energetic and continuously eschatological human subjectivity. In his own words:[740]

> The true pagan Empire, as well as the true pagan subject, are necessarily eschatological. The power which emanates "from there", on which every true Empire rests, is not a banal affirmation of the identity of being with itself. The pagan component in metaphysics is charged with a paradoxical and truly transcendent "energy" which leads much further than the impeccable and unique, yet limited power of faith. This is made especially clear in the critical moments of the unfolding of being, in radical eschatological moments — only then can pagan metaphysics fully demonstrate its deepest foundations.

Therefore, the new ecstatic orthology might be elaborated within new katechontic, local and indigenous, cultural and civilisational religions of Paganism.[741] Nechkasov has dedicated his entire work *Polemos* (whose title, by the way, refers to the Heraclitean conceptualisation of God as manifesting itself through the confrontation between dualities, in dual dynamism[742]) to outlining the threads of a "Pagan Traditionalism", coming to many intuitions similar to those that I have developed in my work; my "Eurasian Universism" might represent yet another comparative framework, more oriented to astral cosmology, for systematising and orienting the doctrines of such renewed Paganisms which include Mesopotamian-Canaanite Zuism (Sumerian-Semitic Neopaganism) and

---

740 Dugin (2019c), passim.

741 I choose the definition of "Neopaganism" or "contemporary Paganism" provided by the *Merriam-Webster's Encyclopedia of World Religions* which restricts such a descriptor to movements which revive or reinvent the ancient, indigenous, pre-Christian and pre-Islamic religions of Europe (including the vast Eurasian expanse of Russia) and the Middle East, not comprising the indigenous religions (very often uninterrupted since time immemorial, such as Hinduism, Iranian Zoroastrianism, Japanese Shinto, Chinese religions and Siberian Tengrism) of cultures other than these two interconnected geographic areas. See: Doniger (2000), pp. 794-795, entry: *Neo-Paganism*.

742 The Heraclitean maxim *"Polemos* is the father of all things" is evoked in my essay as well, in section 1.1.4.

Egyptian Kemetism (Egyptian Neopaganism) from the Near East, Celtic Druidry (Celtic Neopaganism) and Germanic Heathenry (Germanic Neopaganism) from northern Europe, Baltic Druva (also called Baltuva, Romuva; Baltic Neopaganism), Slavic Rodnovery (Slavic Neopaganism) and Scythian Assianism (Scythian Neopaganism) from eastern Europe, Greek Hellenism (Greek Neopaganism) and Roman-Italic Traditionalism (Roman-Italic Neopaganism) from southern Europe, and others.[743]

Nechkasov affirms that making a "conservative revolution" does not imply the return to the dead forms of the past, but implies reconnecting to the primal source of all divinity, to God, actualising it in the present into new forms to be further projected into the future, thereby onsetting a new tradition, that is a new transmission;[744] this last must be a preservation of fire, not of

---

743 Within Slavic Rodnovery are worth mentioning the two sub-movements of Ringing Cedars' Anastasianism and Ynglism, both seemingly reconnecting to aspects of the *Ura-Linda* mythology, the mytho-history of the *Ingaevones*, the northwestern subgroup of the Germanics (narrowly corresponding to the Anglo-Frisians, Anglo-Saxons, or the Englishmen, possibly also including the Scandinavians), conceived as the offspring of Ing-Frey and Freya (the Wanes, the first powers of the universe, then joined by the Ases/Anses, the spirits of Heaven), and Ynglism more specifically to the *Ynglingasaga* of the Edda. In the *Ura-Linda*, the *Ingaevones* (also called "Frisians" in the same myth) are described as having come from a western land named *Altland*, and are therefore comparable to the western branches of the earliest Aryans, or Indo-Europeans, later joined by the Turanians (the eastern branches of the earliest Aryans, associated to the Ases, and called "Findans" in the myth, whom would be Tacitus' *Herminones* and *Istaevones*) in central-eastern Europe, and are described as the purest offspring of white virgin mothers (symbolised by Freya) impregnated by the supreme God, *Wralda*, and as being "free in God", meaning that they perceive that God and its law is within themselves, whereas the "Findans" (sons of Finda, the yellow mother) are "slaves in God", perceiving themselves as submitted to God and the law of God as something external, and the "Lydans" (sons of Lyda, the black mother) do not have any idea of God and law. Anastasianism, established by Vladimir N. Megre, revolves around the figure of Anastasia (i.e. "Resurrection" in Greek), an archetype of white virgin who teaches that the spirit of God is internality and not externality, and, according to Dugin's interpretations of *Ura-Linda* myths, at the beginning of the 3rd millennium *Wralda* re-infuses its breath (*Od*) into reality, and into the descendants of the "Frisians" in particular, resurrecting "freedom in God". The *Ura-Linda* myth is described and interpreted in: Dugin (1992), pp. 47-64.

744 Nechkasov (2021a), p. 264.

278

ashes.[745] We have seen that in Chinese philosophy tradition is the ever-living transmission of the *Li* through the *li*(s) — the Confucian term for the *Logos* and for "rites" —, which have to be regularly reconfirmed to respond to the forces at play in present contexts by "realising the new by reviewing the old", and that the classical Chinese term for "tradition" is the *Dao* itself — the Taoist term for the principle of the universe and at the same time the flux of reality anchored in it — as the "present arriving from the past for leading forth the essential threads for the future", whose etymology possibly indicates the serpentine slithering of reality which has to be aligned with the order of Heaven through aquiline action, the *Ar* of Indo-European cultures.[746] Similarly, Dugin has adopted a distinction, first introduced by the British historian Mark Sedgwick in his *Against the Modern World* (2009), between "tradition" and "Traditionalism", the former to be intended as cold formalism in the throes of death while the latter as a fiery living work of harkening back to the principles of the Perennial Tradition by using the potent tools provided by postmodern means,[747] or hoisting once again the "saving pillar of the luminous presence" of the spirit, therewith triggering the "luminous reabsorption from the heights" of Heaven, by operating with the radical subjectivity, with the many awoken radical subjects who receive from said heights the "infinite light" for the configurations for a new tradition,[748] for new metaphysics expressed in new ontological vectors and new words.[749] In his systematic program

---

745 Ibidem, p. 374.

746 Supra, sections 1.3.1 and 2.1.2.2.

747 Dugin (2019b), pp. 123-129.

748 Ibidem, p. 159.

749 Ibidem, pp. 175-177. Likewise what I have researched in my essay (section 2.2.1) on the basis of Chinese thought, according to Traditionalist thought words, terms and names, are never haphazard but are (using a definition provided by Dugin at p. 176) "spiritual coagulations" which spell and convey the phenomena of being. In this regard, it is important to note that the Russian term for "Paganism", *yazychestvo*, has broader semantics than its Western counterpart, as its root is the word *yazyk* which means "language", "tongue" but also "folk", "people" (Old Slavonic *yazytsy*); therefore, the Russian term for "Paganism" implies the indigenous religiousness of an ethnicity in strict correlation with the correct practice of the indigenous language of such ethnicity, the Perennial Tradition "expressed in a

for the "new task of philosophy", Dugin calls for, among other things, the creation of an "eschatological council (*sobor*) of solar drops" for gathering all the "submerged lights" represented by the radical subjects.[750] This might take place within the framework of a Pagan onto-theological manifestationist orthology reflecting itself as a socio-political Pagan trifunctionalism aimed at reëstablishing verticalising cosmic hierarchies in Europe. Similarly to what I have theorised in my essay with a transposition of Jiang Qing's Confucian trifunctionalism as an all-encompassing Eurasian trifunctionalism articulated into a three-tiered system comprising ① noöcrats linked to the generative power of Heaven from which they draw divine ideas, ② aristocrats as the allocators of the heavenly orders they are given by the former, and ③ democrats linked to the receptive power of the Earth, of matter, which they work with the aim of concretising the divine forms of Heaven,[751] Dugin himself theorises the reconstruction of a social trifunctionalism within the Fourth Political Theory, constituted by ① *brahmana*-philosophers with René Guénon as their tutelary saint, ② *kshatriya*-militants with Julius Evola as their tutelary saint, and ③ *vaishya*-farmers with Mircea Eliade as their tutelary saint, emphasising the need to forsake the globalised cities, the urban hubs and networks of haywire demons[752] of the Western and Westernised industrial civilisation, the degenerate melting-pots functioning as the ganglia of the dissolving techno-

---

people in their native, ancestral, original language", a religion in the truest sense of the word in that it re-links together the people, and relinks the people to the supreme God of the universe via such people's own conceptualisations of it. Cf. Nechkasov (2021b), pp. 335-336; also see: Nechkasov & Arnold (2022), passim.

750 Dugin (2019b), p. 319.

751 Supra, sections 4.3 and 4.4.

752 The phenomena of Western modernity-postmodernity appear as unanimated technological machineries only to non-Traditionalist eyes; a Traditionalist sees such epoch as the dark heart of the Cosmic Midnight, when the God of Heaven and its gods have completely withdrawn from reality and the world is sunken in the hypochthonic dimension, and technological machineries are filled by the unbridled demons of the Great Mother. Men move by train and by car, which are her worms and her beetles, listen to such demons' cacophonic laments passed as "music", and the demons themselves are pleased by the noise of industries and are nourished by the labour aimed at limitless production and consumption. Cf. Nechkasov (2021a), pp. 142-143, 171 & 373.

financial machination of Western modernity, for a return to the land and a re-rooting onto the Earth of gentilitially and threefoldly reorganised folks living in harmony with the patterns of Heaven.[753]

---

753 Dugin (2021b), pp. 98-103. Nechkasov informs us that the trifunctional system is being proposed in Russia within Rodnovery as the three *verv'*, plural *vervi* (literally "ropes", "strings", "lines"), namely the *volkhvy* ("shamans", "mages"; represented by the colour white), the *kniazy* ("dukes"; represented by the colour red) and the *smerdy* ("farmers"; represented by the colour black). He also mentions the historical trifunctional system of the Ossetes, a Caucasian population descending from the Scythians of the Alan tribes, as constituted by the *alagata*, the *akhsartagkata*, and the *borata*; Ossetian trifunctionalism was considered the most paradigmatic among the Indo-European ones by Georges Dumézil. Cf. Nechkasov (2021a), pp. 84-85.

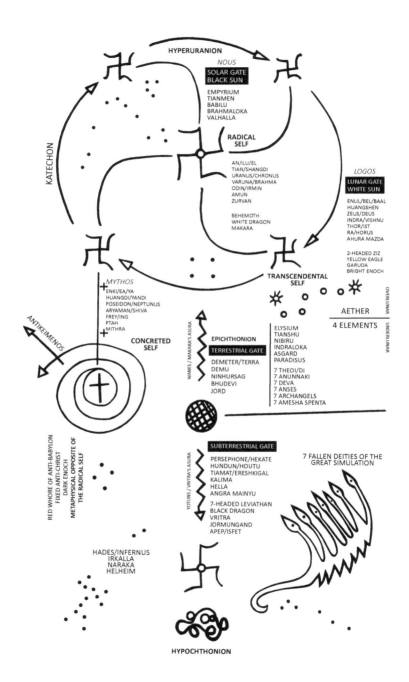

HYPERURANION

NOUS

SOLAR GATE
BLACK SUN

EMPYRIUM
TIANMEN
BABILU
BRAHMALOKA
VALHALLA

RADICAL
SELF

AN/ILU/EL
TIAN/SHANGDI
URANUS/CHRONUS
VARUNA/BRAHMA
ODIN/IRMIN
AMUN
ZURVAN

BEHEMOTH
WHITE DRAGON
MAKARA

KATECHON

LOGOS

LUNAR GATE
WHITE SUN

ENLIL/BEL/BAAL
HUANGSHEN
ZEUS/DEUS
INDRA/VISHNU
THOR/IST
RA/HORUS
AHURA MAZDA

2-HEADED ZIZ
YELLOW EAGLE
GARUDA
BRIGHT ENOCH

TRANSCENDENTAL
SELF

AETHER

4 ELEMENTS

OVERLUNAR

UNDERLUNAR

MYTHOS

ENKI/EA/YA
HUANGDI/YANDI
POSEIDON/NEPTUNUS
ARYAMAN/SHIVA
FREY/ING
PTAH
MITHRA

ANTIKEIMENOS

CONCRETED
SELF

WANES / MAKARA'S ASURA

EPICHTHONION

TERRESTRIAL GATE

DEMETER/TERRA
DEMU
NINHURSAG
BHUDEVI
JORD

ELYSIUM
TIANSHU
NIBIRU
INDRALOKA
ASGARD
PARADISUS

7 THEOI/DI
7 ANUNNAKI
7 DEVA
7 ANSES
7 ARCHANGELS
7 AMESHA SPENTA

RED WHORE OF ANTI-BABYLON
FIXED ANTI-CHRIST
DARK ENOCH
METAPHYSICAL OPPOSITE OF
THE RADICAL SELF

YOTUNS / VRITRA'S ASURA

SUBTERRESTRIAL GATE

PERSEPHONE/HEKATE
HUNDUN/HOUTU
TIAMAT/ERESHKIGAL
KALIMA
HELLA
ANGRA MAINYU

7-HEADED LEVIATHAN
BLACK DRAGON
VRITRA
JORMUNGAND
APEP/ISFET

7 FALLEN DEITIES OF THE
GREAT SIMULATION

HADES/INFERNUS
IRKALLA
NARAKA
HELHEIM

HYPOCHTHONION

282

The scheme on the foregoing page is a proposal of the Pagan manifestationist orthological cosmic map, also including a representation of the cosmological error produced by Christian theology and creationism. ① The centripetal cycle of the *Katechon* of the metaphysical principle of the North Pole, the God of the Hyperuranion (*Draco*, Behemoth), of Babylon, and of the radical self, when projected onto the Earth is reflected as the circle of the Arctic Pole, extending to the katechontic power of the Eurasian landmass, centred in the smaller circle of Gardarika-Russia, as described by Aleksandr Dugin following Gaston Géorgel, while outside of the circle of the Arctic Pole — whose borders are kept by ② the rotation of the sevenfold spirit of God, the seven deities of *Ursa Major* and *Ursa Minor*, led by the two-headed *Ziz*, Sandalphon-Metatron, the Bright Enoch, the transcendental self — there is ③ the "outer darkness" governed by the metaphysical principle of the South Pole, projected onto the Earth as the circle of the Antarctic Pole, extending to the southern hemisphere of the Earth and centred in the smaller Mediterranean-Egyptian circle, which contains some elements of the northern circle, such as the concept of the heavenly trinity of God included in the illustration.[754] ④ The deception of the fixed cross, that is the fixion in the earthly space-time — historicised as linear time —, and in particular in the outer darkness, of the second (spiritual, transcendental) and third (incarnated) aspects of the manifestation of the first (wholly transcendent) aspect of God, is an operation carried out by the metaphysical opposite of God itself and of the radical self,[755] that is to say, the operation of the Whore of Anti-Babylon and the Anti-Christ, the Dark Enoch (*Crux, Canis Major* and *Canis Minor*), a concreted self possessed by the metaphysical principle of the South Pole, the Matrix of the Hypochthonion, which sucks the power of the North Pole and simulates its order by producing an inverted Anti-Babylon,

---

754 Note that the projection on Earth of the two circles, that of the North Pole and Gardarika-Russia and that of the South Pole and Mediterranean-Egypt, is not shown in my illustration. They are illustrated in: Dugin (1992), pp. 31 & 92.

755 Dugin (2019b), pp. 173-175.

setting in motion the centrifugal spiral of the *Antikeimenos*, the coils of the seven-headed Leviathan (*Dorado*), which overturns the manifestationist cosmic map of Eurasian orthology, so that: ① the concreted self of the Anti-Christ is placed at the centre, ② the spirit of God of the transcendental self which should link earthly phenomena to heavenly patterns is switched off, and ③ the radical self rotates in the peripheries of the Great Simulation, the Great Parody of the Anti-Babylon.

BIBLIOGRAPHY

Achuthananda, Swami (2018). *The Ascent of Vishnu and the Fall of Brahma*. The Galaxy of Hindu Gods, 2. Brisbane, Queensland: Relianz Communications.

Assasi, Reza (2013). "Swastika: The Forgotten Constellation Representing the Chariot of Mithras". *Ancient Cosmologies and Modern Prophets. Anthropological Notebooks*, XIX(s): 407-418. Ivan Šprajc; Peter Pehani (Eds.). Ljubljana, Slovenia: Slovene Anthropological Society.

Ataç, Mehmet-Ali (2018). *Art and Immortality in the Ancient Near East*. Cambridge, England: Cambridge University Press.

Balbo, Cesare (1836). *Opuscoli per servire alla storia delle città e dei comuni d'Italia*. Charleston, South Carolina: Nabu Press, 2012.

Barberi, Maria Stella (2006). "Lo spazio katechontico da San Paolo a Carl Schmitt". *Religione e violenza. Identità religiosa e conflitto nel mondo contemporaneo*. Giuliana Parotto (Ed.). Trieste, Italy: Edizioni Università di Trieste.

Bargeliotes, Leonidas (1972). "Origen's Dual Doctrine of God and Logos". *Θεολογια/Theologia*, 43(1-2): 202-212. Athens, Greece: Holy Synod of the Church of Greece.

Bell, Daniel A. (2012). "Introduction". Jiang, Qing. *A Confucian Constitutional Order: How China's Ancient Past Can Shape Its Political Future*. Princeton, New Jersey: Princeton University Press.

Bianchi, Daniele (2020). "Julius Evola e il cristianesimo", 3 pts. *EreticaMente*.

Boodberg, Peter (1953). "The Semasiology of Some Primary Confucian Concepts". *Philosophy East and West*, 2: 317-332. Honolulu, Hawaii: University of Hawaii Press.

Chan, Shirley (2011). "Cosmology, Society and Humanity: Tian in the Guodian Texts (Part I)". *Journal of Chinese Philosophy*, 38(s1): 64-77. Leiden, Netherlands: Brill Academic Publishers.

Chan, Shirley (2012). "Cosmology, Society and Humanity: Tian in the Guodian Texts (Part II)". *Journal of Chinese Philosophy*, 39(1): 106-120. Leiden, Netherlands: Brill Academic Publishers.

Chang, Tsung-tung (1988). "Indo-European Vocabulary in Old Chinese: A New Thesis on the Emergence of Chinese Language and Civilization in the Late Neolithic Age". *Sino-Platonic Papers*, 7. Victor H. Mair (Ed.). Philadelphia, Pennsylvania: University of Pennsylvania.

Cox Miller, Patricia (2001). *The Poetry of Thought in Late Antiquity: Essays in Imagination and Religion*. Farnham, England: Ashgate Publishing.

De Martino, Ernesto (1977). *La fine del mondo. Contributo all'analisi delle apocalissi culturali*. Clara Gallini (Ed.). Turin: Einaudi Editore.

Delio, Ilia (2007). "Theology, Metaphysics and the Centrality of Christ". *Theological Studies*, 68(2): 254-273. Paul G. Cowley (Ed.). Thousand Oaks, California: SAGE Publishing; Jesuits of the United States and Canada.

Didier, John C. (2009). "In and Outside the Square: The Sky and the Power of Belief in Ancient China and the World, c. 4500 BC – AD 200", 3 vols. *Sino-Platonic Papers, 192*. Victor H. Mair (Ed.). Philadelphia, Pennsylvania: University of Pennsylvania.

Dugin, Aleksandr (1992). *Rusia, el misterio de Eurasia*. Paraísos perdidos, 3. Arturo Marián (Trans.). Madrid, Spain: Grupo Libros 88.

Dugin, Aleksandr (2010). *Martin Heidegger: The Philosophy of Another Beginning*. Moscow, Russia: Academic Project.

Dugin, Aleksandr (2012). *The Fourth Political Theory*. London, England: Arktos Media.

Dugin, Aleksandr (2016). "The Indo-Europeans". Jafe Arnold (Trans.). Eurasianist Internet Archive. URL: https://eurasianist-archive.com/2016/12/28/the-indo-europeans/

Dugin, Aleksandr (2019a). *Il sole di mezzanotte. Aurora del soggetto radicale*. Milan, Italy: AGA Editrice.

Dugin, Aleksandr (2019b). *Soggetto radicale. Teoria e fenomenologia*. Milan, Italy: AGA Editrice.

Dugin, Aleksandr (2019c). "The Metaphysical Factor in Paganism". Jafe Arnold (Trans.). Eurasianist Internet Archive. The text has been re-published many times over the years; the original version was published in Russian in 1990. URL: https://eurasianist-archive.com/2019/05/17/the-metaphysical-factor-in-paganism/

Dugin, Aleksandr (2020). *Noomachia. Rivolta contro il mondo postmoderno*. Milan, Italy: AGA Editrice.

Dugin, Aleksandr (2021a). "Continuity and Discontinuity of the Five Elements". Circle of the Five Elements, 2. Gavirate, Italy: Corte dei Brut; *Paideuma.tv*.

Dugin, Aleksandr (2021b). *Contro il Grande Reset. Manifesto del Grande Risveglio*. Milan, Italy: AGA Editrice.

Dumézil, Georges (1941). *Jupiter, Mars, Quirinus. Essai sur la conception indo-européenne de la société et sur les origines de Rome*. Paris, France: Éditions Gallimard.

Dumézil, Georges (1974). *Gli dèi dei Germani*. Milan, Italy: Adelphi Edizioni.

Duval, Paul-Marie (1989). "Teutates, Esus, Taranis". *Publications de l'École française de Rome*, 116: 275-287. Rome, Italy: École française de Rome.

Dynda, Jiří (2014). "The Three-Headed One at the Crossroad: A Comparative Study of the Slavic God Triglav". *Studia mythologica Slavica*, 17. Ljubljana, Slovenia: Institute of Slovenian Ethnology.

Eno, Robert (1990). *The Confucian Creation of Heaven: Philosophy and the Defense of Ritual Mastery*. Albany, New York: State University of New York Press.

Espesset, Grégoire (2008). "Latter Han Religious Mass Movements and the Early Daoist Church". *Early Chinese Religion: Part One: Shang Through Han (1250 BC–220 AD)*. John Lagerwey; Marc Kalinowski (Eds.). Leiden, Netherlands: Brill Academic Publishers. Consulted version from the archive HAL-SHS (Sciences de l'Homme et de la Société), French National Centre for Scientific Research.

Evola, Julius (1990). *Il matriarcato nell'opera di J. J. Bachofen. Quaderni di testi evoliani*, 23. Rome, Italy: Fondazione Julius Evola.

Feng, Youlan (1948). *A Short History of Chinese Philosophy*. Derek Bodde (Ed.). New York City, New York: Macmillan.

Ferrario, Giulio (1829). *Il costume antico e moderno o storia del governo, della milizia, della religione, delle arti, scienze ed usanze di tutti i popoli antichi e moderni provata coi monumenta dell'antichità e rappresentata cogli analoghi disegni*, 34 vols. Charleston, South Carolina: Nabu Press, 2012 et seqq.

Fiskesjö, Magnus (2017). "China's Animal Neighbours". *The Art of Neighbouring: Making Relations Across China's Borders*. Martin Saxer; Juan Zhang (Eds.). Amsterdam, Netherlands: Amsterdam University Press.

Frawley, David (2001). *The Rig Veda and the History of India (Rig Veda Bharata Itihasa)*. New Delhi, India: Aditya Prakashan.

Fukuyama, Francis (1992). *La fine della storia e l'ultimo uomo*. Delfo Ceni (Trans.). Milan: Rizzoli Editore.

Fukuyama, Francis (1995). "Confucianism and Democracy". *Journal of Democracy*, 6(2): 20-33. Baltimore, Maryland: Johns Hopkins University Press.

Fukuyama, Francis (2014). *Political Order and Political Decay: From the Industrial Revolution to the Globalization of Democracy*. New York City, New York: Farrar, Straus and Giroux.

Gabrieli, Silvia (2017). "Il potere performativo della Parola Divina nei miti di Creazione del Vicino Oriente Antico". Padua, Italy: Padua Research Archive, University of Padua.

Glass, James M. (1974). "The Philosopher and the Shaman: The Political Vision as Incantation". *Political Theory*, 2(2): 181-196. Thousand Oaks, California: SAGE Publications.

Goblet d'Alviella, Eugène F.A. (1894). *The Migration of Symbols*. London, England: A. Constable & Co.

Guénon, René (1924). *East and West*. Martin Ling (Trans.). Hillsdale, New York: Sophia Perennis, 2004 ed.

Guénon, René (1945). *The Reign of Quantity and the Signs of the Times*. Walter E.C. James (Trans.). Hillsdale, New York: Sophia Perennis, 2001 ed.

Guénon, René (1962). *Symbols of Sacred Science*. Henry D. Fohr (Trans.). Hillsdale, New York: Sophia Perennis, 2004 ed.

Heidegger, Martin (1971). "The Thing". *Poetry, Language, Thought*. Albert Hofstadter (Trans.). New York City, New York: HarperCollins.

Higgins, Luke B. (2010). "A Logos Without Organs: Cosmologies of Transformation in Origen and Deleuze-Guattari". *SubStance*, 39(1): 141-153. Baltimore, Maryland: Johns Hopkins University Press.

Huang, Yong (2007). "Confucian Theology: Three Models". *Religion Compass*, 1(4): 455-478. Brandi Denison (Ed.). New York City: New York: John Wiley & Sons.

Ingram, Alain (2001). "Alexander Dugin: Geopolitics and Neo-Fascism in Post-Soviet Russia". *Political Geography*, 20(8). Amsterdam, Netherlands: Elsevier.

Jakobson, Roman (2010). *Contributions to Comparative Mythology: Studies in Linguistics and Philology, 1972–1982. Selected Writings, VII*. Stephen Rudy (Ed.). Berlin, Germany: Walter de Gruyter.

James, Peter; Van der Sluijs, Marinus Anthony (2008). "Ziggurats, Colors, and Planets: Rawlinson Revisited". *Journal of Cuneiform Studies*, 60: 57-79. Chicago, Illinois: University of Chicago Press.

Jiang, Qing (2009). "Le confucianisme de la «Voie royale», direction pour le politique en Chine contemporaine". Sébastien Billioud (Trans.). *Extrême-Orient Extrême-Occident*, 31. Paris, France: PUV Éditions.

Jullien, François (1995). *The Propensity of Things: Towards a History of Efficacy in China*. Janet Lloyd (Trans.). New York City, New York: Zone Books.

Jullien, François (2016). *Essere o vivere. Il pensiero occidentale e il pensiero cinese in venti contrasti*. Emanuela Magno (Trans.). Milan: Feltrinelli Editore.

Kasak, Enn; Veede, Raul (2001). "Understanding Planets in Ancient Mesopotamia". *Folklore*, 16. Tartu, Estonia: Folk Belief and Media Group of Estonian Literary Museum, Estonian Institute of Folklore.

Kramer, Samuel Noah (1956). "Sumerian Theology and Ethics". *Harvard Theological Review*, 49(1): 45-62. Cambridge, Massachusetts: Harvard Divinity School, Harvard University.

Krikke, Jan (1998). *The Corridor of Space: China, Modernists and the Cybernetic Century*. Amsterdam, Netherlands: Olive Press.

Kushnir, Dmitriy (2016). *Rodnover: The Spirit Within*. Scotts Valley, California: CreateSpace Publishing.

Lacan, Jacques (2007). *Écrits: The First Complete Edition in English*. Bruce Fink (Trans.). New York City, New York: W. W. Norton & Company.

Latham, Robert G. (1851). *The Germania of Tacitus: With Ethnological Dissertations and Notes*. London, England: Taylor, Walton, and Maberly.

Levenda, Peter (Simon) (1977). *Simon Necronomicon*. New York City, New York: Avon Books.

Levenda, Peter (Simon) (2006). *The Gates of the Necronomicon*. New York City, New York: Avon Books.

Lévi, Jean (2007). "The Rite, the Norm and the Dao: Philosophy of Sacrifice and Transcendence of Power in Ancient

China". *Early Chinese Religion: Part One: Shang Through Han (1250 BC–220 AD)*. John Lagerwey; Marc Kalinowski (Eds.). Leiden, Netherlands: Brill Academic Publishers.

Lewis, Mark Edward (1999). *Writing and Authority in Early China*. Albany, New York: State University of New York Press.

Littlewood, Roland; Dein, Simon (2013). "Did Christianity Lead to Schizophrenia? Psychosis, Psychology and Self-Reference". *Transcultural Psychiatry*, 50(3): 397-420. Thousand Oaks, California: SAGE Publishing.

Liu, Li (1999). "Who Were the Ancestors? The Origins of Chinese Ancestral Culture and Racial Myths". *Antiquity*, 73(281): 602-613. Durham, England: Antiquity Publications; Durham University.

Lyon, Bruce (2010). *Cosmologia Occulta*. Rome, Italy: Group24.

Mahony, William K. (1998). *The Artful Universe: An Introduction to the Vedic Religious Imagination*. Albany, New York: State University of New York Press.

Mair, Victor H. (1990a). *Tao Te Ching: The Classic Book of Integrity and the Way*. New York City, New York: Bantam Books.

Mair, Victor H. (1990b). "Old Sinitic *Myag, Old Persian Magus, and English 'Magician'". *Early China*, 15: 27-47. Cambridge, England: Cambridge University Press.

Mair, Victor H. (1995). "Mummies of the Tarim Basin". *Archaeology*, 48(2). Boston, Massachusetts: Archaeological Institute of America.

Mair, Victor H. (2011). "Religious Formations and Intercultural Contacts in Early China". *Dynamics in the History of Religions between Asia and Europe: Encounters, Notions, and Comparative Perspectives*. Volkhard Krech; Marion Steinicke (Eds.). Leiden, Netherlands: Brill Academic Publishers.

Mair, Victor H. (2012). "The Earliest Identifiable Written Chinese Characters". *Archaeology and Language: Indo-European Studies Presented to James P. Mallory*. Martin E. Huld; Karlene

Jones-Bley; Dean Miller; James P. Mallory (Eds.). Washington, D.C.: Institute for the Study of Man.

Makeham, John (2010). *Dao Companion to Neo-Confucian Philosophy*. New York City, New York: Springer Publishing.

Mander, Pietro (2011). "Religione, potere ed organizzazione sociale: il paradigma dell'antica Mesopotamia sumerica ed assiro-babilonese". *Metábasis, VII*(12). Milan, Italy: Mimesis Edizioni.

Medhurst, Walter H. (1847). *A Dissertation on the Theology of the Chinese, with a View to the Elucidation of the Most Appropriate Term for Expressing the Deity, in the Chinese Language*. Shanghai, China: Mission Press.

Milburn, Olivia (2016). *The Spring and Autumn Annals of Master Yan*. Sinica Leidensia, 128. Leiden, Netherlands: Brill Academic Publishers.

Mosbey, John C. (2015). "Russia, Dugin, and Traditionalism in Politics: Political and Theological Placement of the Fourth Political Theory". *Forum on Public Policy: A Journal of the Oxford Round Table*, 2015(2). Oxford, England: Oxford Round Table.

Müller, Ludvig (1877). *Det saakaldte Hagekors's Anvendelse og Betydning i Oldtiden. Avec un resume en francais*. Copenhagen, Denmark: Bianco Lunos Bogtrykkeri.

Nad, Boris (2014). "Face to Face with God/god". *The Fourth Political Theory (4pt.su)*. URL: http://www.4pt.su/en/content/face-face-godgod

Nechkasov, Yevgeny (Askr Svarte) (2021a). *Polemos: The Dawn of Pagan Traditionalism*. Tucson, Arizona: PRAV Publishing.

Nechkasov, Yevgeny (Askr Svarte) (2021b). *Polemos II: Pagan Perspectives*. Tucson, Arizona: PRAV Publishing.

Nechkasov, Yevgeny (Askr Svarte); Arnold, Jafe (2022). "Naming Tradition: The Word and World of Pagandom". *Continental-Conscious*. URL: https://continentalconscious.com/2022/06/13/naming-tradition-the-word-and-world-of-pagandom/

Nobus, Dany (2000). *Jacques Lacan and the Freudian Practice of Psychoanalysis*. London, England: Routledge.

Ownby, David (2009). "Kang Xiaoguang: Social Science, Civil Society, and Confucian Religion". *China Perspectives*, 4(80): 101-111. Hong Kong, China: French Centre for Research on Contemporary China.

Panikkar, Raimon (1993). *The Cosmotheandric Experience: Emerging Religious Consciousness*. Scott Eastham (Ed.). Ossining, New York: Orbis Books.

Pankenier, David W. (1995). "The Cosmo-Political Background of Heaven's Mandate". *Early China*, 20: 121-176. Cambridge, England: Cambridge University Press.

Pankenier, David W. (2004). "A Brief History of Beiji 北极 (Northern Culmen), with an Excursus on the Origin of the Character Di 帝". *Journal of the American Oriental Society*, 124(2): 211-236. Ann Arbor, Michigan: American Oriental Society.

Pankenier, David W. (2009). "Locating True North in Ancient China". *Cosmology Across Cultures. Astronomical Society of the Pacific Conference Series*, 409: 128-137. J.A. Rubiño-Martín; J.A. Belmonte; F. Prada; A. Alberdi (Eds.). San Francisco, California: Astronomical Society of the Pacific.

Pankenier, David W. (2013). *Astrology and Cosmology in Early China: Conforming Earth to Heaven*. Cambridge, England: Cambridge University Press.

Papillon, Serge (2005). "Mythologie sino-européenne". *Sino-Platonic Papers*, 154. Victor H. Mair (Ed.). Philadelphia, Pennsylvania: University of Pennsylvania.

Parpola, Simo (1993). "The Assyrian Tree of Life: Tracing the Origins of Jewish Monotheism and Greek Philosophy". *Journal of Near Eastern Studies*, 52(3). Chicago, Illinois: University of Chicago Press.

Pattberg, Thorsten J. (2009). *The East-West Dichotomy*. LoD Press.

Puett, Michael (2010). "Centering the Realm: Wang Mang, the Zhouli, and Early Chinese Statecraft". *Statecraft and Classical Learning: The Rituals of Zhou in East Asian History*. Benjamin Elman; Martin Kern (Eds.). Leiden, Netherlands: Brill Academic Publishers.

Recalcati, Massimo (2007). *Il miracolo della forma. Per un'estetica psicoanalitica*. Milan, Italy: Bruno Mondadori Editore.

Reiter, Florian C. (Ed.) (2007). *Purposes, Means and Convictions in Daoism: A Berlin Symposium*. Wiesbaden, Germany: Harrassowitz Verlag.

Resta, Caterina (2002). "Ricordare l'origine. Riflessioni geofilosofiche". *DRP Rassegna di Studi e Ricerche*, 4: 11-18. Nicola Aricò (Ed.). Messina, Italy: Casa Editrice Sicania; University of Messina.

Riddle, Mark A. (2011). "Tennō (天皇): The Central Asian Origins of Japan's Solar Kingship". *Sino-Platonic Papers*, 214. Victor H. Mair (Ed.). Philadelphia, Pennsylvania: University of Pennsylvania.

Robinet, Isabelle (2007). "Hundun 混沌 Chaos; Inchoate State". *The Encyclopedia of Taoism*. Fabrizio Pregadio (Ed.). London, England: Routledge.

Rochat de la Vallée, Elisabeth (2012). "Shen (Spirit, Soul) in Chinese Religion and Medicine". *Charles Strong Trust Lectures*. Melbourne, Victoria: Charles Strong Memorial Trust.

Rogers, J.H. (1998). "Origins of the Ancient Constellations: I. The Mesopotamian Traditions". *Journal of the British Astronomical Association*, 108(1). London, England: British Astronomical Association.

Ruina, Francesca (2014). "Lacan e l'estetica del vuoto". *Aperture, 30*. Rome, Italy: Enrico Castelli Gattinara.

Saso, Michael (2009). "In and Outside the Square: The Sky and the Power of Belief in Ancient China and the World, c. 4500 B.C.–A.D. 200 (review)". *China Review International*, 16(4): 491-493. Honolulu, Hawaii: University of Hawaii Press.

Schwartz, Benjamin I. (1973). "On the Absence of Reductionism in Chinese Thought". *Journal of Chinese Philosophy*, 1(1): 27-43. Leiden, Netherlands: Brill Academic Publishers.

Shekhovtsov, Anton (2008). "The Palingenetic Thrust of Russian Neo-Eurasianism: Ideas of Rebirth in Alexander Dugin's Worldview". *Totalitarian Movements and Political Religions*, 9(4): 491-506. Abingdon-on-Thames, England: Taylor & Francis.

Sigurdsson, Geir. (2004). *Learning and Li: The Confucian Process of Humanization Through Ritual Propriety*. Honolulu, Hawaii: University of Hawaii Press.

Sun, Xiaochun; Kistemaker, Jacob (1997). *The Chinese Sky During the Han: Constellating Stars and Society*. Leiden, Netherlands: Brill Academic Publishers.

Teiser, Stephen F. (1996). "The Spirits of Chinese Religion". *Religions of China in Practice*. Donald S. Lopez Jr. (Ed.). Princeton, New Jersey: Princeton University Press.

Tseng, Lillian Lan-ying (2011). *Picturing Heaven in Early China*. Cambridge, Massachusetts: Harvard University Press.

Van den Dungen, Wim (2002). "Amun, the Great God: Hidden, One and Millions". *Sofiatopia*. URL: http://www.sofiatopia.org/maat/amun.htm

Vv.Aa. (1951). *University of California Publications in Semitic Philology*, 11-12. Berkeley, California: University of California Press; Charleston, South Carolina: Nabu Press, 2012 et seqq.

Wallace, Anthony (1956). "Mazeway Resynthesis. A Biocultural Theory of Religious Inspiration". *Transactions of the New York Academy of Sciences*, 18(7): 626-638. New York City, New York: New York Academy of Sciences.

Wang, Mingming (2012). "All Under Heaven (Tianxia): Cosmological Perspectives and Political Ontologies in Pre-Modern China". *HAU: Journal of Ethnographic Theory*, 2(1): 337-383. Chicago, Illinois: University of Chicago Press.

Wei, Julie Lee (2005). "Huangdi and Huntun (The Yellow Emperor and Wonton): A New Hypothesis on Some Figures in Chinese Mythology". *Sino-Platonic Papers*, 163. Victor H. Mair (Ed.). Philadelphia, Pennsylvania: University of Pennsylvania.

Wells, Marnix (2014). *The Pheasant Cap Master and the End of History: Linking Religion to Philosophy in Early China*. St. Petersburg, Florida: Three Pines Press.

Wright, J. Edward (2002). *The Early History of Heaven*. Oxford, England: Oxford University Press.

Yao, Xinzhong (2000). *An Introduction to Confucianism*. Cambridge, England: Cambridge University Press.

Yao, Xinzhong (2010). *Chinese Religion: A Contextual Approach*. London, England: Continuum International Publishing Group.

Young, Linda Martina (2007). *Where Grace May Pass: A Poetics of the Body*. Carpinteria, California: Pacifica Graduate Institute.

Zhang, Longxi (1985). "The 'Tao' and the 'Logos': Notes on Derrida's Critique of Logocentrism". *Critical Inquiry*, 11(3): 385-398. Chicago, Illinois: University of Chicago Press.

Zhao, Tingyang (2011). *The Tianxia System: An Introduction to the Philosophy of a World Institution*. Beijing, China: Renmin University Press.

Zhong, Xinzi (2014). *A Reconstruction of Zhū Xī's Religious Philosophy Inspired by Leibniz: The Natural Theology of Heaven*. Hong Kong, China: Hong Kong Baptist University Institutional Repository.

Zhou, Jixu (2005). "Old Chinese *Tees and Proto-Indo-European *Deus: Similarity in Religious Ideas and Common Source in Linguistics". *Sino-Platonic Papers*, 167. Victor H. Mair (Ed.). Philadelphia, Pennsylvania: University of Pennsylvania.

Ziporyn, Brook. (2008). "Form, Principle, Pattern or Coherence? Li 理 in Chinese Philosophy". *Philosophy Compass*, 3: 1-50. Hoboken, New Jersey: Wiley-Blackwell.

Žižek, Slavoj (2006). *The Parallax View.* Cambridge, Massachusetts: MIT Press.

ENCYCLOPÆDIAS, DICTIONARIES AND COMPILATIONS

Adams, Douglas Q. (1997). *Encyclopedia of Indo-European Culture.* James P. Mallory (Ed.). Abingdon-on-Thames, England: Taylor & Francis.

Allen, Richard Hinckley (1963). *Star Names: Their Lore and Meaning.* Mineola, New York: Dover Publications.

Black, Jeremy; Green, Anthony (1992). *Gods, Demons and Symbols of Ancient Mesopotamia: An Illustrated Dictionary.* Austin, Texas: University of Texas Press.

Bonnefoy, Yves; Doniger, Wendy (Eds.). *Asian Mythologies.* Chicago, Illinois: University of Chicago Press.

Cua, Antonio S. (Ed.) (2013). *Encyclopedia of Chinese Philosophy.* Abingdon-on-Thames, England: Taylor & Francis

De Vaan, Michiel (2008). *Etymological Dictionary of Latin and the other Italic Languages.* Leiden Indo-European Etymological Dictionary Series, 7. Leiden, Netherlands: Brill Academic Publishers.

Doniger, Wendy (Ed.) (2000). *Merriam-Webster's Encyclopedia of World Religions.* Springfield, Massachusetts: Merriam-Webster.

Koch, Rudolf (1955). *The Book of Signs.* Mineola, New York: Dover Publications.

Leeming, David (2005). *The Oxford Companion to World Mythology.* Oxford, England: Oxford University Press.

Mathieu-Colas, Michel (2017). "Dieux slaves et baltes". *Dictionnaire des noms des divinités.* Paris, France: HAL-SHS (Sciences de l'Homme et de la Société), French National Centre for Scientific Research.

Orel, Vladimir E. (2003). *A Handbook of Germanic Etymology*. Leiden, Netherlands: Brill Academic Publishers.

Perkins, Franklin (2016). "Metaphysics in Chinese Philosophy". *The Stanford Encyclopedia of Philosophy*. Edward N. Zalta (Ed.). Stanford, California: Stanford University.

Pianigiani, Ottorino (1907). *Vocabolario etimologico della lingua italiana*. Rome, Italy: Albrighi, Segati & C.

Pokorny, Julius (1959). *Indogermanisches etymologisches Wörterbuch*. Bern, Switzerland: Francke Verlag.

Rendich, Franco (2010). *Dizionario etimologico comparato delle lingue classiche indoeuropee*. Rome, Italy: Palombi Editore.

Watkins, Calvert (Ed.) (2000). *The American Heritage Dictionary of Indo-European Roots*. Boston, Massachusetts: Houghton Mifflin Harcourt, 2nd ed.

Lightning Source UK Ltd.
Milton Keynes UK
UKHW022041090123
415085UK00005B/140

9 781952 671883